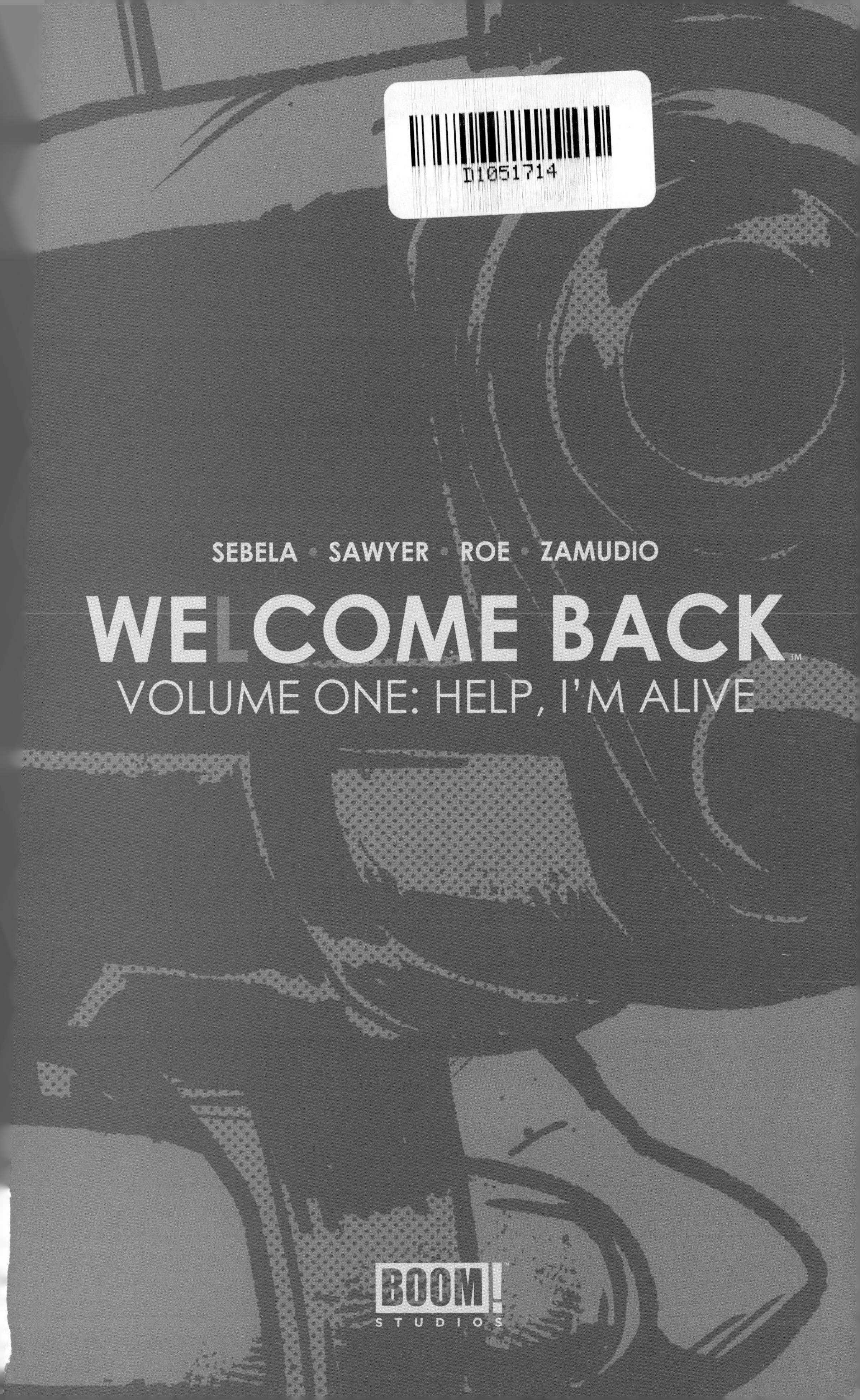

SEBELA • SAWYER • ROE • ZAMUDIO

WELCOME BACK™

VOLUME ONE: HELP, I'M ALIVE

BOOM! STUDIOS

ROSS RICHIE CEO & Founder
MATT GAGNON Editor-in-Chief
FILIP SABLIK President of Publishing & Marketing
STEPHEN CHRISTY President of Development
LANCE KREITER VP of Licensing & Merchandising
PHIL BARBARO VP of Finance
BRYCE CARLSON Managing Editor
MEL CAYLO Marketing Manager
SCOTT NEWMAN Production Design Manager
IRENE BRADISH Operations Manager
CHRISTINE DINH Brand Communications Manager
SIERRA HAHN Senior Editor
DAFNA PLEBAN Editor
SHANNON WATTERS Editor
ERIC HARBURN Editor
WHITNEY LEOPARD Associate Editor

JASMINE AMIRI Associate Editor
CHRIS ROSA Associate Editor
ALEX GALER Assistant Editor
CAMERON CHITTOCK Assistant Editor
MARY GUMPORT Assistant Editor
KELSEY DIETERICH Production Designer
JILLIAN CRAB Production Designer
KARA LEOPARD Production Designer
MICHELLE ANKLEY Production Design Assistant
AARON FERRARA Operations Coordinator
ELIZABETH LOUGHRIDGE Accounting Coordinator
JOSÉ MEZA Sales Assistant
JAMES ARRIOLA Mailroom Assistant
STEPHANIE HOCUTT Marketing Assistant
SAM KUSEK Direct Market Representative
HILLARY LEVI Executive Assistant

BOOM! STUDIOS

WELCOME BACK Volume One, February 2016. Published by BOOM! Studios, a division of Boom Entertainment, Inc. Welcome Back is ™ & © 2016 Christopher Sebela & Jonathan Brandon Sawyer. Originally published in single magazine form as WELCOME BACK No. 1-4. ™ & © 2015 Christopher Sebela & Jonathan Brandon Sawyer. All rights reserved. BOOM! Studios™ and the BOOM! Studios logo are trademarks of Boom Entertainment, Inc., registered in various countries and categories. All characters, events, and institutions depicted herein are fictional. Any similarity between any of the names, characters, persons, events, and/or institutions in this publication to actual names, characters, and persons, whether living or dead, events, and/or institutions is unintended and purely coincidental. BOOM! Studios does not read or accept unsolicited submissions of ideas, stories, or artwork.

A catalog record of this book is available from OCLC and from the BOOM! Studios website, www.boom-studios.com, on the Librarians page.

BOOM! Studios, 5670 Wilshire Boulevard, Suite 450, Los Angeles, CA 90036-5679.
Printed in USA. First Printing.

ISBN: 978-1-60886-855-1, eISBN: 978-1-61398-526-7

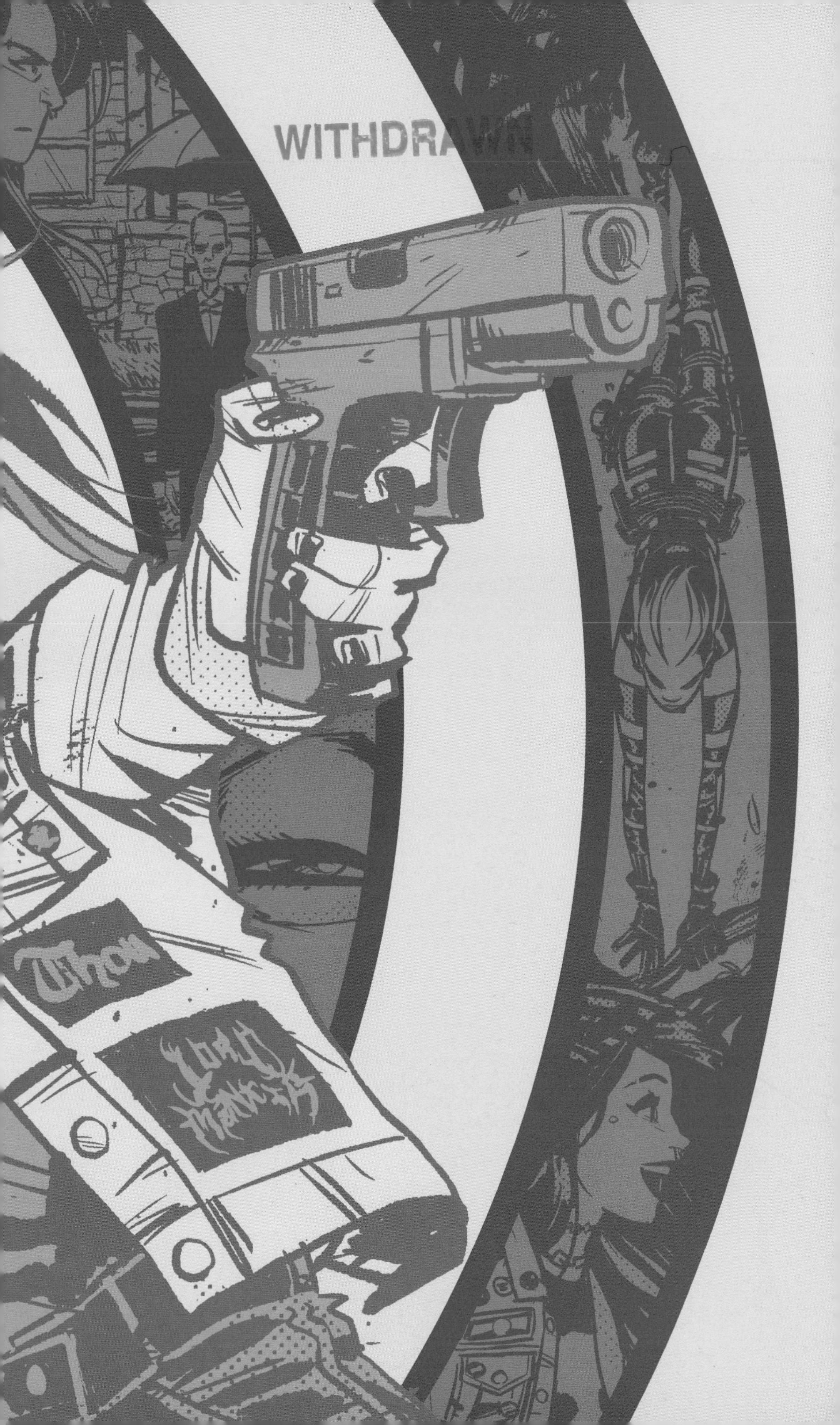

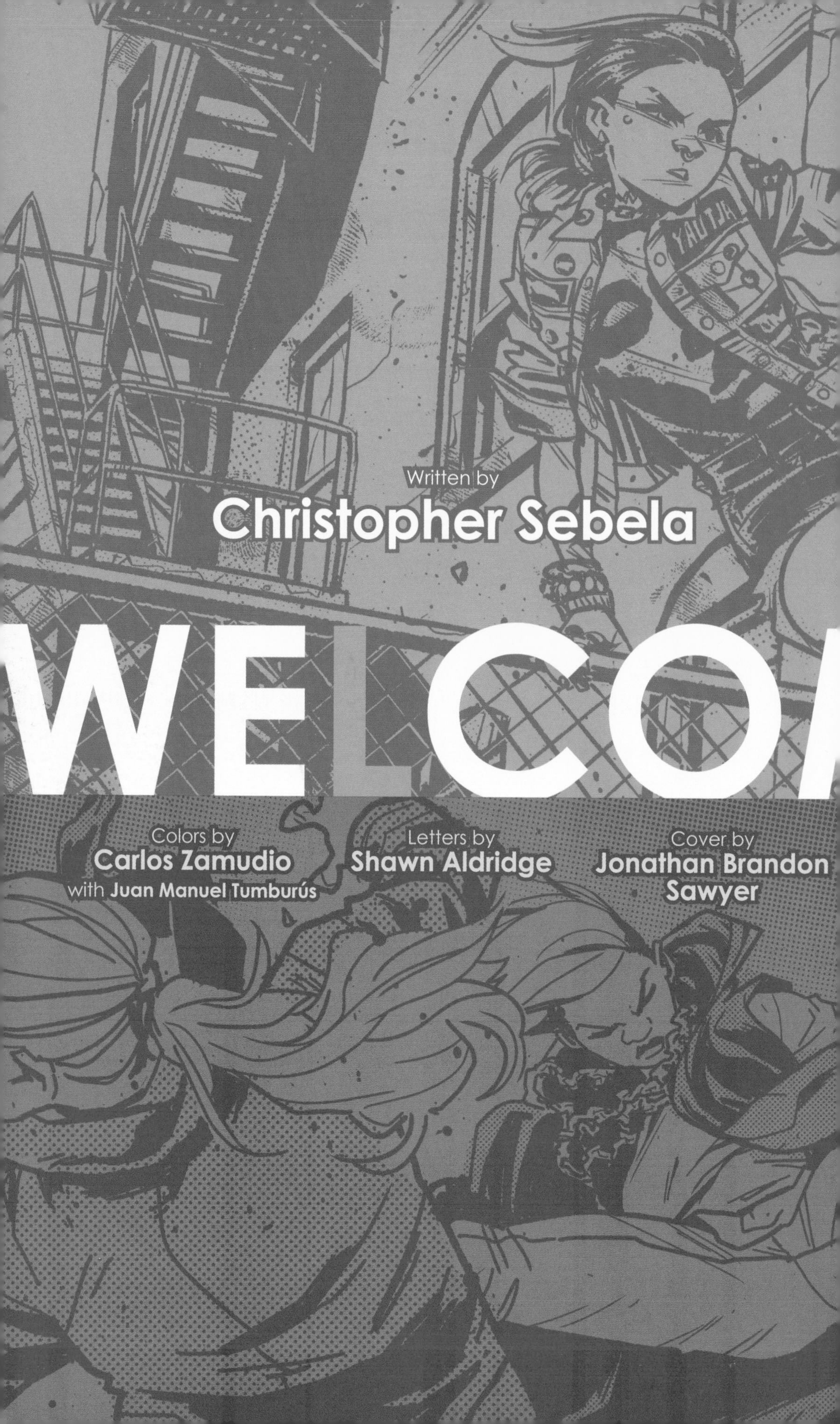

Written by

Christopher Sebela

WELCO

Colors by
Carlos Zamudio
with **Juan Manuel Tumburús**

Letters by
Shawn Aldridge

Cover by
Jonathan Brandon Sawyer

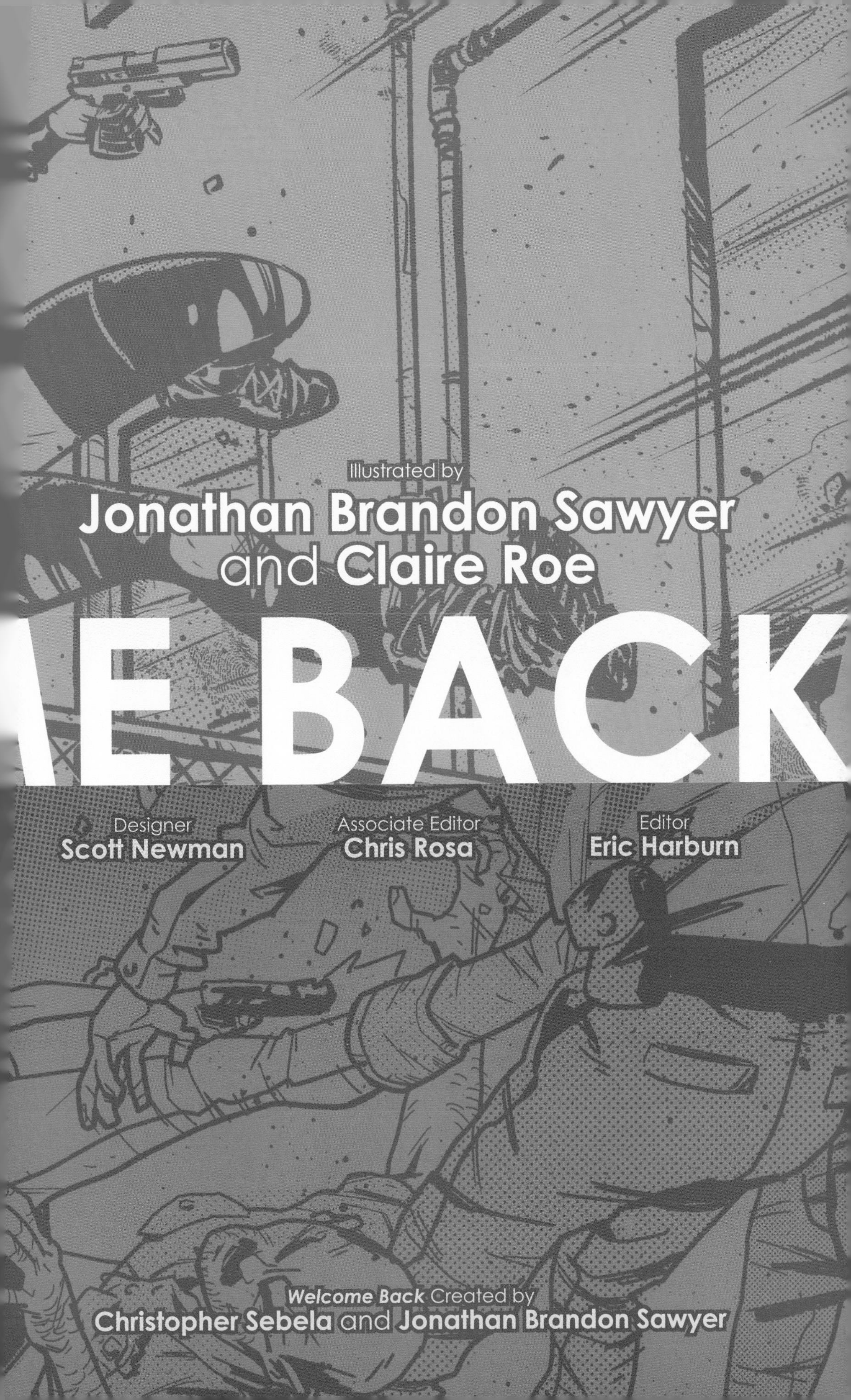

Illustrated by
Jonathan Brandon Sawyer
and **Claire Roe**

E BACK

Designer
Scott Newman

Associate Editor
Chris Rosa

Editor
Eric Harburn

Welcome Back Created by
Christopher Sebela and **Jonathan Brandon Sawyer**

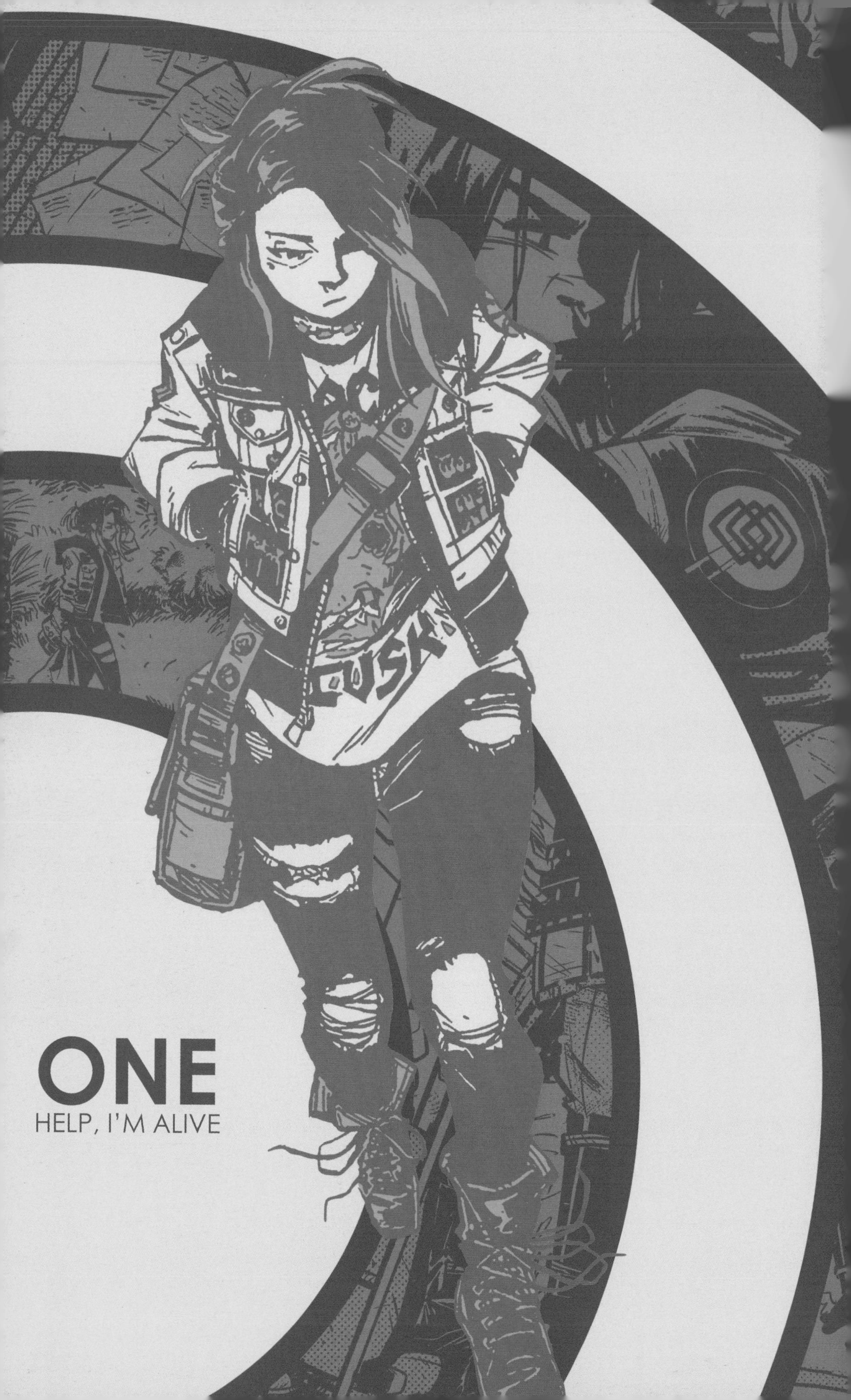

ONE
HELP, I'M ALIVE

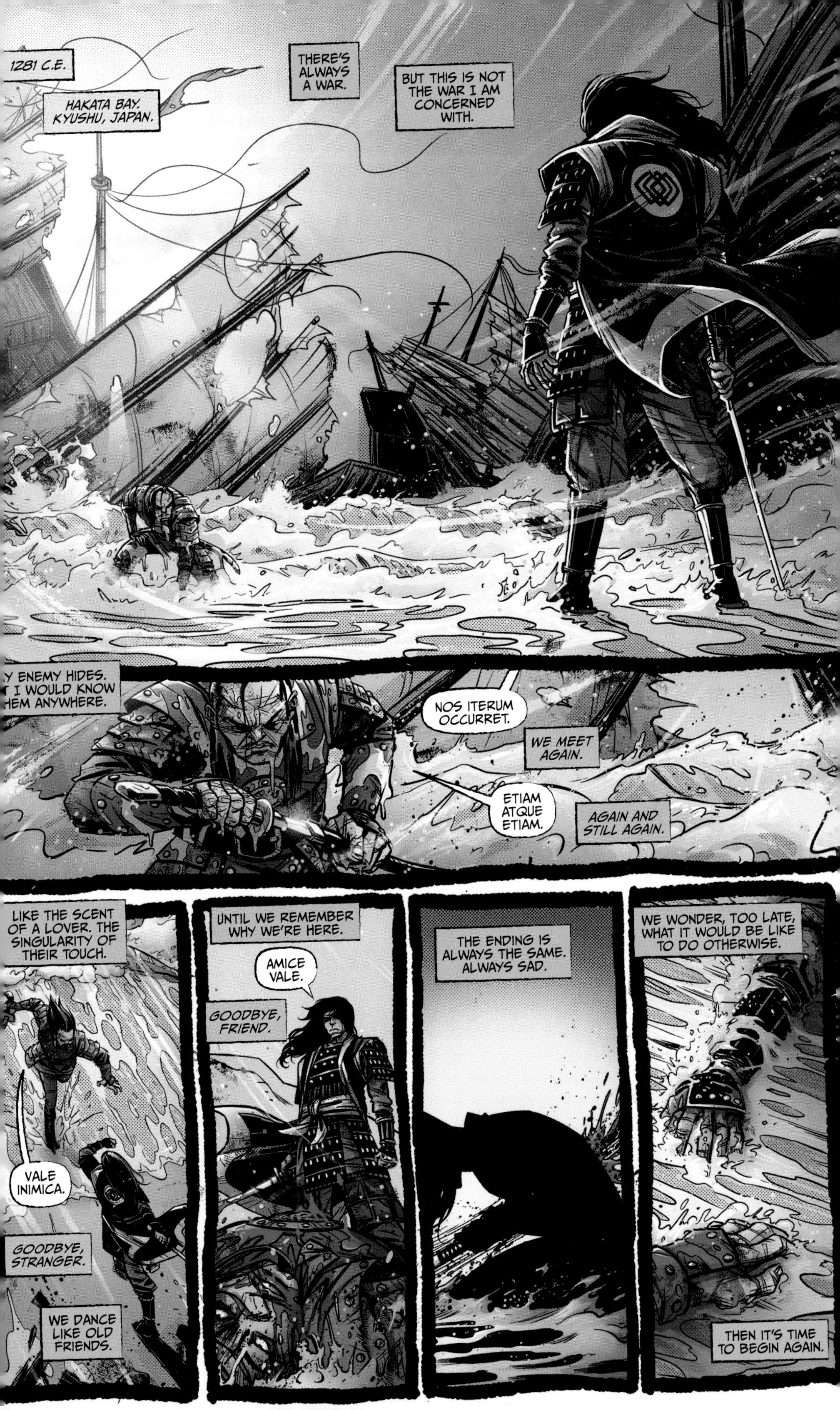
1281 C.E.
HAKATA BAY. KYUSHU, JAPAN.
THERE'S ALWAYS A WAR.
BUT THIS IS NOT THE WAR I AM CONCERNED WITH.
Y ENEMY HIDES. I WOULD KNOW HEM ANYWHERE.
NOS ITERUM OCCURRET.
WE MEET AGAIN.
ETIAM ATQUE ETIAM.
AGAIN AND STILL AGAIN.
LIKE THE SCENT OF A LOVER. THE SINGULARITY OF THEIR TOUCH.
VALE INIMICA.
GOODBYE, STRANGER.
WE DANCE LIKE OLD FRIENDS.
UNTIL WE REMEMBER WHY WE'RE HERE.
AMICE VALE.
GOODBYE, FRIEND.
THE ENDING IS ALWAYS THE SAME. ALWAYS SAD.
WE WONDER, TOO LATE, WHAT IT WOULD BE LIKE TO DO OTHERWISE.
THEN IT'S TIME TO BEGIN AGAIN.

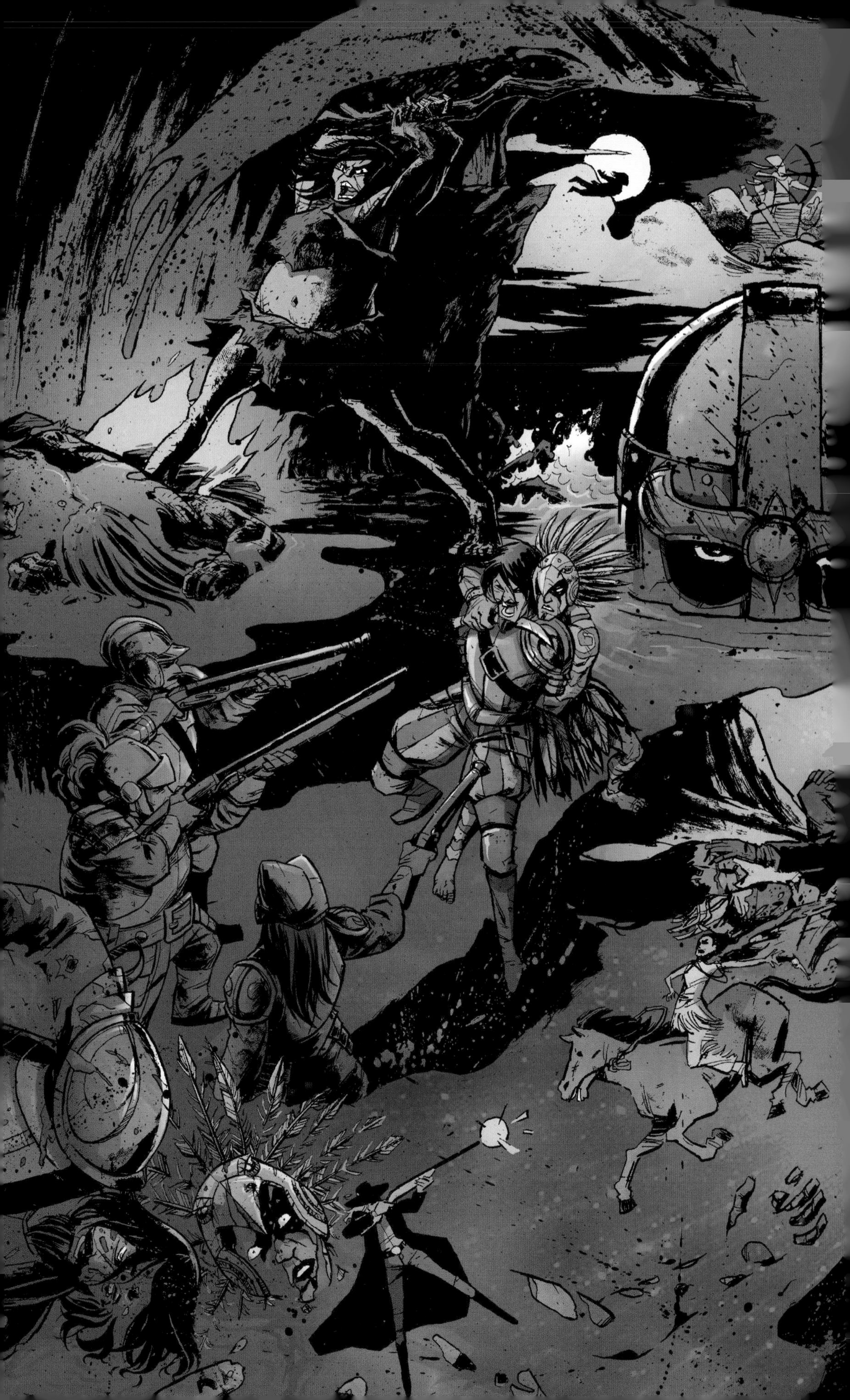

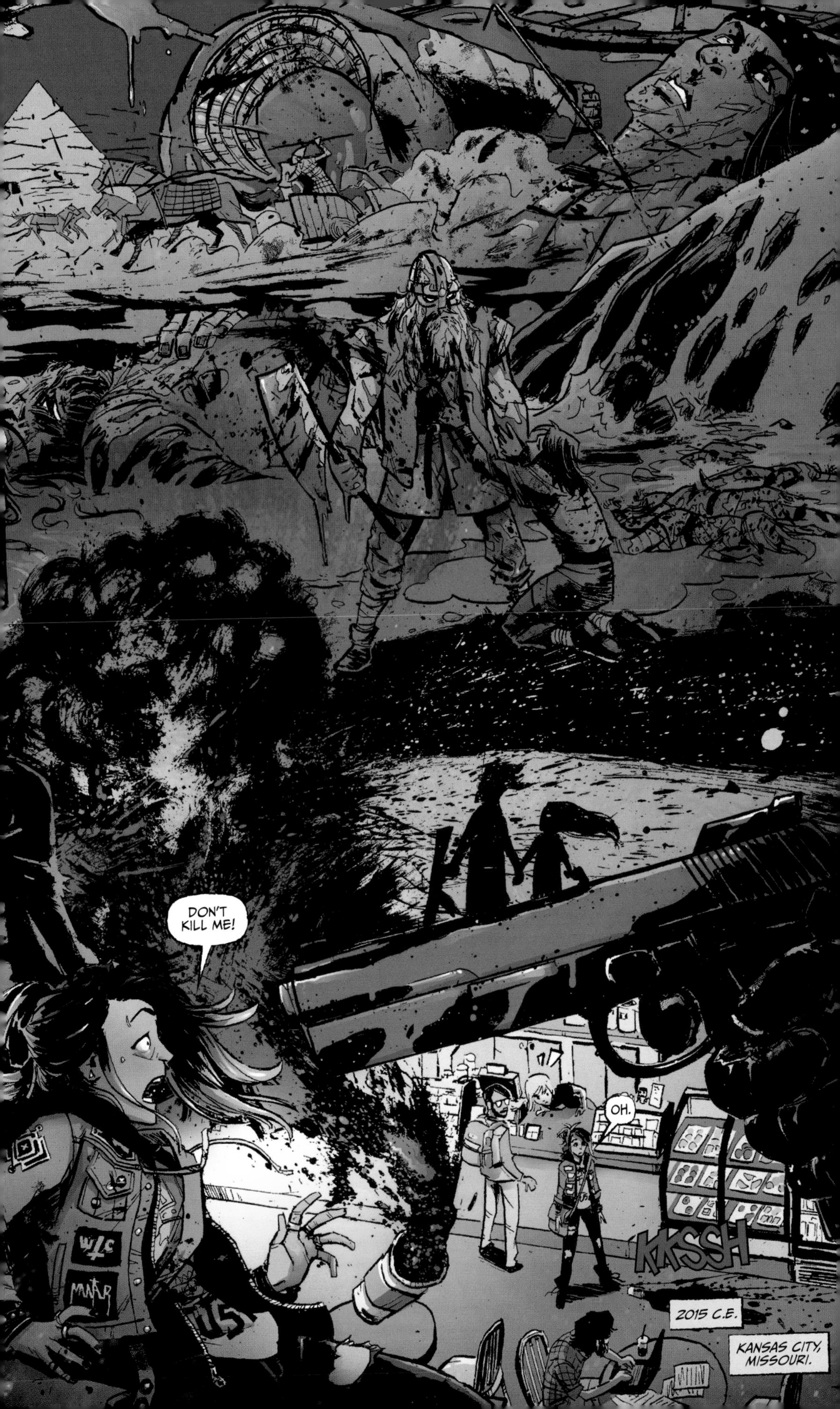
DON'T KILL ME!
OH.
KKSSH
2015 C.E.
KANSAS CITY, MISSOURI.

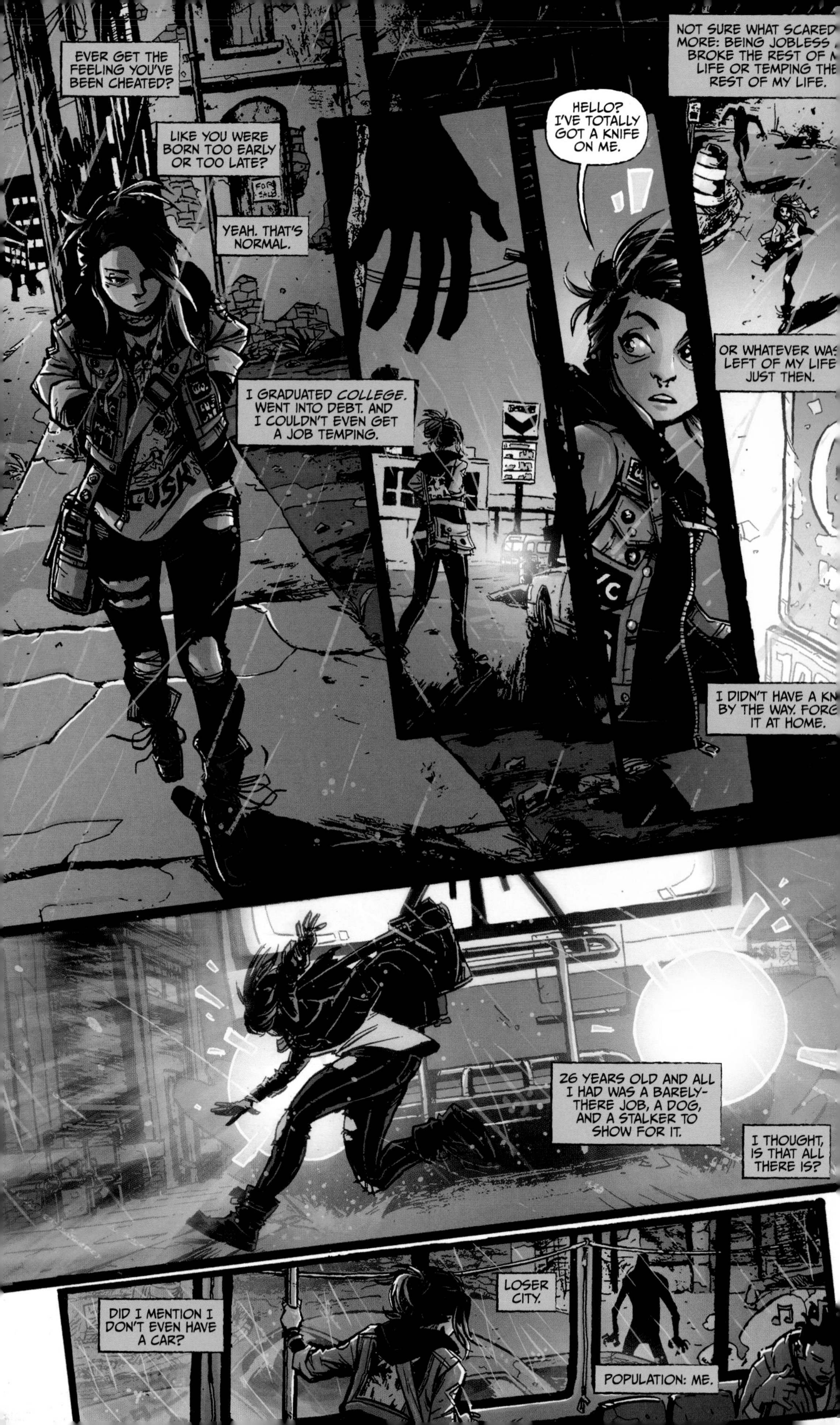
EVER GET THE FEELING YOU'VE BEEN CHEATED?
LIKE YOU WERE BORN TOO EARLY OR TOO LATE?
YEAH. THAT'S NORMAL.
I GRADUATED *COLLEGE*. WENT INTO DEBT. AND I COULDN'T EVEN GET A JOB TEMPING.
HELLO? I'VE TOTALLY GOT A KNIFE ON ME.
NOT SURE WHAT SCARED MORE: BEING JOBLESS BROKE THE REST OF LIFE OR TEMPING THE REST OF MY LIFE.
OR WHATEVER WAS LEFT OF MY LIFE JUST THEN.
I DIDN'T HAVE A KN BY THE WAY. FORG IT AT HOME.
26 YEARS OLD AND ALL I HAD WAS A BARELY-THERE JOB, A DOG, AND A STALKER TO SHOW FOR IT.
I THOUGHT, IS THAT ALL THERE IS?
DID I MENTION I DON'T EVEN HAVE A CAR?
LOSER CITY.
POPULATION: ME.

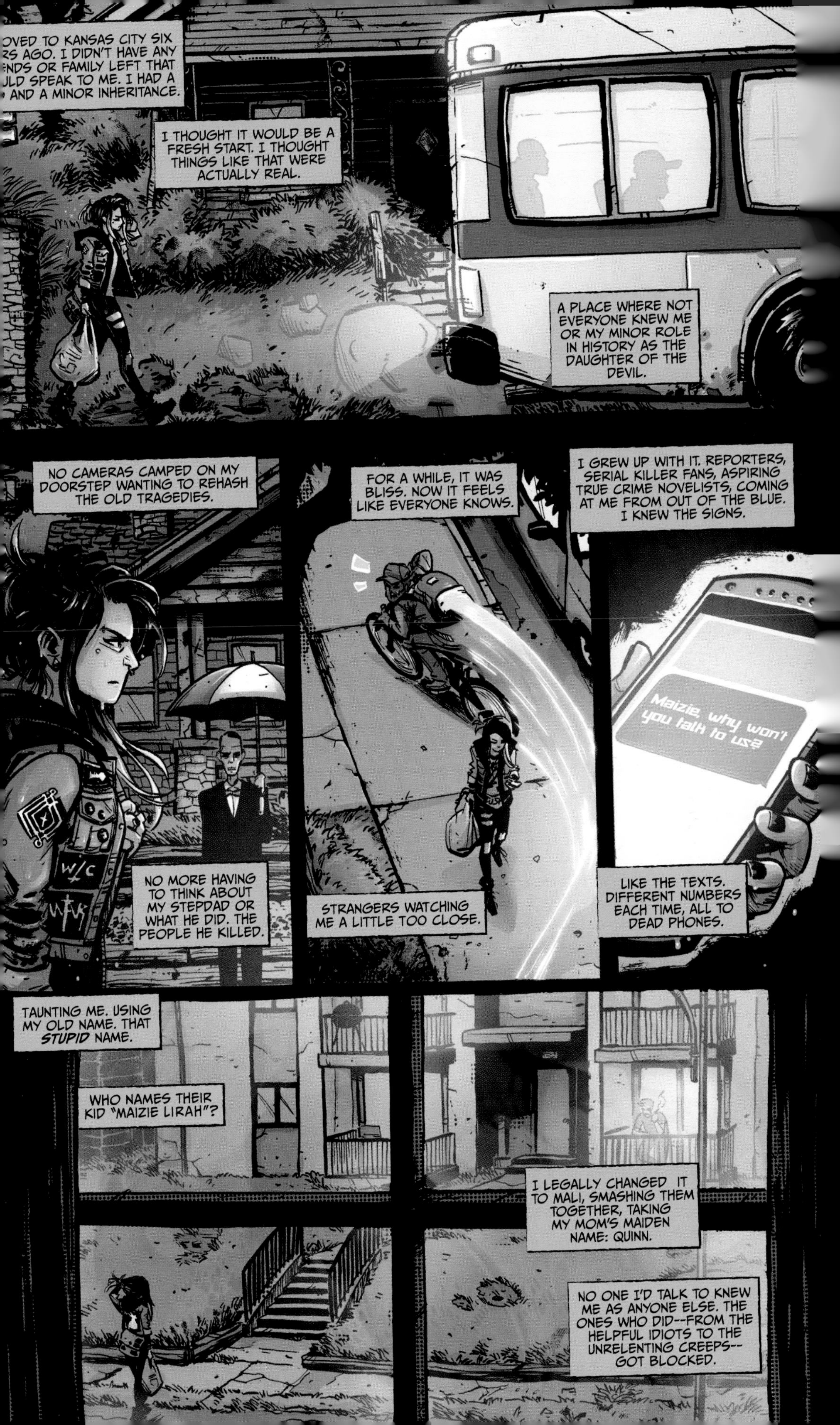
OVED TO KANSAS CITY SIX
RS AGO. I DIDN'T HAVE ANY
ENDS OR FAMILY LEFT THAT
ULD SPEAK TO ME. I HAD A
AND A MINOR INHERITANCE.
I THOUGHT IT WOULD BE A FRESH START. I THOUGHT THINGS LIKE THAT WERE ACTUALLY REAL.
A PLACE WHERE NOT EVERYONE KNEW ME OR MY MINOR ROLE IN HISTORY AS THE DAUGHTER OF THE DEVIL.
NO CAMERAS CAMPED ON MY DOORSTEP WANTING TO REHASH THE OLD TRAGEDIES.
NO MORE HAVING TO THINK ABOUT MY STEPDAD OR WHAT HE DID. THE PEOPLE HE KILLED.
FOR A WHILE, IT WAS BLISS. NOW IT FEELS LIKE EVERYONE KNOWS.
STRANGERS WATCHING ME A LITTLE TOO CLOSE.
I GREW UP WITH IT. REPORTERS, SERIAL KILLER FANS, ASPIRING TRUE CRIME NOVELISTS, COMING AT ME FROM OUT OF THE BLUE. I KNEW THE SIGNS.
Maizie, why won't you talk to us?
LIKE THE TEXTS. DIFFERENT NUMBERS EACH TIME, ALL TO DEAD PHONES.
TAUNTING ME. USING MY OLD NAME. THAT *STUPID* NAME.
WHO NAMES THEIR KID "MAIZIE LIRAH"?
I LEGALLY CHANGED IT TO MALI, SMASHING THEM TOGETHER, TAKING MY MOM'S MAIDEN NAME: QUINN.
NO ONE I'D TALK TO KNEW ME AS ANYONE ELSE. THE ONES WHO DID--FROM THE HELPFUL IDIOTS TO THE UNRELENTING CREEPS--GOT BLOCKED.

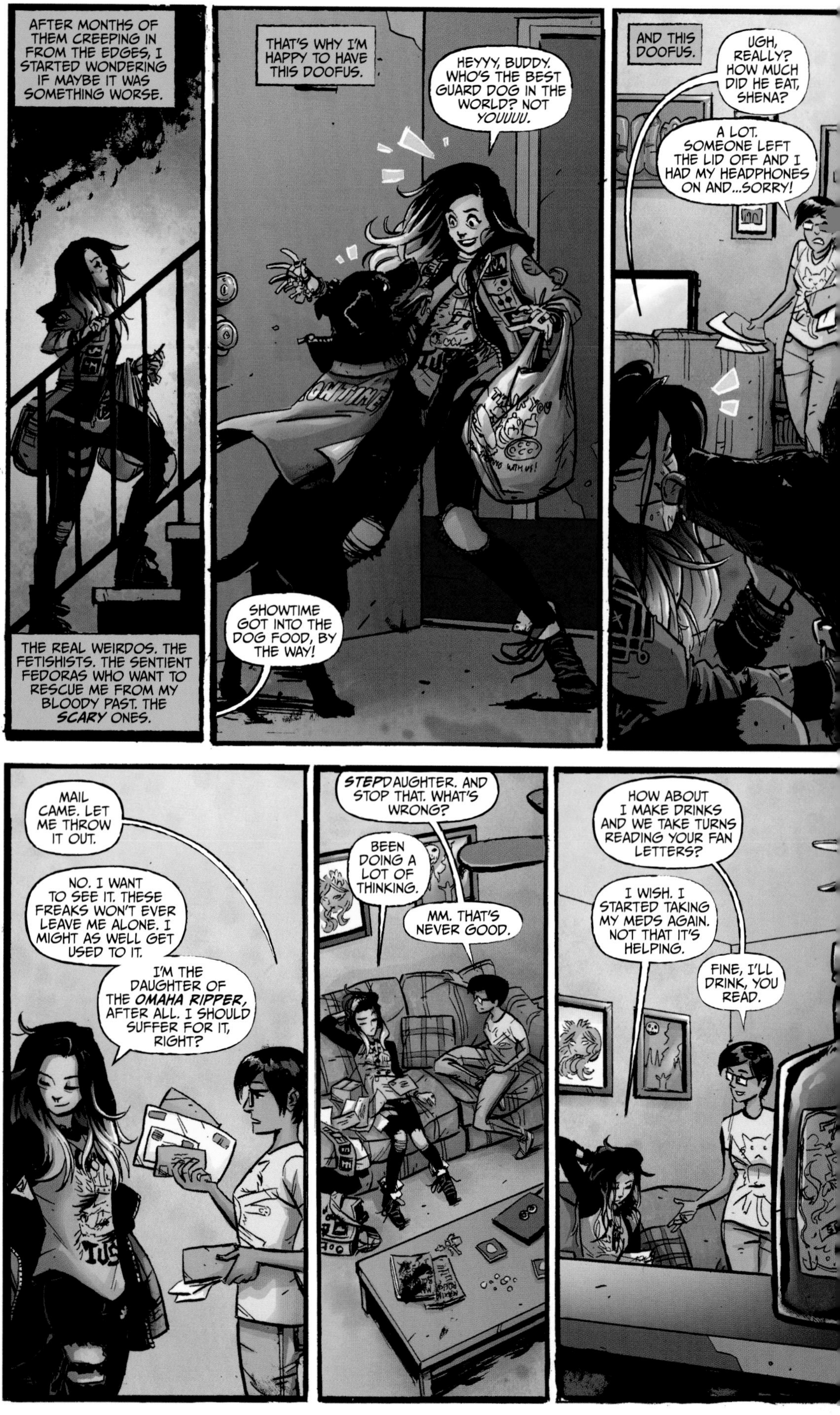
AFTER MONTHS OF THEM CREEPING IN FROM THE EDGES, I STARTED WONDERING IF MAYBE IT WAS SOMETHING WORSE.
THE REAL WEIRDOS. THE FETISHISTS. THE SENTIENT FEDORAS WHO WANT TO RESCUE ME FROM MY BLOODY PAST. THE SCARY ONES.
THAT'S WHY I'M HAPPY TO HAVE THIS DOOFUS.
HEYYY, BUDDY. WHO'S THE BEST GUARD DOG IN THE WORLD? NOT YOUUUU.
SHOWTIME GOT INTO THE DOG FOOD, BY THE WAY!
AND THIS DOOFUS.
UGH, REALLY? HOW MUCH DID HE EAT, SHENA?
A LOT. SOMEONE LEFT THE LID OFF AND I HAD MY HEADPHONES ON AND...SORRY!
MAIL CAME. LET ME THROW IT OUT.
NO. I WANT TO SEE IT. THESE FREAKS WON'T EVER LEAVE ME ALONE. I MIGHT AS WELL GET USED TO IT.
I'M THE DAUGHTER OF THE OMAHA RIPPER, AFTER ALL. I SHOULD SUFFER FOR IT, RIGHT?
STEPDAUGHTER. AND STOP THAT. WHAT'S WRONG?
BEEN DOING A LOT OF THINKING.
MM. THAT'S NEVER GOOD.
HOW ABOUT I MAKE DRINKS AND WE TAKE TURNS READING YOUR FAN LETTERS?
I WISH. I STARTED TAKING MY MEDS AGAIN. NOT THAT IT'S HELPING.
FINE, I'LL DRINK, YOU READ.

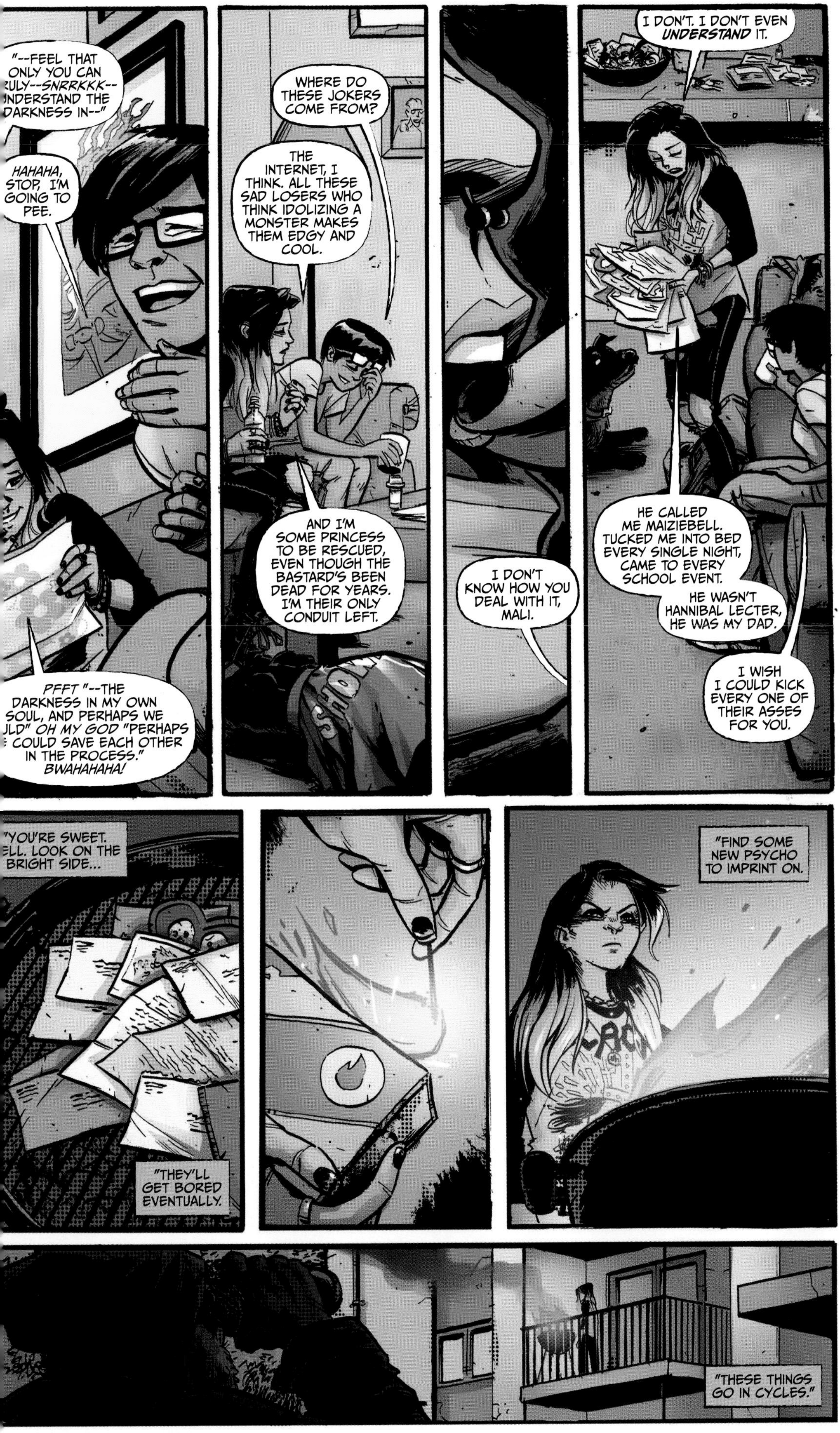
"--FEEL THAT ONLY YOU CAN RULY--SNRRKKK-- UNDERSTAND THE DARKNESS IN--"
HAHAHA, STOP, I'M GOING TO PEE.
PFFT "--THE DARKNESS IN MY OWN SOUL, AND PERHAPS WE ULD" OH MY GOD "PERHAPS E COULD SAVE EACH OTHER IN THE PROCESS." BWAHAHAHA!
WHERE DO THESE JOKERS COME FROM?
THE INTERNET, I THINK. ALL THESE SAD LOSERS WHO THINK IDOLIZING A MONSTER MAKES THEM EDGY AND COOL.
AND I'M SOME PRINCESS TO BE RESCUED, EVEN THOUGH THE BASTARD'S BEEN DEAD FOR YEARS. I'M THEIR ONLY CONDUIT LEFT.
I DON'T KNOW HOW YOU DEAL WITH IT, MALI.
I DON'T. I DON'T EVEN UNDERSTAND IT.
HE CALLED ME MAIZIEBELL. TUCKED ME INTO BED EVERY SINGLE NIGHT, CAME TO EVERY SCHOOL EVENT.
HE WASN'T HANNIBAL LECTER, HE WAS MY DAD.
I WISH I COULD KICK EVERY ONE OF THEIR ASSES FOR YOU.
"YOU'RE SWEET. ELL. LOOK ON THE BRIGHT SIDE...
"THEY'LL GET BORED EVENTUALLY.
"FIND SOME NEW PSYCHO TO IMPRINT ON.
"THESE THINGS GO IN CYCLES."

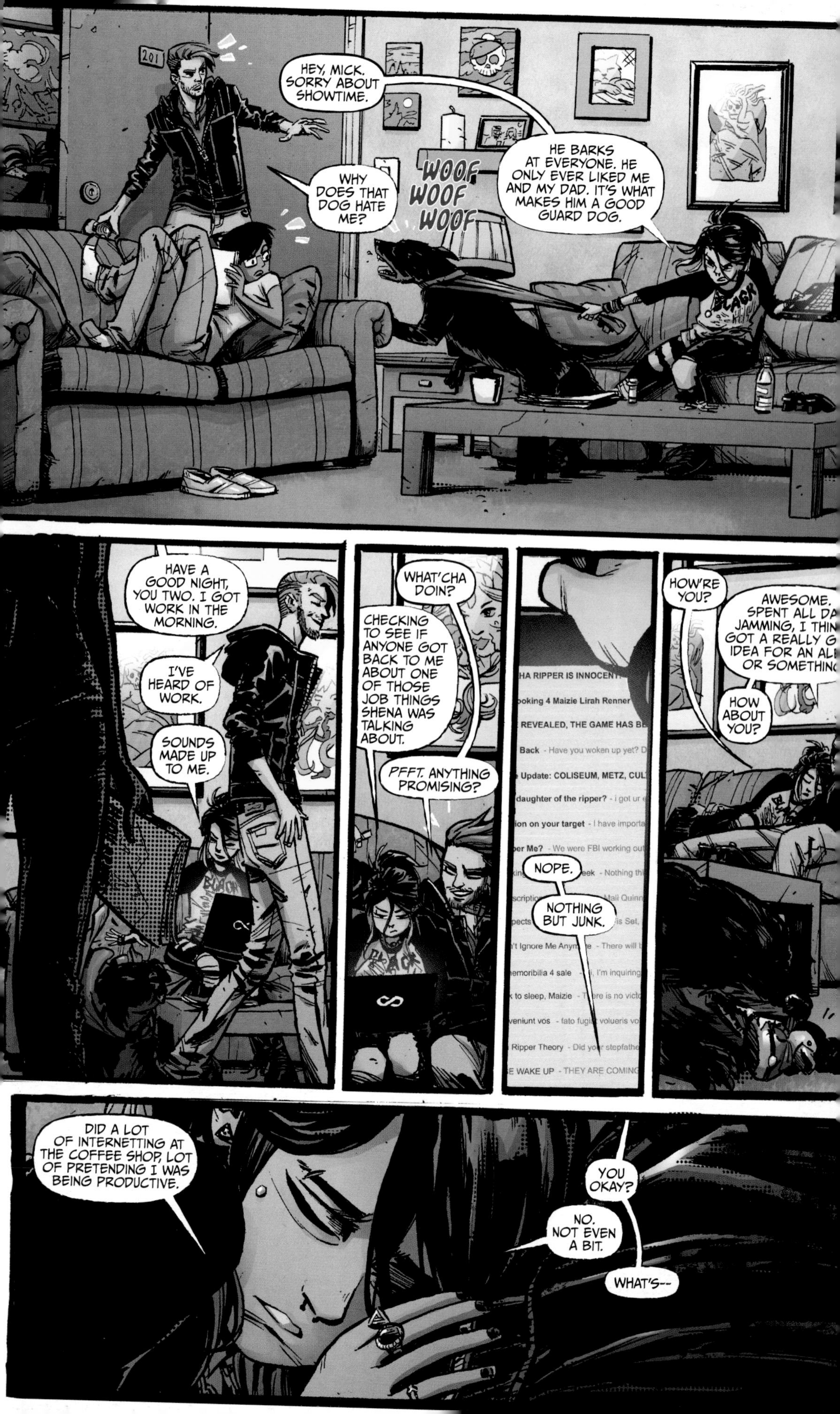
201
HEY, MICK. SORRY ABOUT SHOWTIME.
WHY DOES THAT DOG HATE ME?
WOOF WOOF WOOF
HE BARKS AT EVERYONE. HE ONLY EVER LIKED ME AND MY DAD. IT'S WHAT MAKES HIM A GOOD GUARD DOG.
BLACK
HAVE A GOOD NIGHT, YOU TWO. I GOT WORK IN THE MORNING.
I'VE HEARD OF WORK.
SOUNDS MADE UP TO ME.
WHAT'CHA DOIN?
CHECKING TO SEE IF ANYONE GOT BACK TO ME ABOUT ONE OF THOSE JOB THINGS SHENA WAS TALKING ABOUT.
PFFT. ANYTHING PROMISING?
CHA RIPPER IS INNOCENT
ooking 4 Maizie Lirah Renner
REVEALED, THE GAME HAS BE
Back - Have you woken up yet? D
e Update: COLISEUM, METZ, CUL
daughter of the ripper? - i got ur e
ion on your target - I have importa
per Me? - We were FBI working out
eek - Nothing thi
scription
Mail Quinn
pects
is Set,
n't Ignore Me Anym
e - There will b
nemoribilia 4 sale
I'm inquiring
k to sleep, Maizie
ere is no victo
veniunt vos - fato fugiat volueris vo
Ripper Theory - Did your stepfathe
E WAKE UP - THEY ARE COMING
NOPE.
NOTHING BUT JUNK.
HOW'RE YOU?
AWESOME. SPENT ALL DA JAMMING, I THIN GOT A REALLY G IDEA FOR AN AL OR SOMETHIN
HOW ABOUT YOU?
DID A LOT OF INTERNETTING AT THE COFFEE SHOP, LOT OF PRETENDING I WAS BEING PRODUCTIVE.
YOU OKAY?
NO. NOT EVEN A BIT.
WHAT'S--

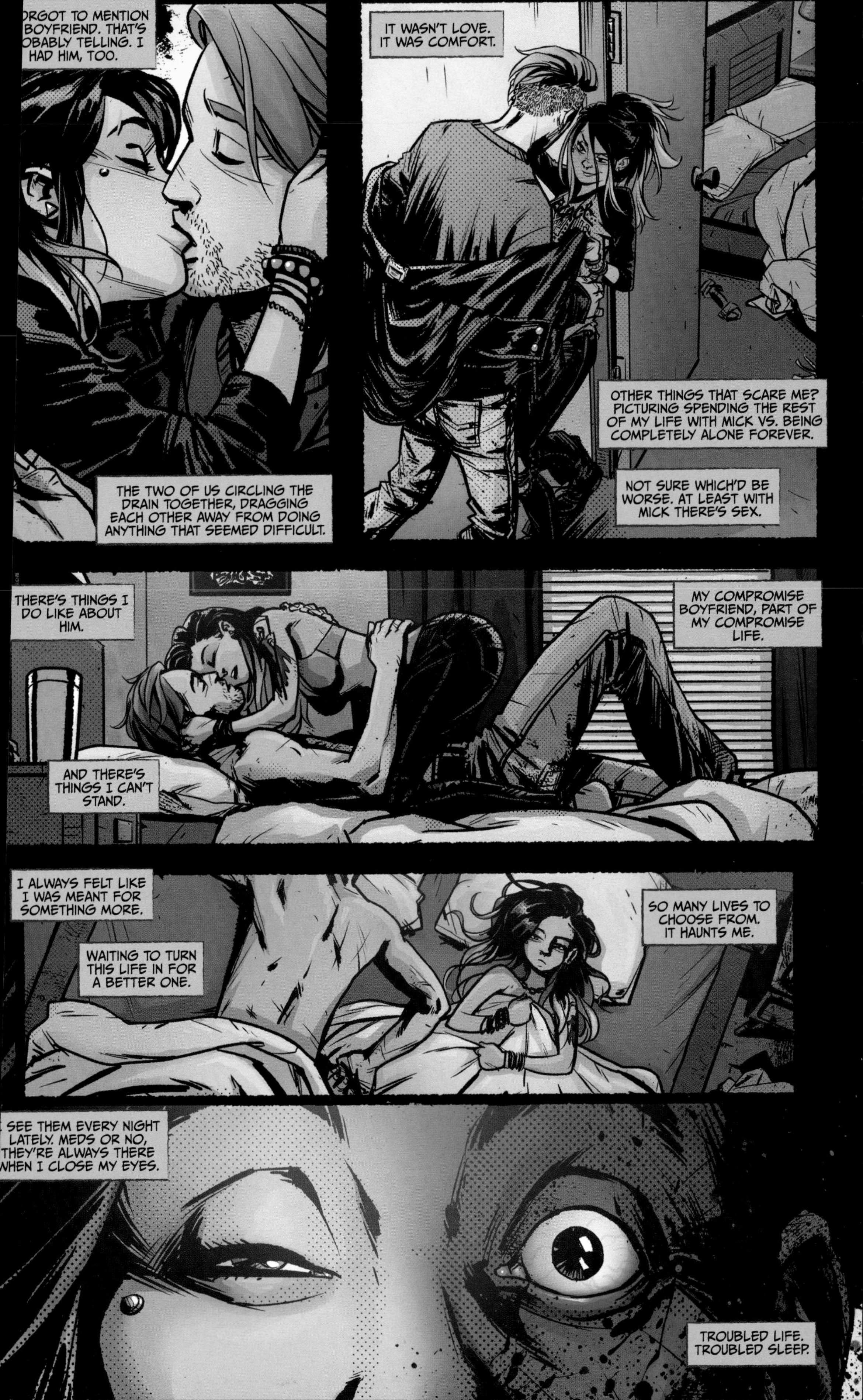
ORGOT TO MENTION BOYFRIEND. THAT'S OBABLY TELLING. I HAD HIM, TOO.
THE TWO OF US CIRCLING THE DRAIN TOGETHER, DRAGGING EACH OTHER AWAY FROM DOING ANYTHING THAT SEEMED DIFFICULT.
IT WASN'T LOVE. IT WAS COMFORT.
OTHER THINGS THAT SCARE ME? PICTURING SPENDING THE REST OF MY LIFE WITH MICK VS. BEING COMPLETELY ALONE FOREVER.
NOT SURE WHICH'D BE WORSE. AT LEAST WITH MICK THERE'S SEX.
THERE'S THINGS I DO LIKE ABOUT HIM.
AND THERE'S THINGS I CAN'T STAND.
MY COMPROMISE BOYFRIEND, PART OF MY COMPROMISE LIFE.
I ALWAYS FELT LIKE I WAS MEANT FOR SOMETHING MORE.
WAITING TO TURN THIS LIFE IN FOR A BETTER ONE.
SO MANY LIVES TO CHOOSE FROM. IT HAUNTS ME.
SEE THEM EVERY NIGHT LATELY. MEDS OR NO, THEY'RE ALWAYS THERE WHEN I CLOSE MY EYES.
TROUBLED LIFE. TROUBLED SLEEP.

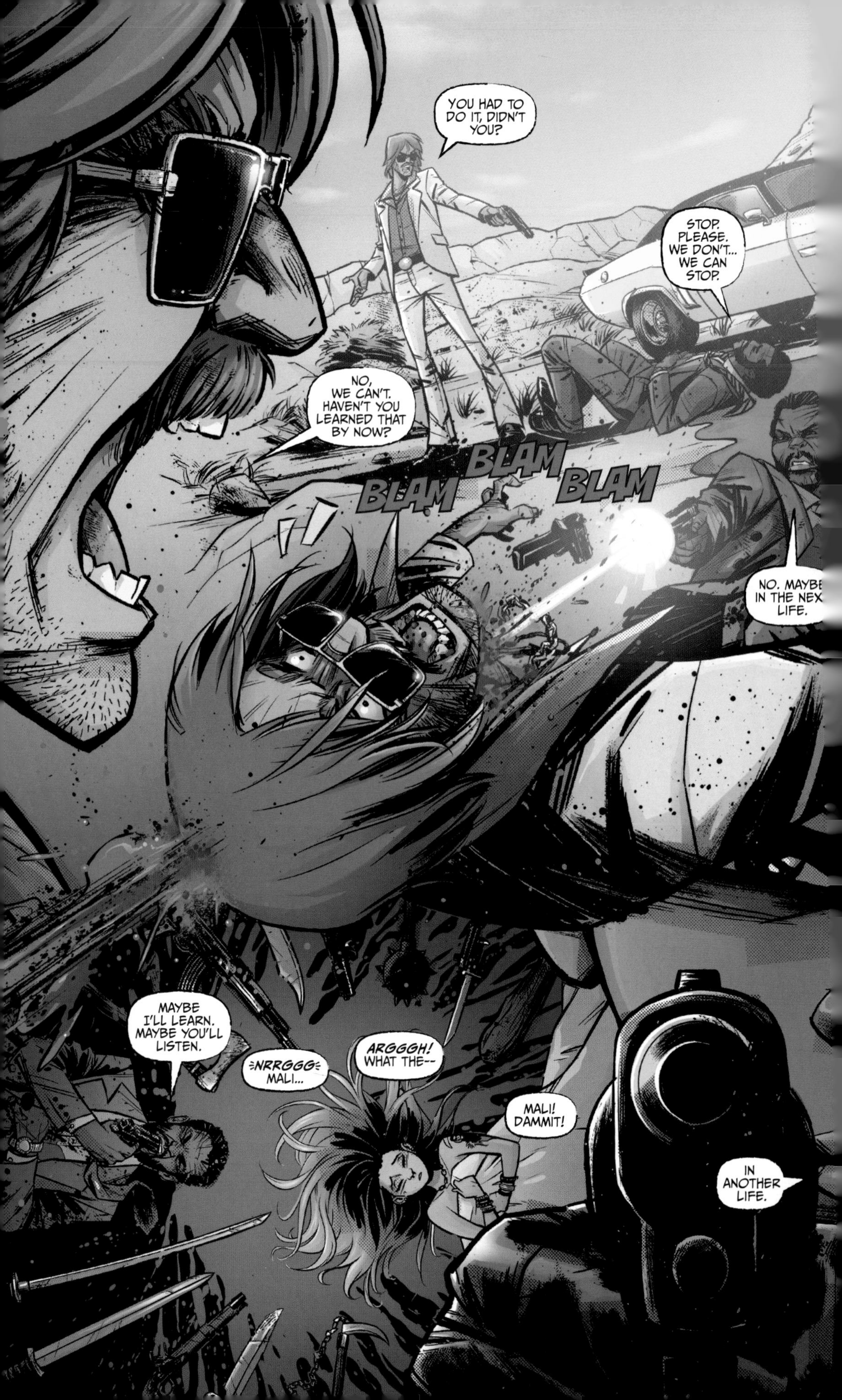
YOU HAD TO DO IT, DIDN'T YOU?
STOP. PLEASE. WE DON'T... WE CAN STOP.
NO, WE CAN'T. HAVEN'T YOU LEARNED THAT BY NOW?
BLAM BLAM BLAM BLAM
NO. MAYBE IN THE NEX LIFE.
MAYBE I'LL LEARN. MAYBE YOU'LL LISTEN.
NRRGGG MALI...
ARGGGH! WHAT THE--
MALI! DAMMIT!
IN ANOTHER LIFE.

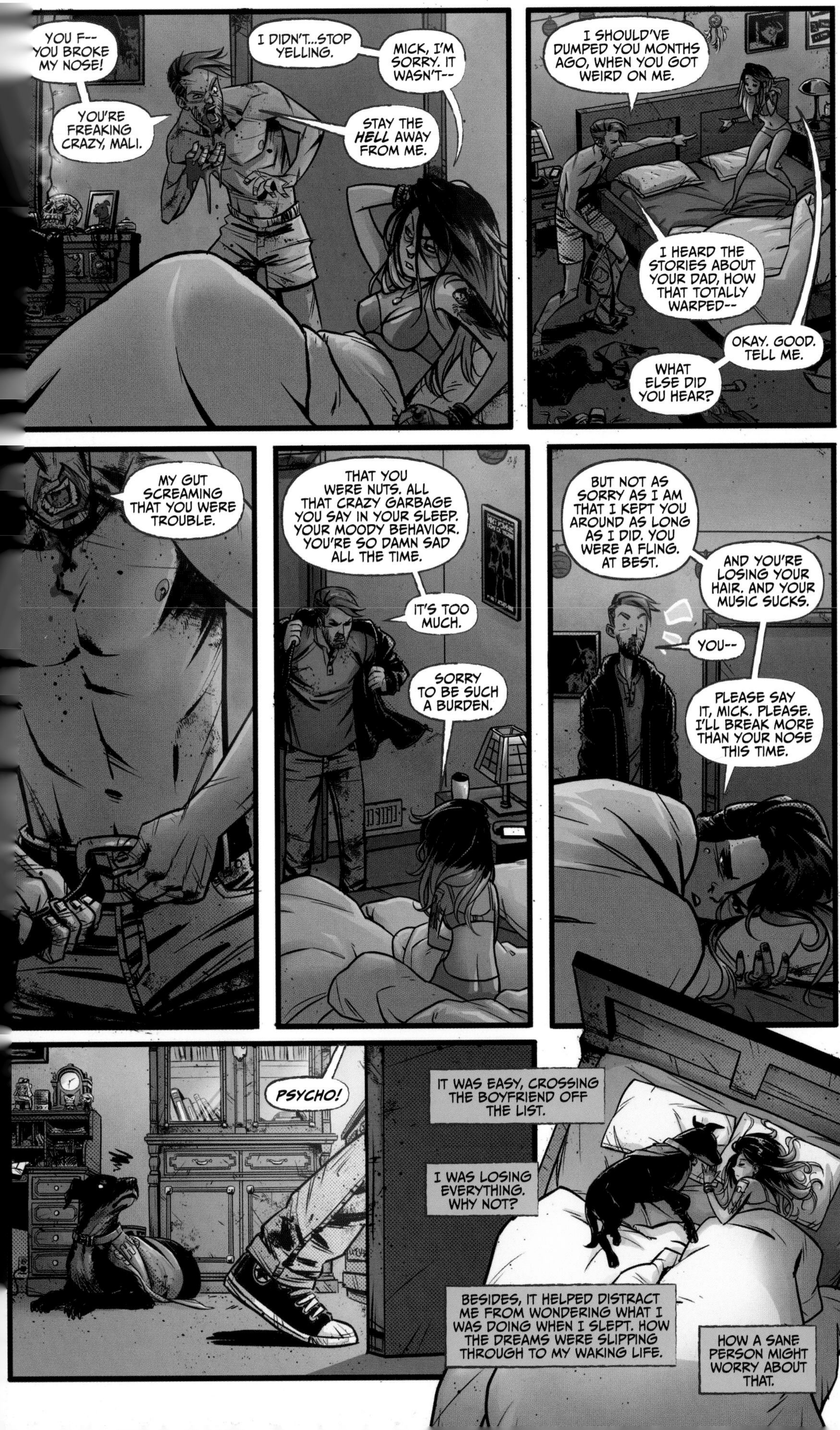
YOU F-- YOU BROKE MY NOSE!
YOU'RE FREAKING CRAZY, MALI.
I DIDN'T...STOP YELLING.
MICK, I'M SORRY. IT WASN'T--
STAY THE HELL AWAY FROM ME.
I SHOULD'VE DUMPED YOU MONTHS AGO, WHEN YOU GOT WEIRD ON ME.
I HEARD THE STORIES ABOUT YOUR DAD, HOW THAT TOTALLY WARPED--
OKAY. GOOD. TELL ME.
WHAT ELSE DID YOU HEAR?
MY GUT SCREAMING THAT YOU WERE TROUBLE.
THAT YOU WERE NUTS. ALL THAT CRAZY GARBAGE YOU SAY IN YOUR SLEEP. YOUR MOODY BEHAVIOR. YOU'RE SO DAMN SAD ALL THE TIME.
IT'S TOO MUCH.
SORRY TO BE SUCH A BURDEN.
BUT NOT AS SORRY AS I AM THAT I KEPT YOU AROUND AS LONG AS I DID. YOU WERE A FLING. AT BEST.
AND YOU'RE LOSING YOUR HAIR. AND YOUR MUSIC SUCKS.
YOU--
PLEASE SAY IT, MICK. PLEASE. I'LL BREAK MORE THAN YOUR NOSE THIS TIME.
PSYCHO!
IT WAS EASY, CROSSING THE BOYFRIEND OFF THE LIST.
I WAS LOSING EVERYTHING. WHY NOT?
BESIDES, IT HELPED DISTRACT ME FROM WONDERING WHAT I WAS DOING WHEN I SLEPT. HOW THE DREAMS WERE SLIPPING THROUGH TO MY WAKING LIFE.
HOW A SANE PERSON MIGHT WORRY ABOUT THAT.

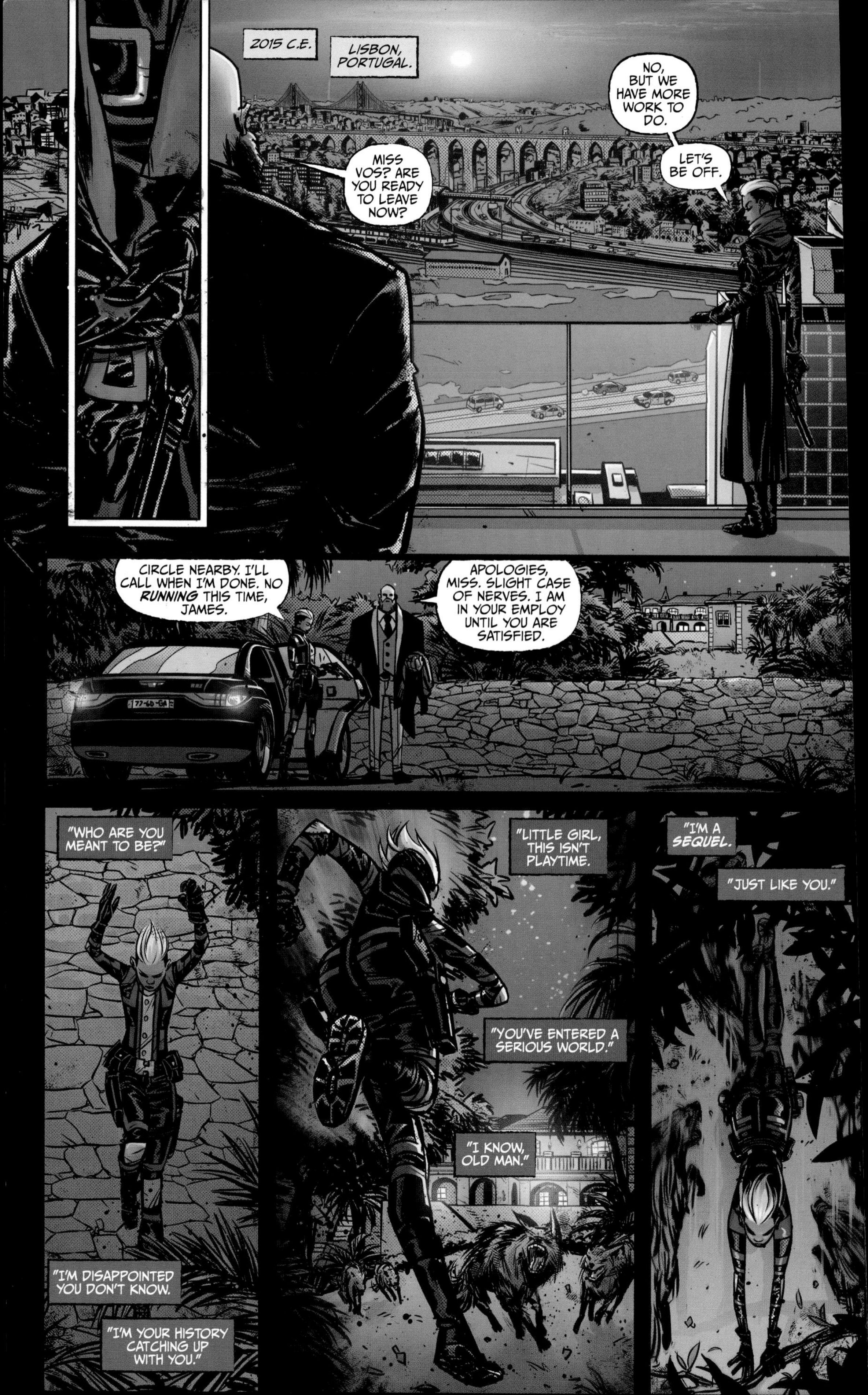
2015 C.E.
LISBON, PORTUGAL.
MISS VOS? ARE YOU READY TO LEAVE NOW?
NO, BUT WE HAVE MORE WORK TO DO.
LET'S BE OFF.
CIRCLE NEARBY. I'LL CALL WHEN I'M DONE. NO *RUNNING* THIS TIME, JAMES.
APOLOGIES, MISS. SLIGHT CASE OF NERVES. I AM IN YOUR EMPLOY UNTIL YOU ARE SATISFIED.
"WHO ARE YOU MEANT TO BE?"
"I'M DISAPPOINTED YOU DON'T KNOW.
"I'M YOUR HISTORY CATCHING UP WITH YOU."
"LITTLE GIRL, THIS ISN'T PLAYTIME.
"YOU'VE ENTERED A SERIOUS WORLD."
"I KNOW, OLD MAN."
"I'M A *SEQUEL*.
"JUST LIKE YOU."

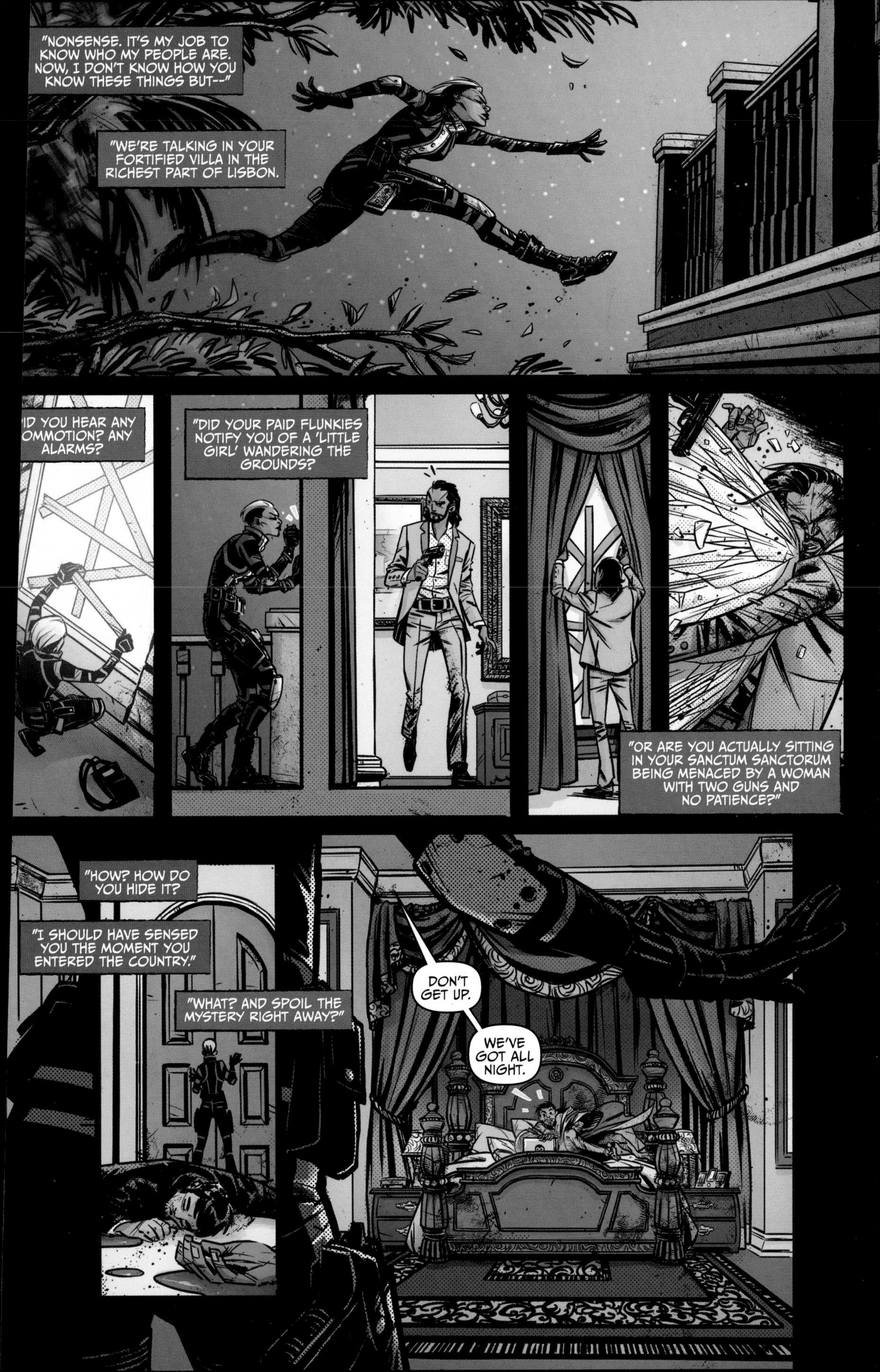
"NONSENSE. IT'S MY JOB TO KNOW WHO MY PEOPLE ARE. NOW, I DON'T KNOW HOW YOU KNOW THESE THINGS BUT--"
"WE'RE TALKING IN YOUR FORTIFIED VILLA IN THE RICHEST PART OF LISBON.
ID YOU HEAR ANY OMMOTION? ANY ALARMS?
"DID YOUR PAID FLUNKIES NOTIFY YOU OF A 'LITTLE GIRL' WANDERING THE GROUNDS?
"OR ARE YOU ACTUALLY SITTING IN YOUR SANCTUM SANCTORUM BEING MENACED BY A WOMAN WITH TWO GUNS AND NO PATIENCE?"
"HOW? HOW DO YOU HIDE IT?
"I SHOULD HAVE SENSED YOU THE MOMENT YOU ENTERED THE COUNTRY."
"WHAT? AND SPOIL THE MYSTERY RIGHT AWAY?"
DON'T GET UP.
WE'VE GOT ALL NIGHT.

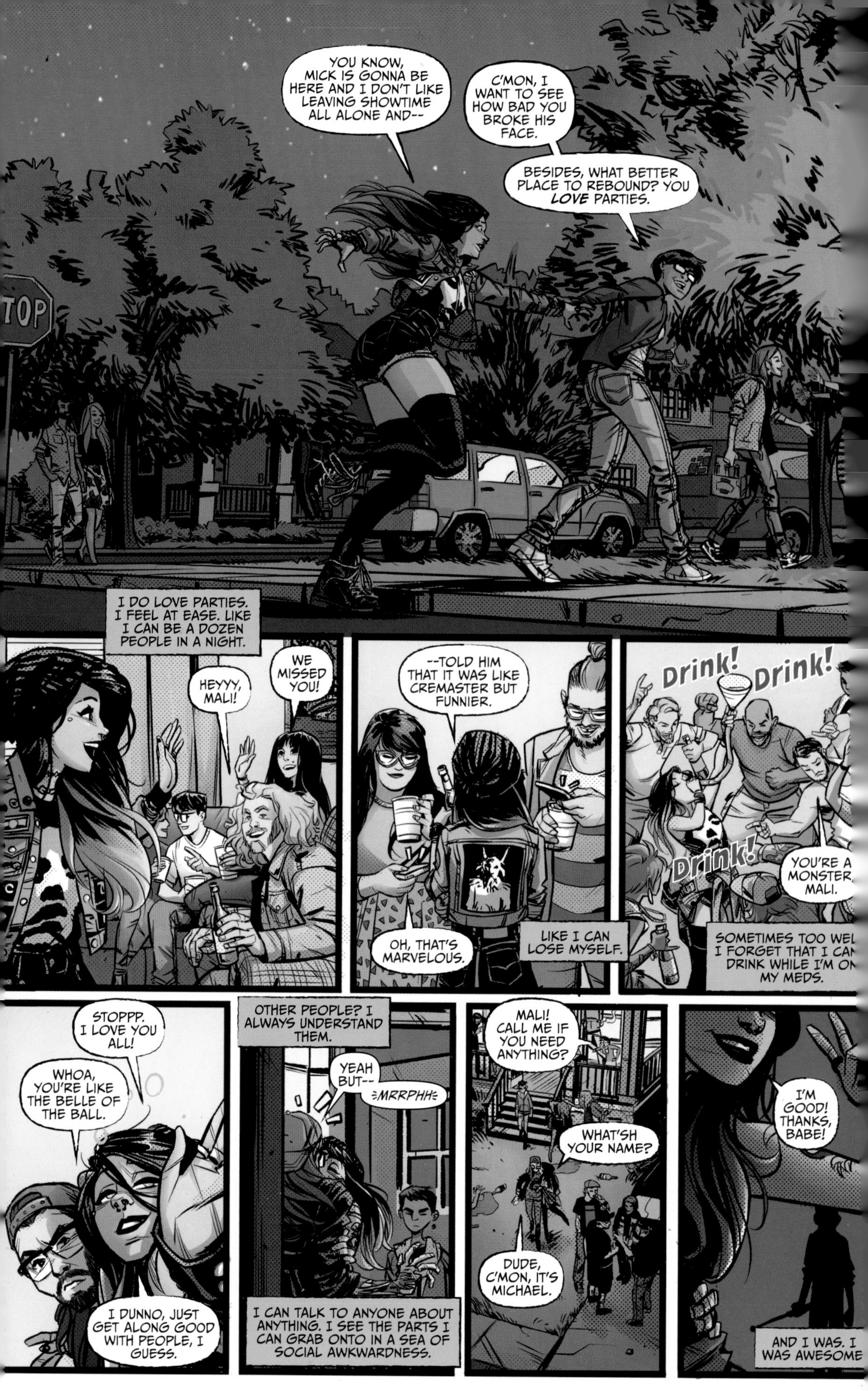
YOU KNOW, MICK IS GONNA BE HERE AND I DON'T LIKE LEAVING SHOWTIME ALL ALONE AND--
C'MON, I WANT TO SEE HOW BAD YOU BROKE HIS FACE.
BESIDES, WHAT BETTER PLACE TO REBOUND? YOU *LOVE* PARTIES.
TOP
I DO LOVE PARTIES. I FEEL AT EASE. LIKE I CAN BE A DOZEN PEOPLE IN A NIGHT.
HEYYY, MALI!
WE MISSED YOU!
--TOLD HIM THAT IT WAS LIKE CREMASTER BUT FUNNIER.
OH, THAT'S MARVELOUS.
LIKE I CAN LOSE MYSELF.
Drink!
Drink!
Drink!
YOU'RE A MONSTER, MALI.
SOMETIMES TOO WEL
I FORGET THAT I CAN
DRINK WHILE I'M ON MY MEDS.
STOPPP. I LOVE YOU ALL!
WHOA, YOU'RE LIKE THE BELLE OF THE BALL.
I DUNNO, JUST GET ALONG GOOD WITH PEOPLE, I GUESS.
OTHER PEOPLE? I ALWAYS UNDERSTAND THEM.
YEAH BUT--
MRRPHH
I CAN TALK TO ANYONE ABOUT ANYTHING. I SEE THE PARTS I CAN GRAB ONTO IN A SEA OF SOCIAL AWKWARDNESS.
MALI! CALL ME IF YOU NEED ANYTHING?
WHAT'SH YOUR NAME?
DUDE, C'MON, IT'S MICHAEL.
I'M GOOD! THANKS, BABE!
AND I WAS. I WAS AWESOME

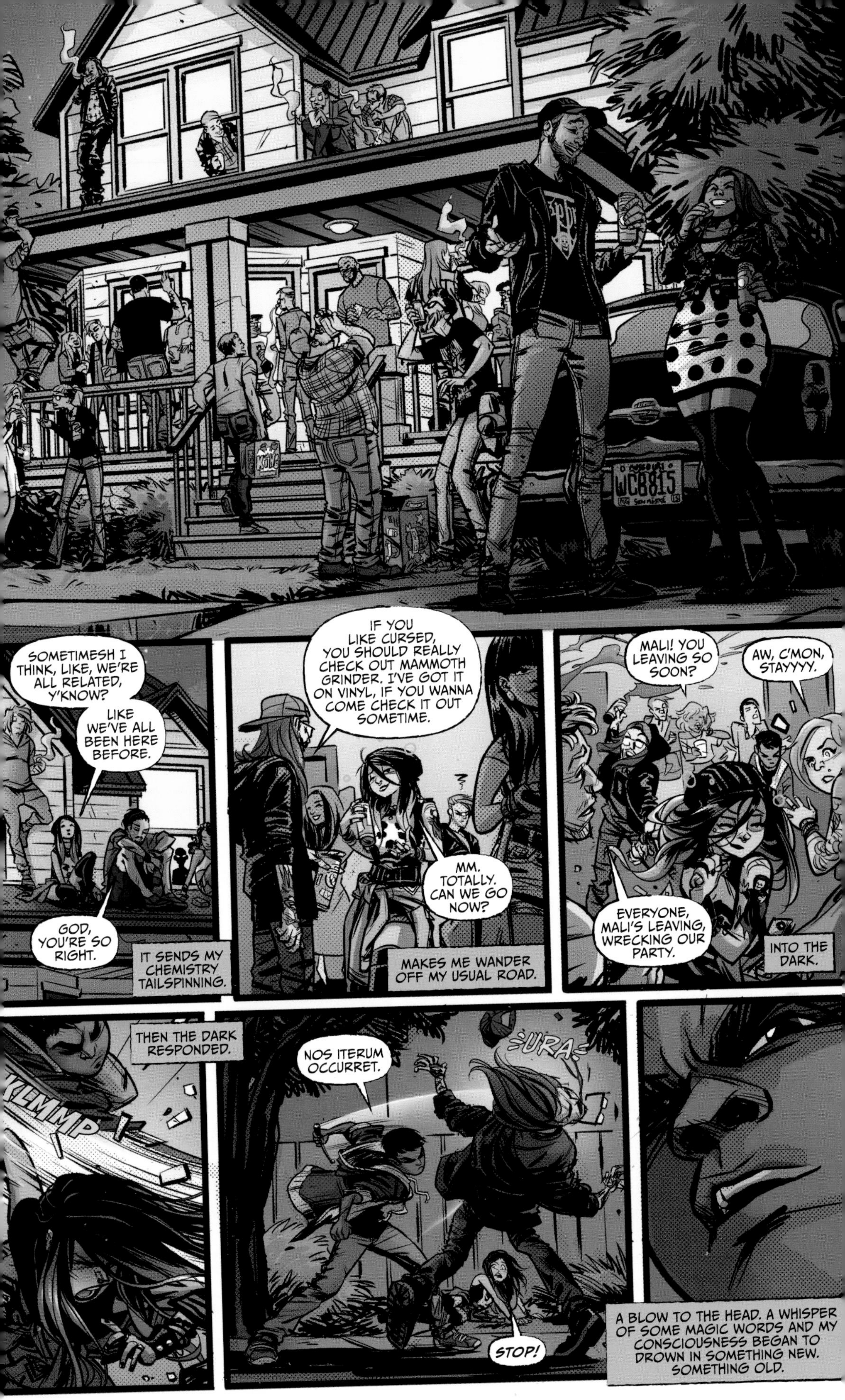
SOMETIMESH I THINK, LIKE, WE'RE ALL RELATED, Y'KNOW?
LIKE WE'VE ALL BEEN HERE BEFORE.
GOD, YOU'RE SO RIGHT.
IT SENDS MY CHEMISTRY TAILSPINNING.
IF YOU LIKE CURSED, YOU SHOULD REALLY CHECK OUT MAMMOTH GRINDER. I'VE GOT IT ON VINYL, IF YOU WANNA COME CHECK IT OUT SOMETIME.
MM. TOTALLY. CAN WE GO NOW?
MAKES ME WANDER OFF MY USUAL ROAD.
MALI! YOU LEAVING SO SOON?
AW, C'MON, STAYYYY.
EVERYONE, MALI'S LEAVING, WRECKING OUR PARTY.
INTO THE DARK.
THEN THE DARK RESPONDED.
KLMMP
NOS ITERUM OCCURRET.
URA
STOP!
A BLOW TO THE HEAD. A WHISPER OF SOME MAGIC WORDS AND MY CONSCIOUSNESS BEGAN TO DROWN IN SOMETHING NEW. SOMETHING OLD.

NICE SCIMITAR. NOW, THE CRUSADES? *THOSE* WERE FUN. THAT'S WHERE WE FIRST MET, Y'KNOW.

LOVELY. ARE YOU GOING TO BEGIN THE TORTURE ANYTIME SOON?

OH, COME NOW. I'M NOT GOING TO TORTURE YOU. WE BOTH KNOW THAT'S A WASTE OF TIME.

YOU'RE JUST GOING TO TELL ME WHAT I WANT TO KNOW SO I WON'T *KILL* YOU, MAKE YOU START ALL OVER, LOSE ALL YOUR PRECIOUS *STUFF*.

AND IF I WANT TO DIE?

YOU'D HAVE DONE IT YEARS AGO.

LEADERSHIP PERKS. YOU BARTER YOUR POSITION INTO LIVING A LONG, HEALTHY LIFE THE REST OF US CAN'T.

WHAT ARE YOU--STOP THAT THIS INSTANT.

THIS USED TO BE YOURS, RIGHT?

ALL OF THIS STUFF. YOU'RE TAKING IT WITH YOU WHEN YOU GO, AREN'T YOU?

THAT'S CHEATING. I LIKE IT.

YOU'RE STILL A SIMPLE CHILD. YOU DON'T KNOW WHAT IT MEANS TO BE ONE OF US.

YOU TREAT IT LIKE A GAME. LIKE A LARK.

YOU'RE RIGHT. I DO. BUT I KNOW WHAT THIS IS.

A NEVER-ENDING WAR.

AND I'M YOUR ENEM STORMING YC BEACHES.

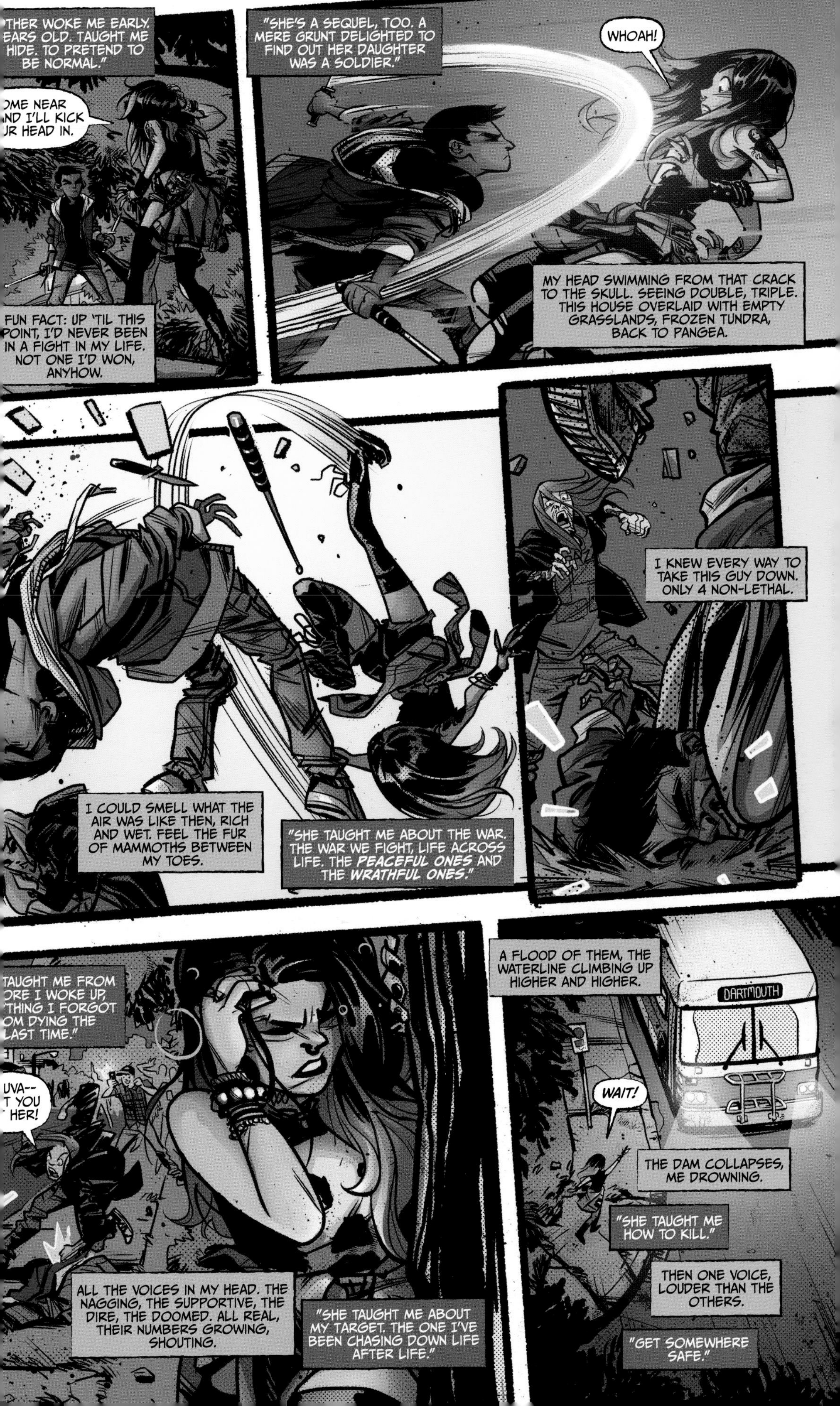

THER WOKE ME EARLY. EARS OLD. TAUGHT ME HIDE. TO PRETEND TO BE NORMAL."
OME NEAR ND I'LL KICK JR HEAD IN.
FUN FACT: UP 'TIL THIS POINT, I'D NEVER BEEN IN A FIGHT IN MY LIFE. NOT ONE I'D WON, ANYHOW.
"SHE'S A SEQUEL, TOO. A MERE GRUNT DELIGHTED TO FIND OUT HER DAUGHTER WAS A SOLDIER."
WHOAH!
MY HEAD SWIMMING FROM THAT CRACK TO THE SKULL. SEEING DOUBLE, TRIPLE. THIS HOUSE OVERLAID WITH EMPTY GRASSLANDS, FROZEN TUNDRA, BACK TO PANGEA.
I COULD SMELL WHAT THE AIR WAS LIKE THEN, RICH AND WET. FEEL THE FUR OF MAMMOTHS BETWEEN MY TOES.
"SHE TAUGHT ME ABOUT THE WAR. THE WAR WE FIGHT, LIFE ACROSS LIFE. THE *PEACEFUL ONES* AND THE *WRATHFUL ONES*."
I KNEW EVERY WAY TO TAKE THIS GUY DOWN. ONLY 4 NON-LETHAL.
TAUGHT ME FROM ORE I WOKE UP, 'THING I FORGOT OM DYING THE LAST TIME."
UVA-- T YOU HER!
ALL THE VOICES IN MY HEAD. THE NAGGING, THE SUPPORTIVE, THE DIRE, THE DOOMED. ALL REAL, THEIR NUMBERS GROWING, SHOUTING.
"SHE TAUGHT ME ABOUT MY TARGET. THE ONE I'VE BEEN CHASING DOWN LIFE AFTER LIFE."
A FLOOD OF THEM, THE WATERLINE CLIMBING UP HIGHER AND HIGHER.
DARTMOUTH
WAIT!
THE DAM COLLAPSES, ME DROWNING.
"SHE TAUGHT ME HOW TO KILL."
THEN ONE VOICE, LOUDER THAN THE OTHERS.
"GET SOMEWHERE SAFE."

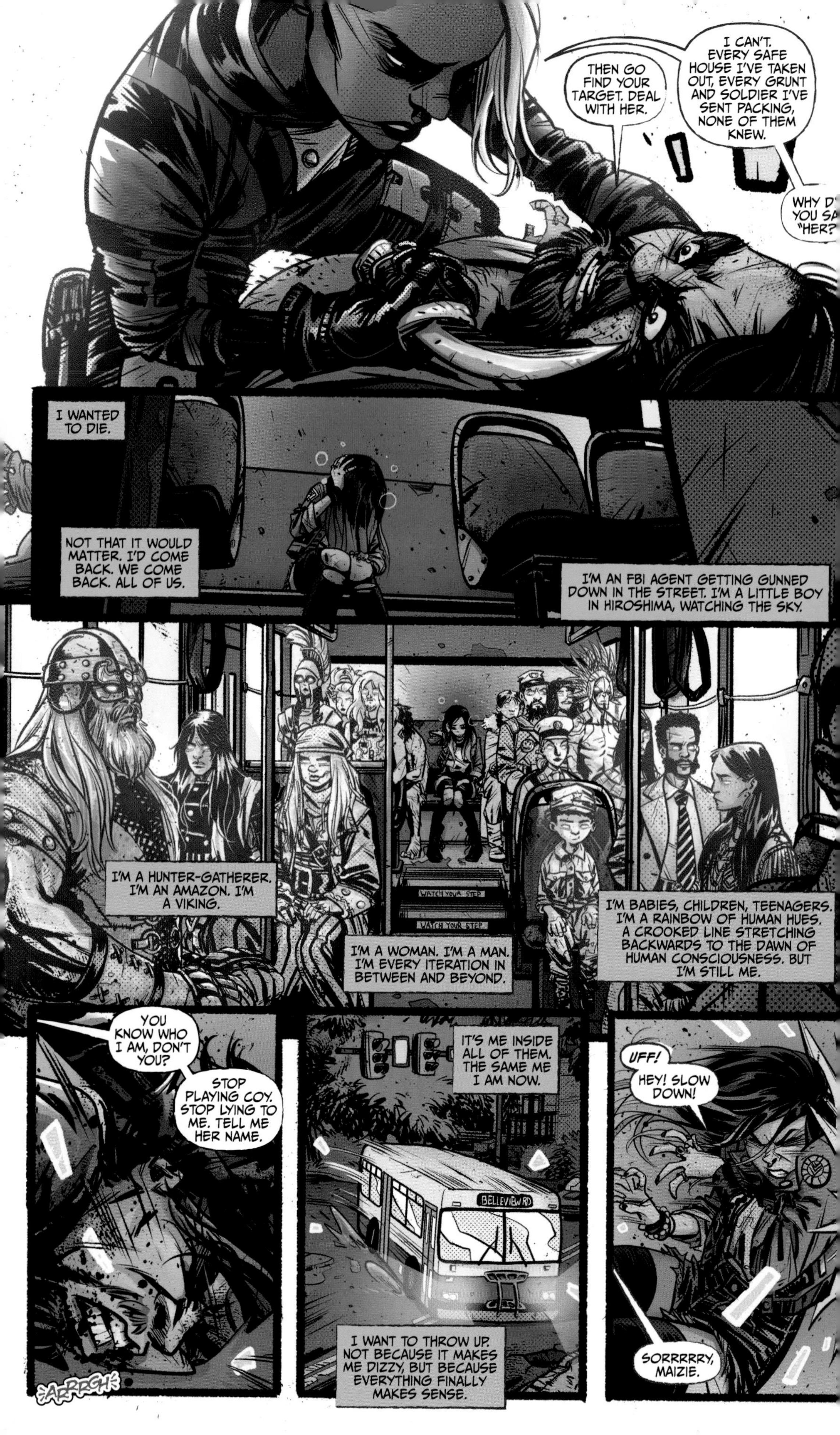
THEN GO FIND YOUR TARGET. DEAL WITH HER.
I CAN'T. EVERY SAFE HOUSE I'VE TAKEN OUT, EVERY GRUNT AND SOLDIER I'VE SENT PACKING, NONE OF THEM KNEW.
WHY D' YOU SA "HER?
I WANTED TO DIE.
NOT THAT IT WOULD MATTER. I'D COME BACK. WE COME BACK. ALL OF US.
I'M AN FBI AGENT GETTING GUNNED DOWN IN THE STREET. I'M A LITTLE BOY IN HIROSHIMA, WATCHING THE SKY.
I'M A HUNTER-GATHERER. I'M AN AMAZON. I'M A VIKING.
WATCH YOUR STEP
WATCH YOUR STEP
I'M A WOMAN. I'M A MAN. I'M EVERY ITERATION IN BETWEEN AND BEYOND.
I'M BABIES, CHILDREN, TEENAGERS. I'M A RAINBOW OF HUMAN HUES. A CROOKED LINE STRETCHING BACKWARDS TO THE DAWN OF HUMAN CONSCIOUSNESS. BUT I'M STILL ME.
YOU KNOW WHO I AM, DON'T YOU?
STOP PLAYING COY. STOP LYING TO ME. TELL ME HER NAME.
ARRRGH
IT'S ME INSIDE ALL OF THEM. THE SAME ME I AM NOW.
BELLEVIEW RD
I WANT TO THROW UP. NOT BECAUSE IT MAKES ME DIZZY, BUT BECAUSE EVERYTHING FINALLY MAKES SENSE.
UFF!
HEY! SLOW DOWN!
SORRRRRY, MAIZIE.

IT'S A FUNNY THING ABOUT US. HOW WE ALL CLUMP TOGETHER, LIKE FATE GIVES US A SUPPORT SYSTEM.

LIKE FAMILIES. LIKE *YOUR* FAMILY.

I VISITED THEM TODAY.

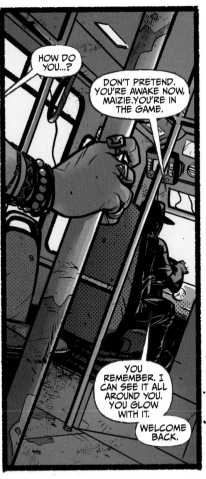

HOW DO YOU...?

DON'T PRETEND. YOU'RE AWAKE NOW, MAIZIE. YOU'RE IN THE GAME.

YOU REMEMBER. I CAN SEE IT ALL AROUND YOU. YOU GLOW WITH IT.

WELCOME BACK.

WHAT HAVE YOU DONE? TELL ME!

YOU FIRST, OLD MAN. A NAME. A LOCATION.

BLOOD FOR BLOOD.

NOW YOU DIE.

THE WATERS RECEDED. THEY ALWAYS DO.

WATCH YOUR ST

BEATEN BACK, VIOLENTLY. A LANGUAGE I QUICKLY REALIZED I'M FLUENT IN.

SCREEE

WE KNOW WHO SHE IS. WHERE SHE IS.

JUST AS WE KNOW WHO YOU ARE.

WE'VE ALWAYS KNOWN.

YOU FIRST.

I OPEN MY MOUTH TO SPEAK IT BACK TO HIM.

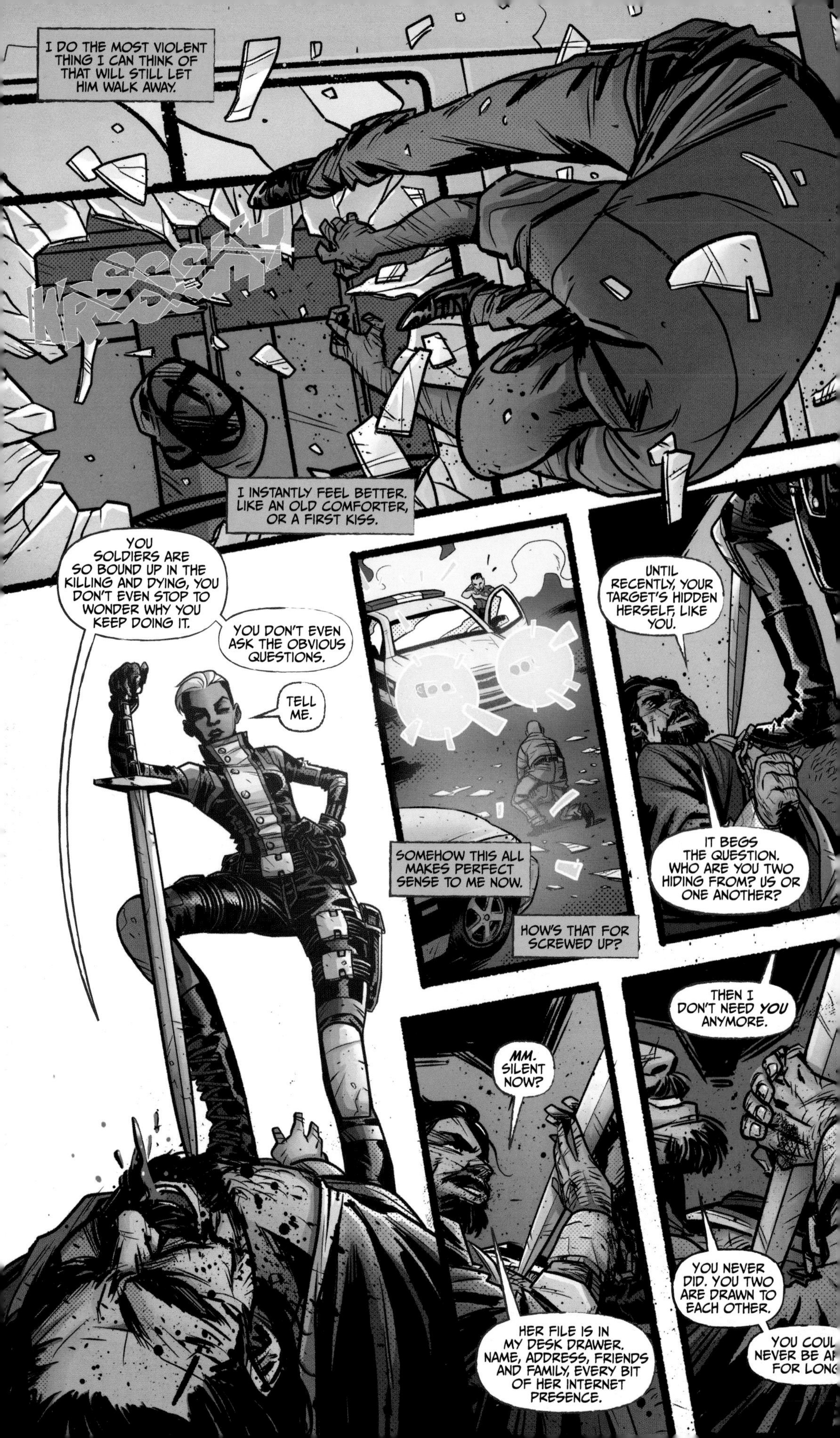

I DO THE MOST VIOLENT THING I CAN THINK OF THAT WILL STILL LET HIM WALK AWAY.
KRSSSHH
I INSTANTLY FEEL BETTER. LIKE AN OLD COMFORTER, OR A FIRST KISS.
YOU SOLDIERS ARE SO BOUND UP IN THE KILLING AND DYING, YOU DON'T EVEN STOP TO WONDER WHY YOU KEEP DOING IT.
YOU DON'T EVEN ASK THE OBVIOUS QUESTIONS.
TELL ME.
SOMEHOW THIS ALL MAKES PERFECT SENSE TO ME NOW.
HOW'S THAT FOR SCREWED UP?
UNTIL RECENTLY, YOUR TARGET'S HIDDEN HERSELF, LIKE YOU.
IT BEGS THE QUESTION. WHO ARE YOU TWO HIDING FROM? US OR ONE ANOTHER?
MM. SILENT NOW?
HER FILE IS IN MY DESK DRAWER. NAME, ADDRESS, FRIENDS AND FAMILY, EVERY BIT OF HER INTERNET PRESENCE.
THEN I DON'T NEED *YOU* ANYMORE.
YOU NEVER DID. YOU TWO ARE DRAWN TO EACH OTHER.
YOU COUL NEVER BE A FOR LONG

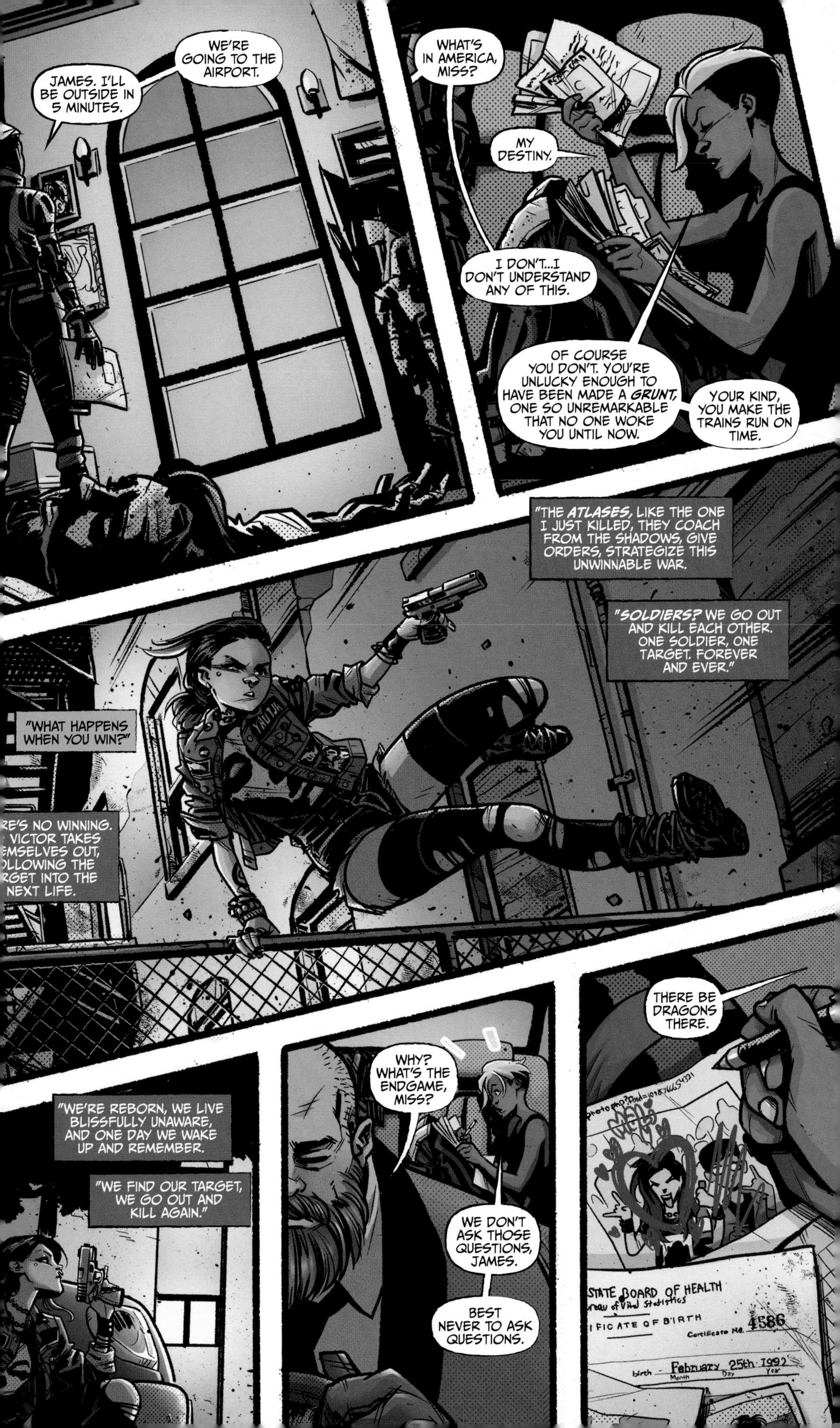

JAMES. I'LL BE OUTSIDE IN 5 MINUTES.
WE'RE GOING TO THE AIRPORT.
WHAT'S IN AMERICA, MISS?
MY DESTINY.
I DON'T...I DON'T UNDERSTAND ANY OF THIS.
OF COURSE YOU DON'T. YOU'RE UNLUCKY ENOUGH TO HAVE BEEN MADE A GRUNT, ONE SO UNREMARKABLE THAT NO ONE WOKE YOU UNTIL NOW.
YOUR KIND, YOU MAKE THE TRAINS RUN ON TIME.
"THE ATLASES, LIKE THE ONE I JUST KILLED, THEY COACH FROM THE SHADOWS, GIVE ORDERS, STRATEGIZE THIS UNWINNABLE WAR.
"SOLDIERS? WE GO OUT AND KILL EACH OTHER. ONE SOLDIER, ONE TARGET. FOREVER AND EVER."
"WHAT HAPPENS WHEN YOU WIN?"
RE'S NO WINNING. VICTOR TAKES EMSELVES OUT, OLLOWING THE RGET INTO THE NEXT LIFE.
"WE'RE REBORN, WE LIVE BLISSFULLY UNAWARE, AND ONE DAY WE WAKE UP AND REMEMBER.
"WE FIND OUR TARGET, WE GO OUT AND KILL AGAIN."
WHY? WHAT'S THE ENDGAME, MISS?
WE DON'T ASK THOSE QUESTIONS, JAMES.
BEST NEVER TO ASK QUESTIONS.
THERE BE DRAGONS THERE.
STATE BOARD OF HEALTH
IFICATE OF BIRTH
Certificate No. 4586
February 25th 1992

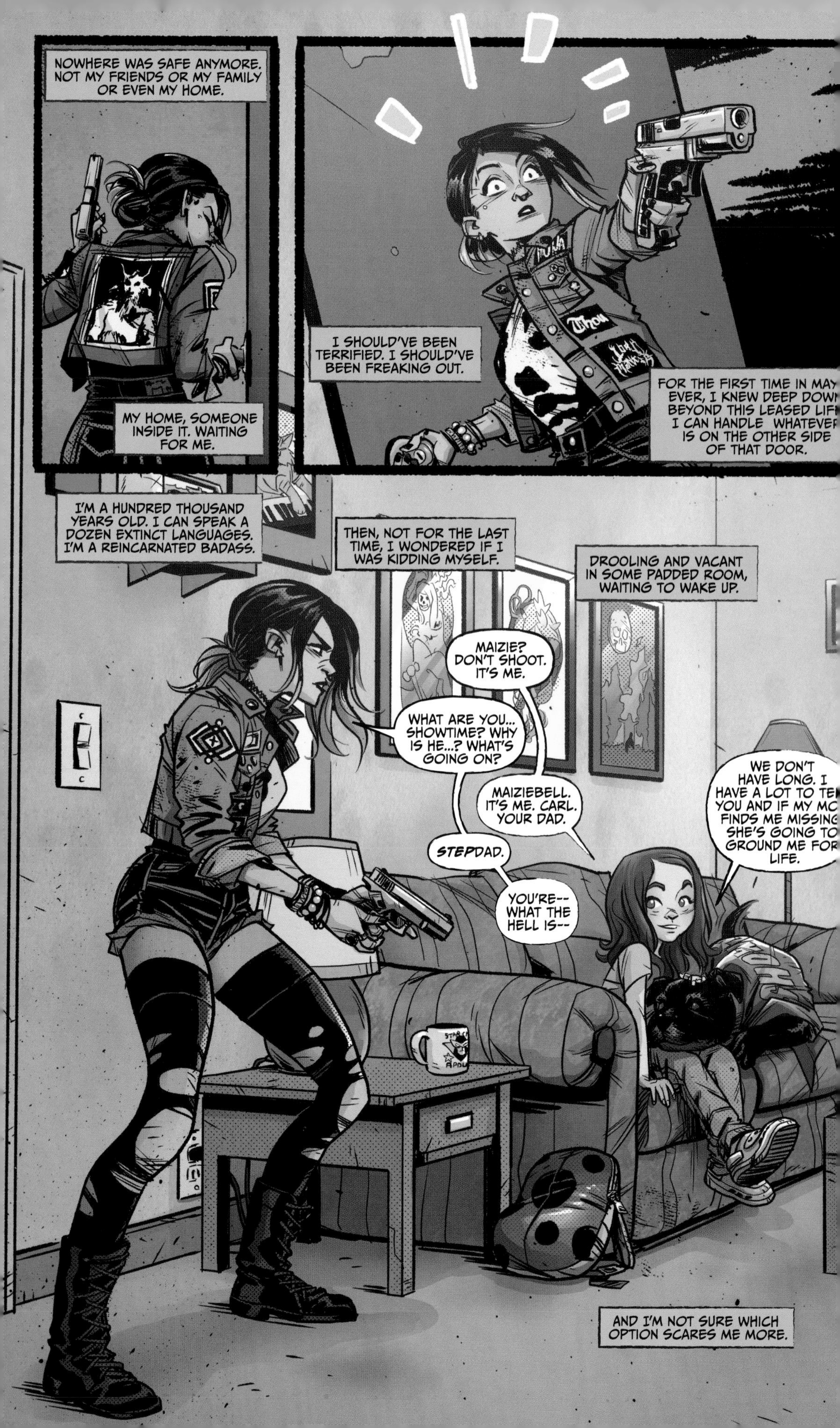

NOWHERE WAS SAFE ANYMORE. NOT MY FRIENDS OR MY FAMILY OR EVEN MY HOME.
MY HOME, SOMEONE INSIDE IT. WAITING FOR ME.
I SHOULD'VE BEEN TERRIFIED. I SHOULD'VE BEEN FREAKING OUT.
FOR THE FIRST TIME IN MAY EVER, I KNEW DEEP DOWN BEYOND THIS LEASED LIFE I CAN HANDLE WHATEVER IS ON THE OTHER SIDE OF THAT DOOR.
I'M A HUNDRED THOUSAND YEARS OLD. I CAN SPEAK A DOZEN EXTINCT LANGUAGES. I'M A REINCARNATED BADASS.
THEN, NOT FOR THE LAST TIME, I WONDERED IF I WAS KIDDING MYSELF.
DROOLING AND VACANT IN SOME PADDED ROOM, WAITING TO WAKE UP.
MAIZIE? DON'T SHOOT. IT'S ME.
WHAT ARE YOU... SHOWTIME? WHY IS HE...? WHAT'S GOING ON?
MAIZIEBELL. IT'S ME. CARL. YOUR DAD.
STEPDAD.
YOU'RE-- WHAT THE HELL IS--
WE DON'T HAVE LONG. I HAVE A LOT TO TE YOU AND IF MY MO FINDS ME MISSING SHE'S GOING TO GROUND ME FOR LIFE.
AND I'M NOT SURE WHICH OPTION SCARES ME MORE.

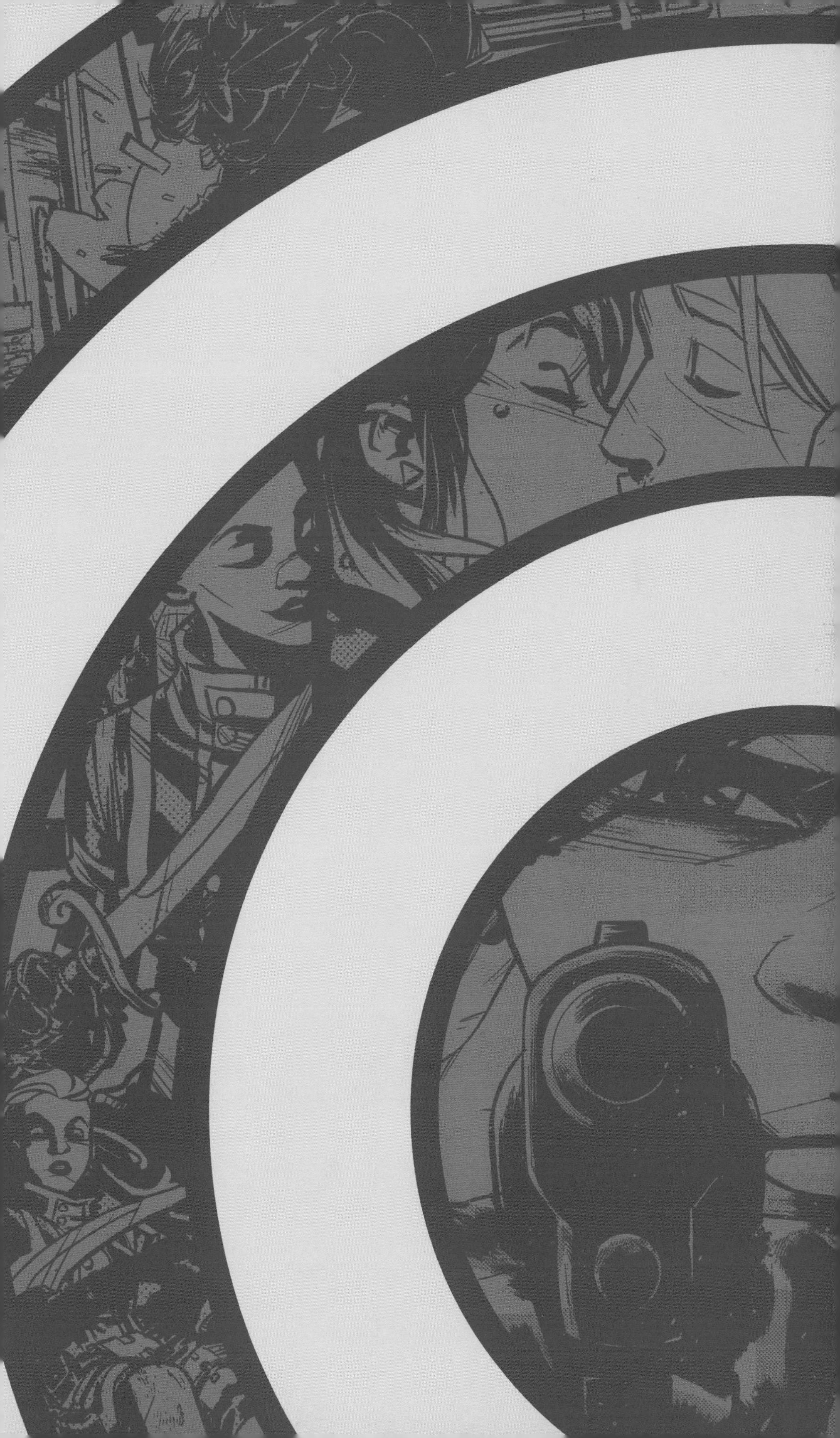

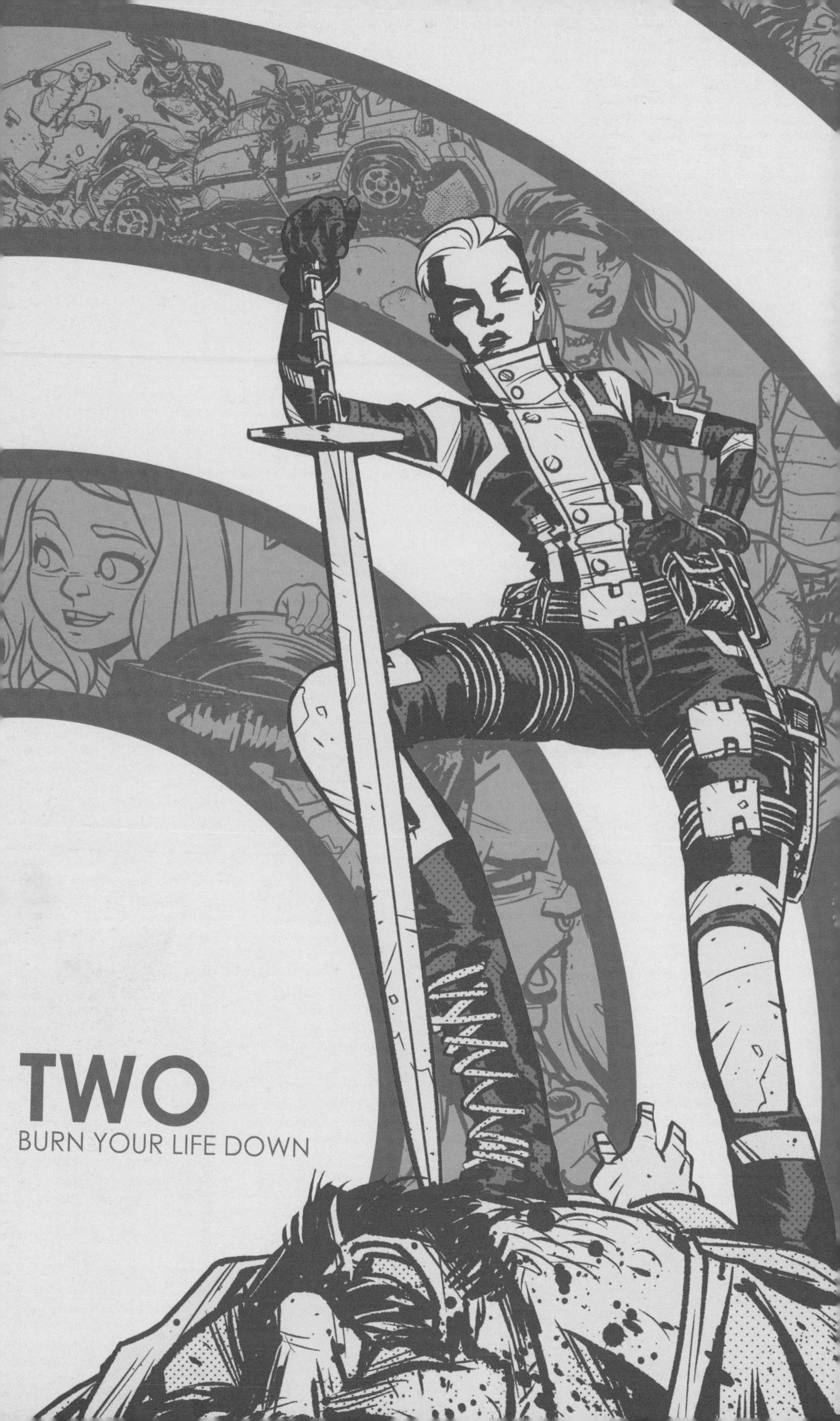

TWO

BURN YOUR LIFE DOWN

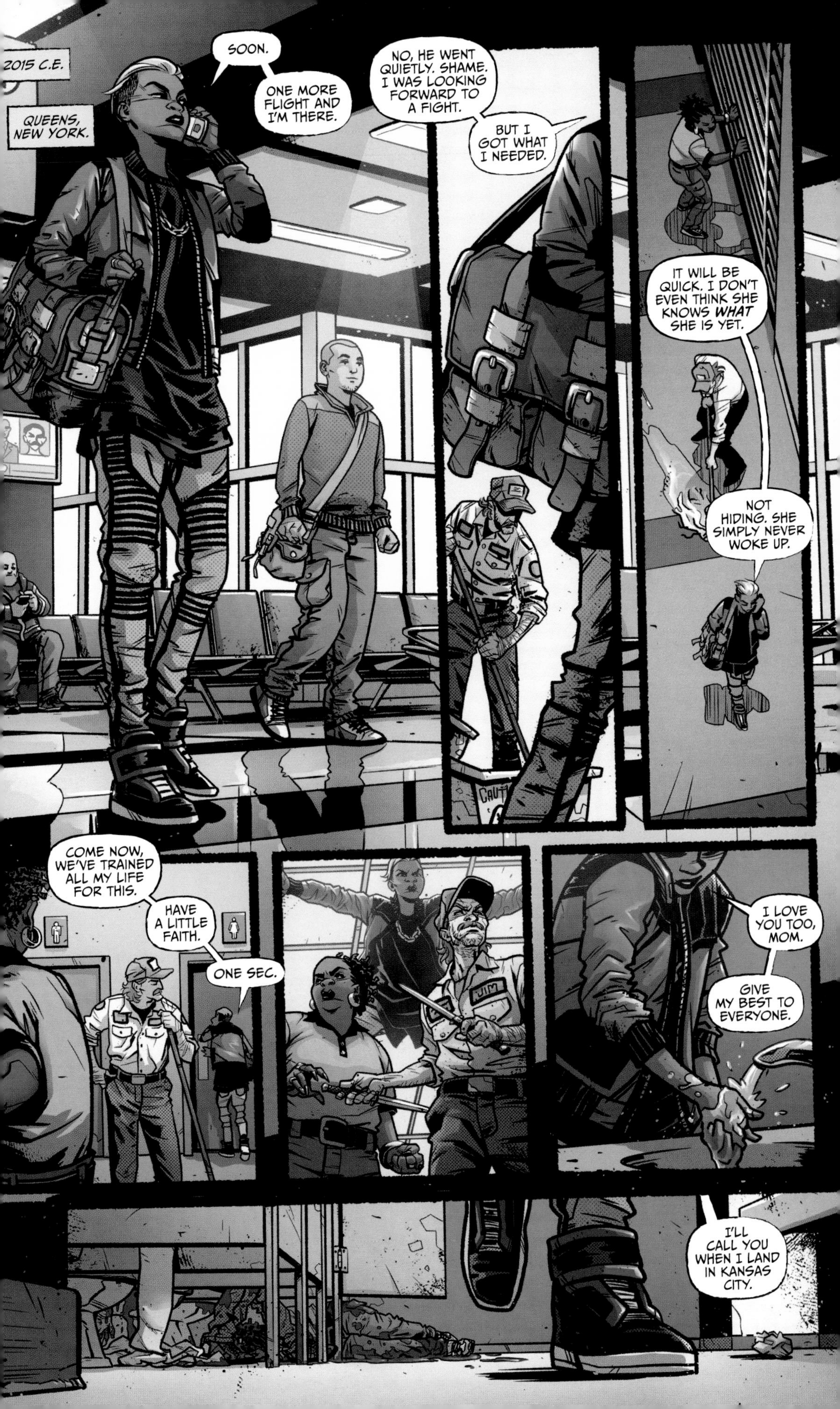
2015 C.E.
QUEENS, NEW YORK.
SOON.
ONE MORE FLIGHT AND I'M THERE.
NO, HE WENT QUIETLY. SHAME. I WAS LOOKING FORWARD TO A FIGHT.
BUT I GOT WHAT I NEEDED.
IT WILL BE QUICK. I DON'T EVEN THINK SHE KNOWS *WHAT* SHE IS YET.
NOT HIDING. SHE SIMPLY NEVER WOKE UP.
COME NOW, WE'VE TRAINED ALL MY LIFE FOR THIS.
HAVE A LITTLE FAITH.
ONE SEC.
JIM
I LOVE YOU TOO, MOM.
GIVE MY BEST TO EVERYONE.
I'LL CALL YOU WHEN I LAND IN KANSAS CITY.

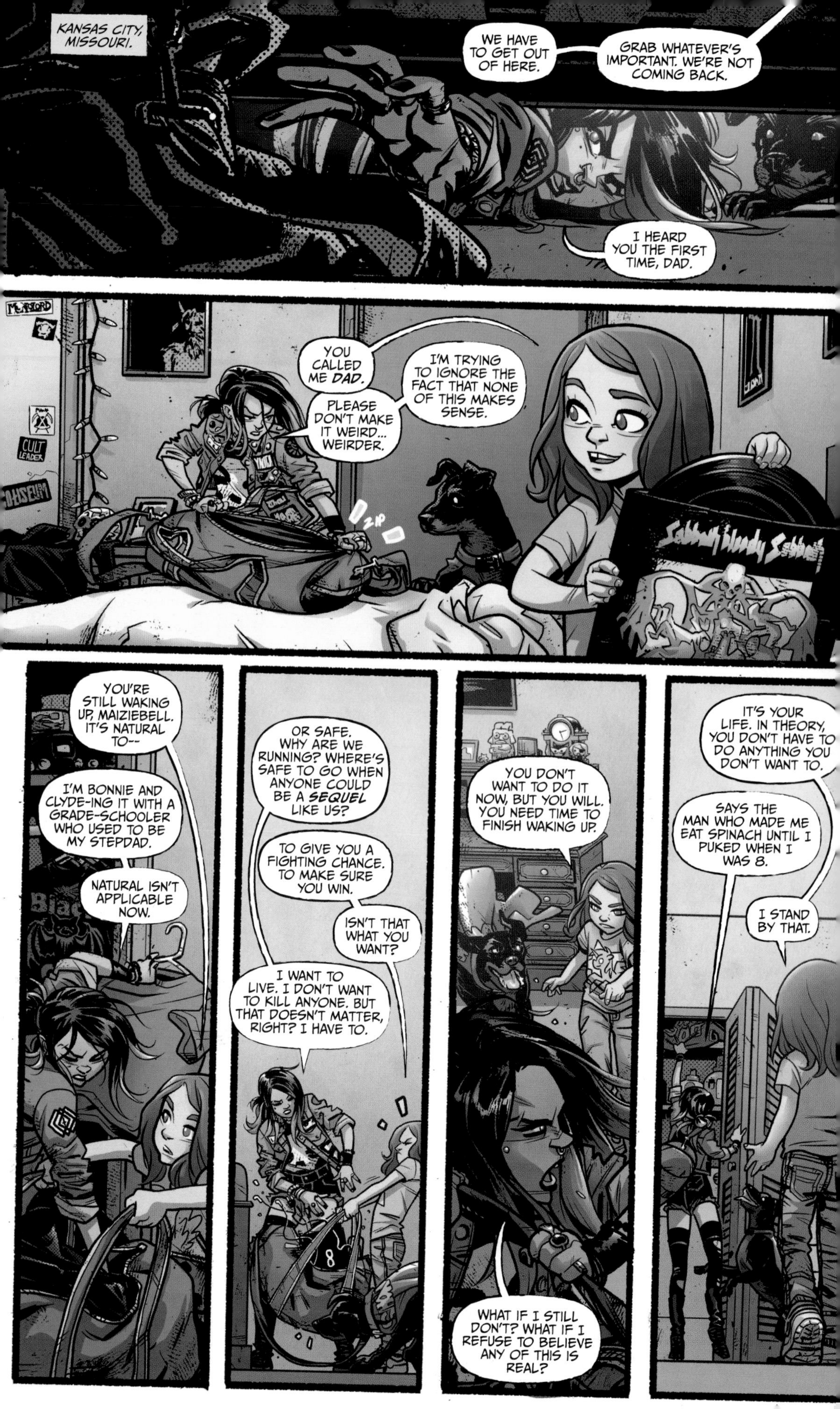
KANSAS CITY, MISSOURI.
WE HAVE TO GET OUT OF HERE.
GRAB WHATEVER'S IMPORTANT. WE'RE NOT COMING BACK.
I HEARD YOU THE FIRST TIME, DAD.
YOU CALLED ME DAD.
PLEASE DON'T MAKE IT WEIRD... WEIRDER.
I'M TRYING TO IGNORE THE FACT THAT NONE OF THIS MAKES SENSE.
ZIP
YOU'RE STILL WAKING UP, MAIZIEBELL. IT'S NATURAL TO--
I'M BONNIE AND CLYDE-ING IT WITH A GRADE-SCHOOLER WHO USED TO BE MY STEPDAD.
NATURAL ISN'T APPLICABLE NOW.
OR SAFE. WHY ARE WE RUNNING? WHERE'S SAFE TO GO WHEN ANYONE COULD BE A SEQUEL LIKE US?
TO GIVE YOU A FIGHTING CHANCE. TO MAKE SURE YOU WIN.
ISN'T THAT WHAT YOU WANT?
I WANT TO LIVE. I DON'T WANT TO KILL ANYONE. BUT THAT DOESN'T MATTER, RIGHT? I HAVE TO.
YOU DON'T WANT TO DO IT NOW, BUT YOU WILL. YOU NEED TIME TO FINISH WAKING UP.
WHAT IF I STILL DON'T? WHAT IF I REFUSE TO BELIEVE ANY OF THIS IS REAL?
IT'S YOUR LIFE. IN THEORY, YOU DON'T HAVE TO DO ANYTHING YOU DON'T WANT TO.
SAYS THE MAN WHO MADE ME EAT SPINACH UNTIL I PUKED WHEN I WAS 8.
I STAND BY THAT.

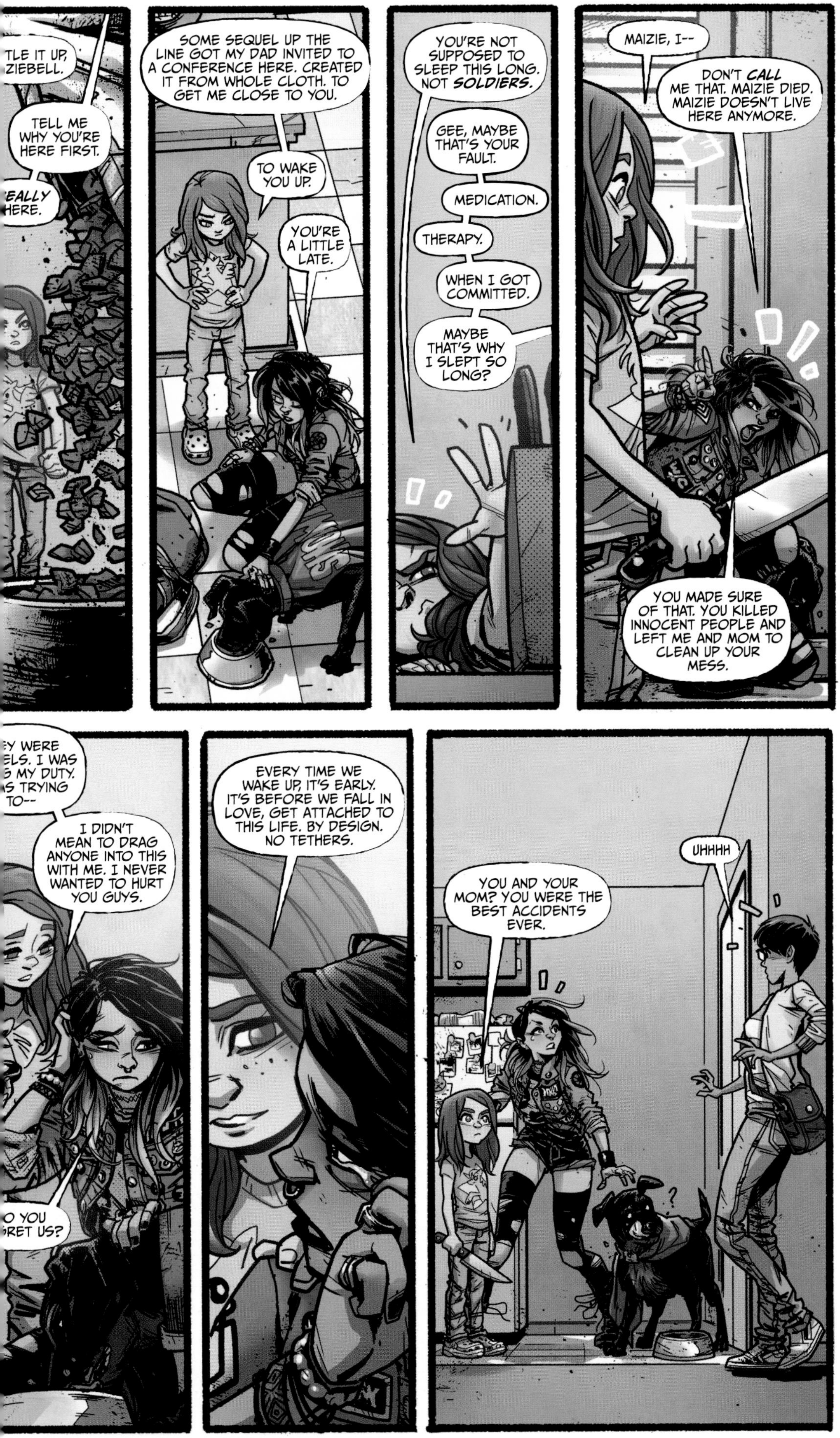
TLE IT UP, ZIEBELL.
TELL ME WHY YOU'RE HERE FIRST.
EALLY HERE.
SOME SEQUEL UP THE LINE GOT MY DAD INVITED TO A CONFERENCE HERE. CREATED IT FROM WHOLE CLOTH. TO GET ME CLOSE TO YOU.
TO WAKE YOU UP.
YOU'RE A LITTLE LATE.
YOU'RE NOT SUPPOSED TO SLEEP THIS LONG. NOT SOLDIERS.
GEE, MAYBE THAT'S YOUR FAULT.
MEDICATION.
THERAPY.
WHEN I GOT COMMITTED.
MAYBE THAT'S WHY I SLEPT SO LONG?
MAIZIE, I--
DON'T CALL ME THAT. MAIZIE DIED. MAIZIE DOESN'T LIVE HERE ANYMORE.
YOU MADE SURE OF THAT. YOU KILLED INNOCENT PEOPLE AND LEFT ME AND MOM TO CLEAN UP YOUR MESS.
EY WERE ELS. I WAS G MY DUTY. S TRYING TO--
I DIDN'T MEAN TO DRAG ANYONE INTO THIS WITH ME. I NEVER WANTED TO HURT YOU GUYS.
O YOU RET US?
EVERY TIME WE WAKE UP, IT'S EARLY. IT'S BEFORE WE FALL IN LOVE, GET ATTACHED TO THIS LIFE. BY DESIGN. NO TETHERS.
YOU AND YOUR MOM? YOU WERE THE BEST ACCIDENTS EVER.
UHHHH

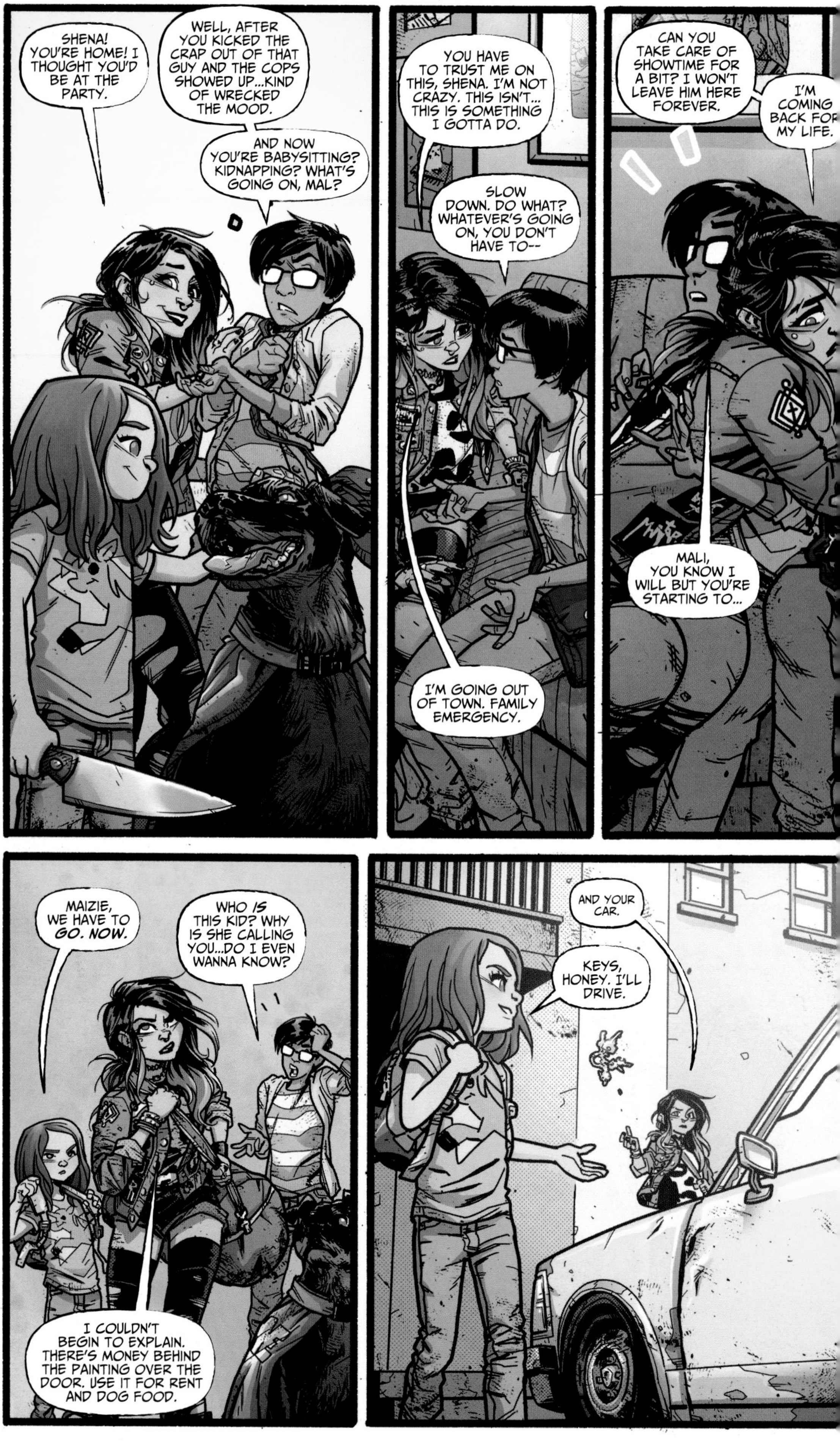
SHENA! YOU'RE HOME! I THOUGHT YOU'D BE AT THE PARTY.
WELL, AFTER YOU KICKED THE CRAP OUT OF THAT GUY AND THE COPS SHOWED UP...KIND OF WRECKED THE MOOD.
AND NOW YOU'RE BABYSITTING? KIDNAPPING? WHAT'S GOING ON, MAL?
YOU HAVE TO TRUST ME ON THIS, SHENA. I'M NOT CRAZY. THIS ISN'T... THIS IS SOMETHING I GOTTA DO.
SLOW DOWN. DO WHAT? WHATEVER'S GOING ON, YOU DON'T HAVE TO--
I'M GOING OUT OF TOWN. FAMILY EMERGENCY.
CAN YOU TAKE CARE OF SHOWTIME FOR A BIT? I WON'T LEAVE HIM HERE FOREVER.
I'M COMING BACK FOR MY LIFE.
MALI, YOU KNOW I WILL BUT YOU'RE STARTING TO...
MAIZIE, WE HAVE TO GO. NOW.
WHO IS THIS KID? WHY IS SHE CALLING YOU...DO I EVEN WANNA KNOW?
I COULDN'T BEGIN TO EXPLAIN. THERE'S MONEY BEHIND THE PAINTING OVER THE DOOR. USE IT FOR RENT AND DOG FOOD.
AND YOUR CAR.
KEYS, HONEY. I'LL DRIVE.

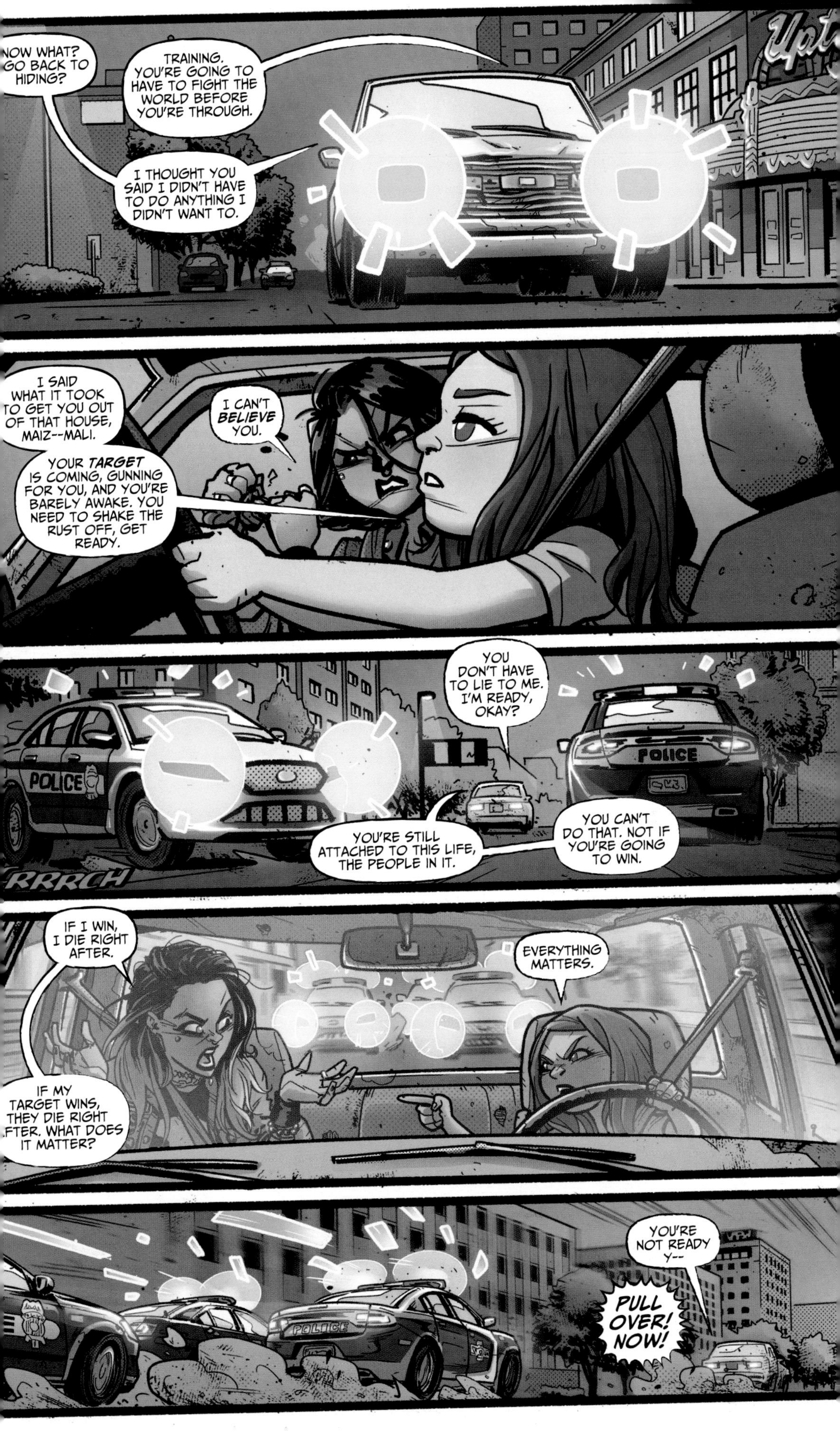

NOW WHAT? GO BACK TO HIDING?
TRAINING. YOU'RE GOING TO HAVE TO FIGHT THE WORLD BEFORE YOU'RE THROUGH.
I THOUGHT YOU SAID I DIDN'T HAVE TO DO ANYTHING I DIDN'T WANT TO.
I SAID WHAT IT TOOK TO GET YOU OUT OF THAT HOUSE, MAIZ--MALI.
I CAN'T BELIEVE YOU.
YOUR TARGET IS COMING, GUNNING FOR YOU, AND YOU'RE BARELY AWAKE. YOU NEED TO SHAKE THE RUST OFF, GET READY.
POLICE
YOU DON'T HAVE TO LIE TO ME. I'M READY, OKAY?
POLICE
RRRCH
YOU'RE STILL ATTACHED TO THIS LIFE, THE PEOPLE IN IT.
YOU CAN'T DO THAT. NOT IF YOU'RE GOING TO WIN.
IF I WIN, I DIE RIGHT AFTER.
EVERYTHING MATTERS.
IF MY TARGET WINS, THEY DIE RIGHT FTER. WHAT DOES IT MATTER?
POLICE
YOU'RE NOT READY Y--
PULL OVER! NOW!

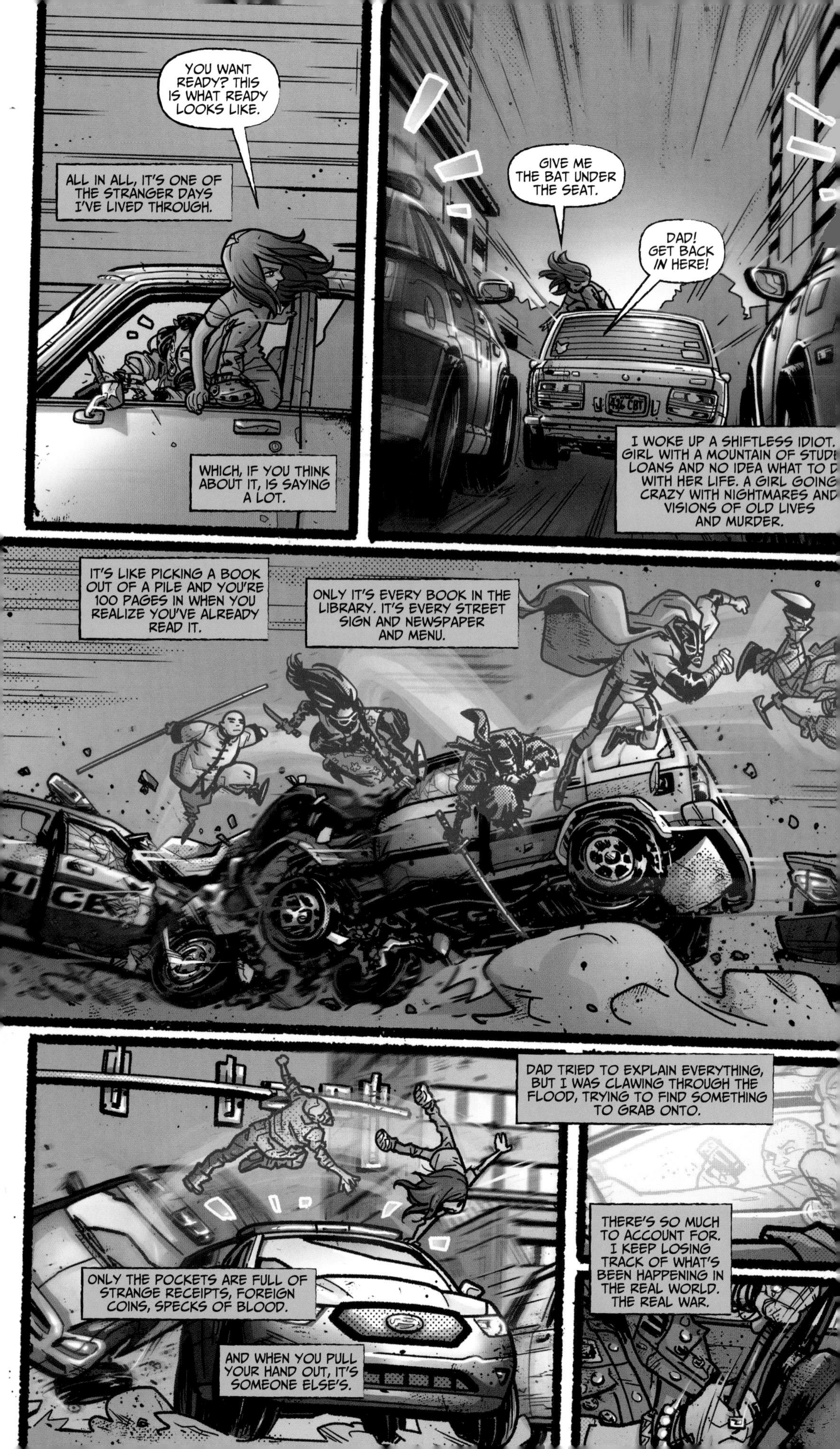
YOU WANT READY? THIS IS WHAT READY LOOKS LIKE.
ALL IN ALL, IT'S ONE OF THE STRANGER DAYS I'VE LIVED THROUGH.
WHICH, IF YOU THINK ABOUT IT, IS SAYING A LOT.
GIVE ME THE BAT UNDER THE SEAT.
DAD! GET BACK IN HERE!
I WOKE UP A SHIFTLESS IDIOT. GIRL WITH A MOUNTAIN OF STUDE LOANS AND NO IDEA WHAT TO D WITH HER LIFE. A GIRL GOING CRAZY WITH NIGHTMARES AND VISIONS OF OLD LIVES AND MURDER.
IT'S LIKE PICKING A BOOK OUT OF A PILE AND YOU'RE 100 PAGES IN WHEN YOU REALIZE YOU'VE ALREADY READ IT.
ONLY IT'S EVERY BOOK IN THE LIBRARY. IT'S EVERY STREET SIGN AND NEWSPAPER AND MENU.
ONLY THE POCKETS ARE FULL OF STRANGE RECEIPTS, FOREIGN COINS, SPECKS OF BLOOD.
AND WHEN YOU PULL YOUR HAND OUT, IT'S SOMEONE ELSE'S.
DAD TRIED TO EXPLAIN EVERYTHING, BUT I WAS CLAWING THROUGH THE FLOOD, TRYING TO FIND SOMETHING TO GRAB ONTO.
THERE'S SO MUCH TO ACCOUNT FOR. I KEEP LOSING TRACK OF WHAT'S BEEN HAPPENING IN THE REAL WORLD. THE REAL WAR.

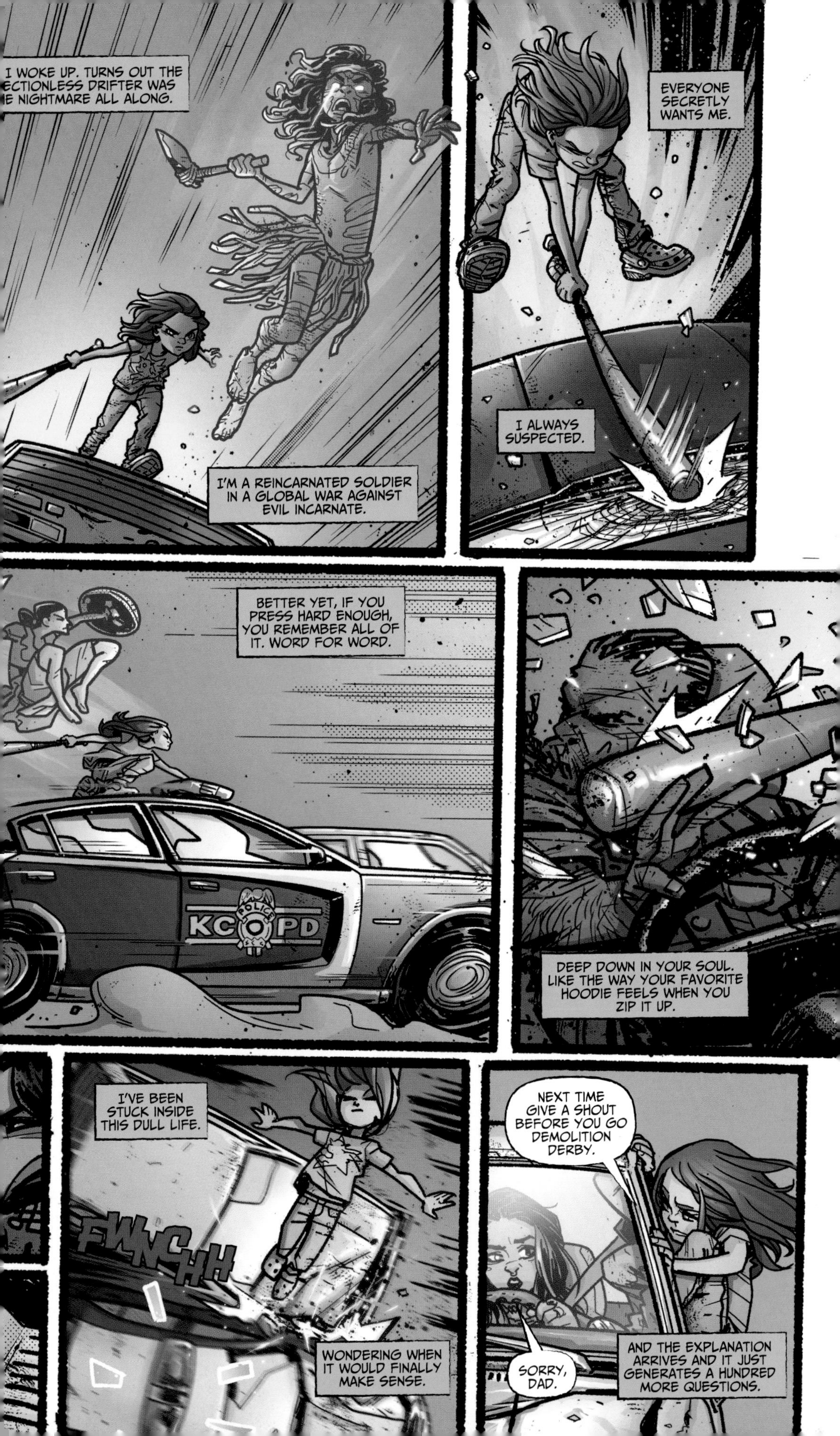

I WOKE UP. TURNS OUT THE
ECTIONLESS DRIFTER WAS
E NIGHTMARE ALL ALONG.
I'M A REINCARNATED SOLDIER IN A GLOBAL WAR AGAINST EVIL INCARNATE.
EVERYONE SECRETLY WANTS ME.
I ALWAYS SUSPECTED.
BETTER YET, IF YOU PRESS HARD ENOUGH, YOU REMEMBER ALL OF IT. WORD FOR WORD.
KC POLICE PD
DEEP DOWN IN YOUR SOUL. LIKE THE WAY YOUR FAVORITE HOODIE FEELS WHEN YOU ZIP IT UP.
I'VE BEEN STUCK INSIDE THIS DULL LIFE.
FWNCHH
WONDERING WHEN IT WOULD FINALLY MAKE SENSE.
NEXT TIME GIVE A SHOUT BEFORE YOU GO DEMOLITION DERBY.
SORRY, DAD.
AND THE EXPLANATION ARRIVES AND IT JUST GENERATES A HUNDRED MORE QUESTIONS.

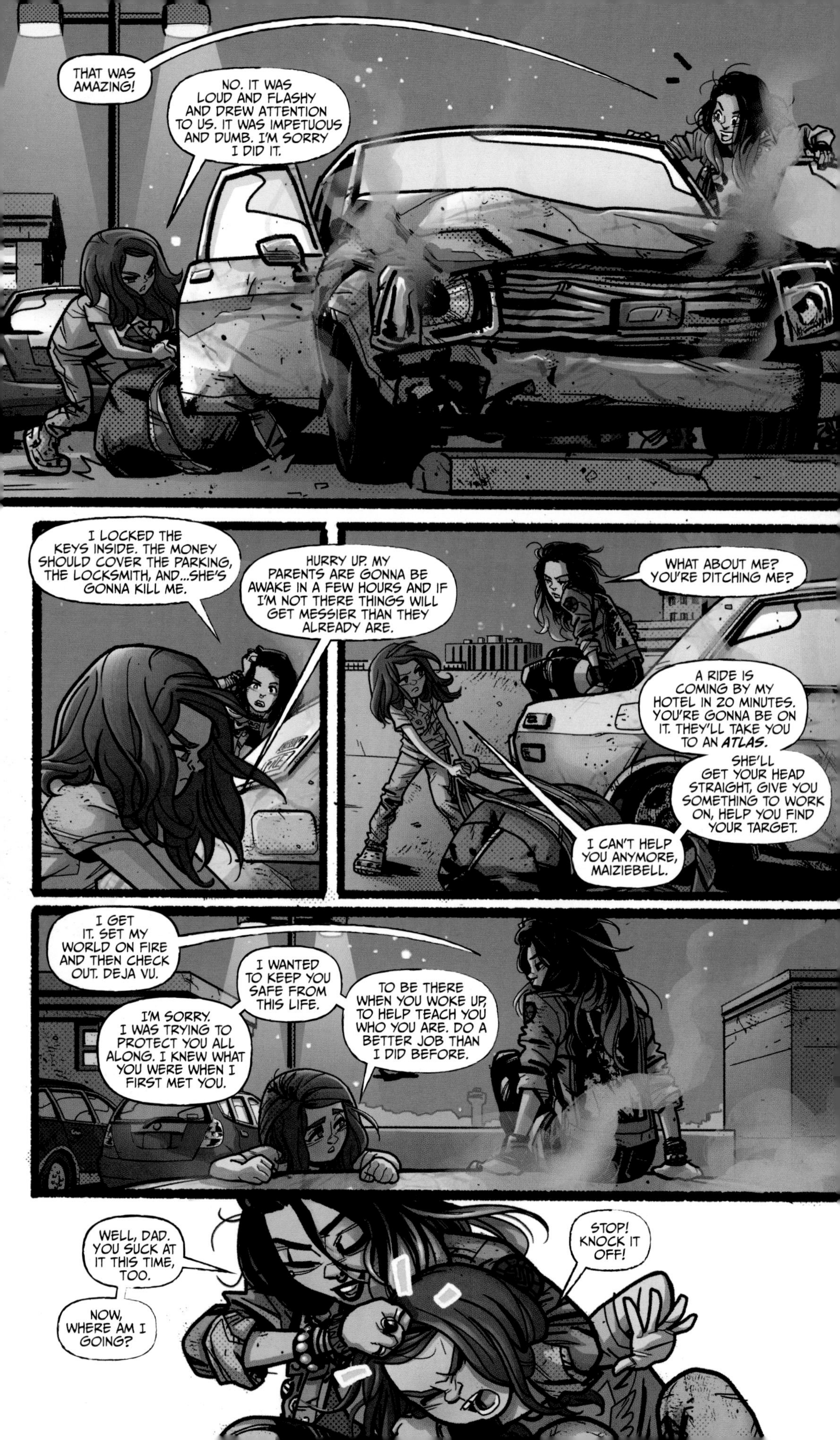
THAT WAS AMAZING!
NO. IT WAS LOUD AND FLASHY AND DREW ATTENTION TO US. IT WAS IMPETUOUS AND DUMB. I'M SORRY I DID IT.
I LOCKED THE KEYS INSIDE. THE MONEY SHOULD COVER THE PARKING, THE LOCKSMITH, AND...SHE'S GONNA KILL ME.
HURRY UP. MY PARENTS ARE GONNA BE AWAKE IN A FEW HOURS AND IF I'M NOT THERE THINGS WILL GET MESSIER THAN THEY ALREADY ARE.
WHAT ABOUT ME? YOU'RE DITCHING ME?
A RIDE IS COMING BY MY HOTEL IN 20 MINUTES. YOU'RE GONNA BE ON IT. THEY'LL TAKE YOU TO AN ATLAS.
SHE'LL GET YOUR HEAD STRAIGHT, GIVE YOU SOMETHING TO WORK ON, HELP YOU FIND YOUR TARGET.
I CAN'T HELP YOU ANYMORE, MAIZIEBELL.
I GET IT. SET MY WORLD ON FIRE AND THEN CHECK OUT. DEJA VU.
I'M SORRY. I WAS TRYING TO PROTECT YOU ALL ALONG. I KNEW WHAT YOU WERE WHEN I FIRST MET YOU.
I WANTED TO KEEP YOU SAFE FROM THIS LIFE.
TO BE THERE WHEN YOU WOKE UP, TO HELP TEACH YOU WHO YOU ARE. DO A BETTER JOB THAN I DID BEFORE.
WELL, DAD. YOU SUCK AT IT THIS TIME, TOO.
NOW, WHERE AM I GOING?
STOP! KNOCK IT OFF!

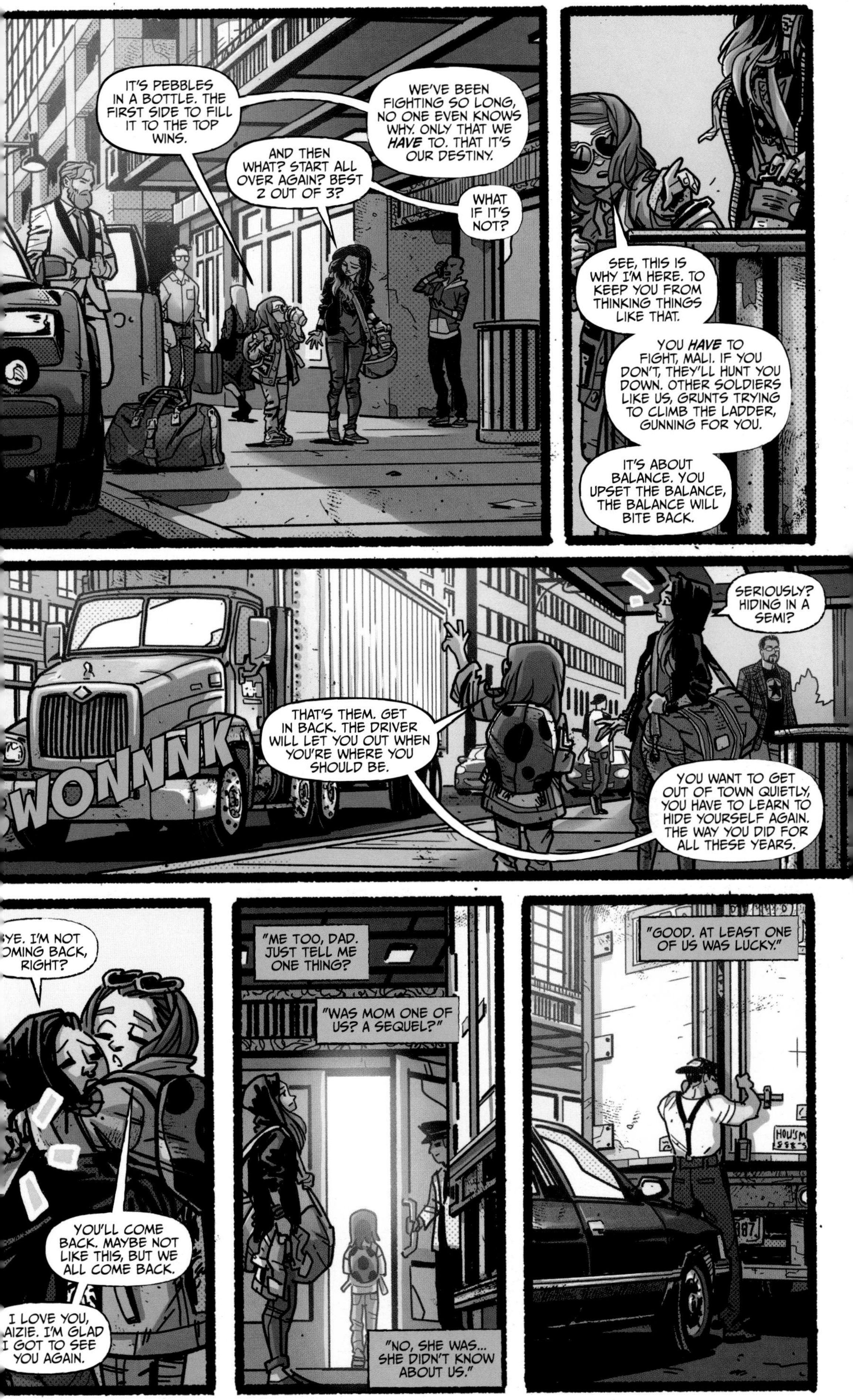
IT'S PEBBLES IN A BOTTLE. THE FIRST SIDE TO FILL IT TO THE TOP WINS.
WE'VE BEEN FIGHTING SO LONG, NO ONE EVEN KNOWS WHY. ONLY THAT WE *HAVE* TO. THAT IT'S OUR DESTINY.
AND THEN WHAT? START ALL OVER AGAIN? BEST 2 OUT OF 3?
WHAT IF IT'S NOT?
SEE, THIS IS WHY I'M HERE. TO KEEP YOU FROM THINKING THINGS LIKE THAT.
YOU *HAVE* TO FIGHT, MALI. IF YOU DON'T, THEY'LL HUNT YOU DOWN. OTHER SOLDIERS LIKE US, GRUNTS TRYING TO CLIMB THE LADDER, GUNNING FOR YOU.
IT'S ABOUT BALANCE. YOU UPSET THE BALANCE, THE BALANCE WILL BITE BACK.
WONNNK
SERIOUSLY? HIDING IN A SEMI?
THAT'S THEM. GET IN BACK. THE DRIVER WILL LET YOU OUT WHEN YOU'RE WHERE YOU SHOULD BE.
YOU WANT TO GET OUT OF TOWN QUIETLY, YOU HAVE TO LEARN TO HIDE YOURSELF AGAIN. THE WAY YOU DID FOR ALL THESE YEARS.
YE. I'M NOT OMING BACK, RIGHT?
YOU'LL COME BACK. MAYBE NOT LIKE THIS, BUT WE ALL COME BACK.
I LOVE YOU, AIZIE. I'M GLAD I GOT TO SEE YOU AGAIN.
"ME TOO, DAD. JUST TELL ME ONE THING?
"WAS MOM ONE OF US? A SEQUEL?"
"NO, SHE WAS... SHE DIDN'T KNOW ABOUT US."
"GOOD. AT LEAST ONE OF US WAS LUCKY."

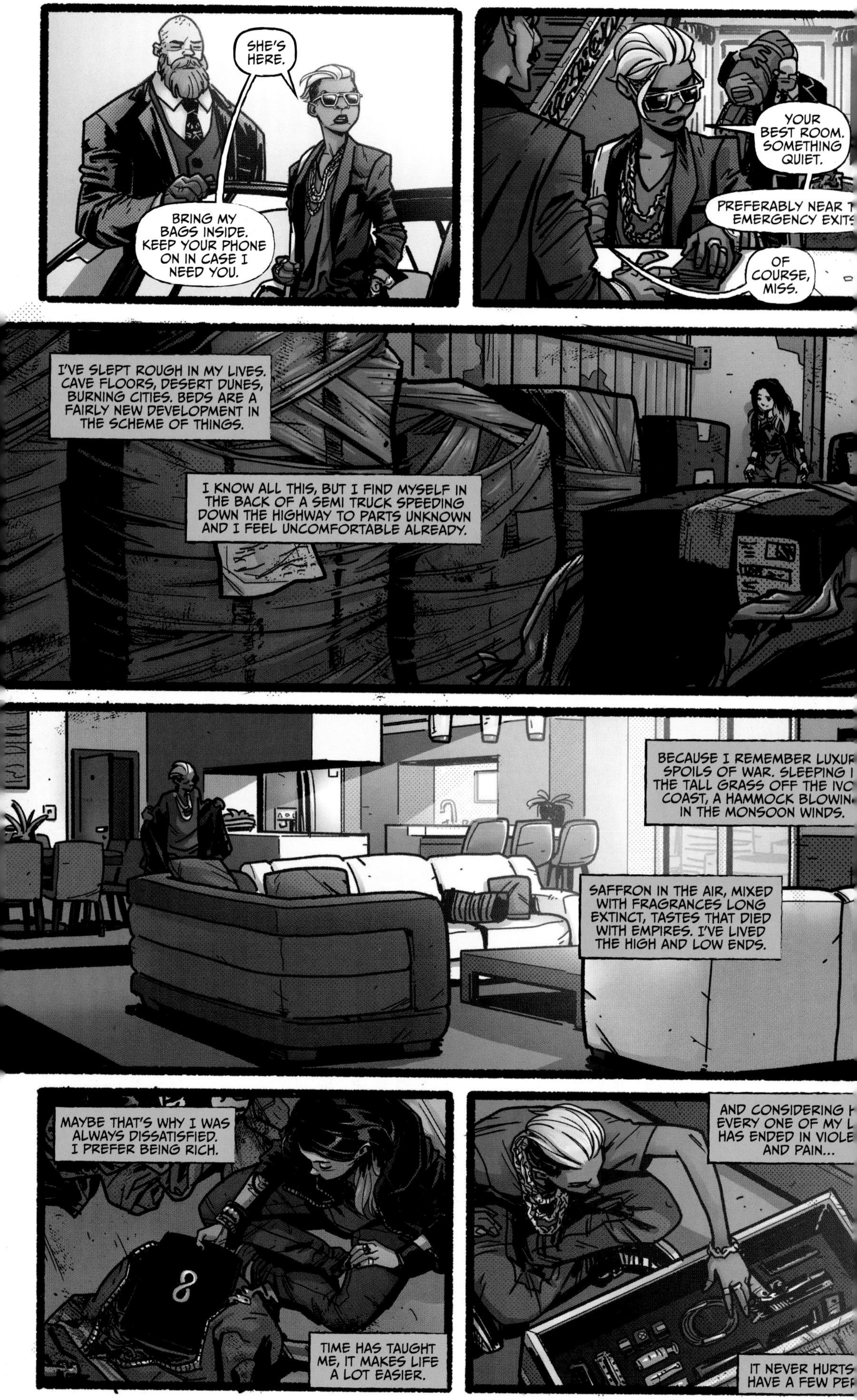
SHE'S HERE.
BRING MY BAGS INSIDE. KEEP YOUR PHONE ON IN CASE I NEED YOU.
YOUR BEST ROOM. SOMETHING QUIET.
PREFERABLY NEAR T EMERGENCY EXITS
OF COURSE, MISS.
I'VE SLEPT ROUGH IN MY LIVES. CAVE FLOORS, DESERT DUNES, BURNING CITIES. BEDS ARE A FAIRLY NEW DEVELOPMENT IN THE SCHEME OF THINGS.
I KNOW ALL THIS, BUT I FIND MYSELF IN THE BACK OF A SEMI TRUCK SPEEDING DOWN THE HIGHWAY TO PARTS UNKNOWN AND I FEEL UNCOMFORTABLE ALREADY.
BECAUSE I REMEMBER LUXUR SPOILS OF WAR. SLEEPING I THE TALL GRASS OFF THE IVO COAST, A HAMMOCK BLOWIN IN THE MONSOON WINDS.
SAFFRON IN THE AIR, MIXED WITH FRAGRANCES LONG EXTINCT, TASTES THAT DIED WITH EMPIRES. I'VE LIVED THE HIGH AND LOW ENDS.
MAYBE THAT'S WHY I WAS ALWAYS DISSATISFIED. I PREFER BEING RICH.
TIME HAS TAUGHT ME, IT MAKES LIFE A LOT EASIER.
AND CONSIDERING H EVERY ONE OF MY L HAS ENDED IN VIOLE AND PAIN...
IT NEVER HURTS HAVE A FEW PER

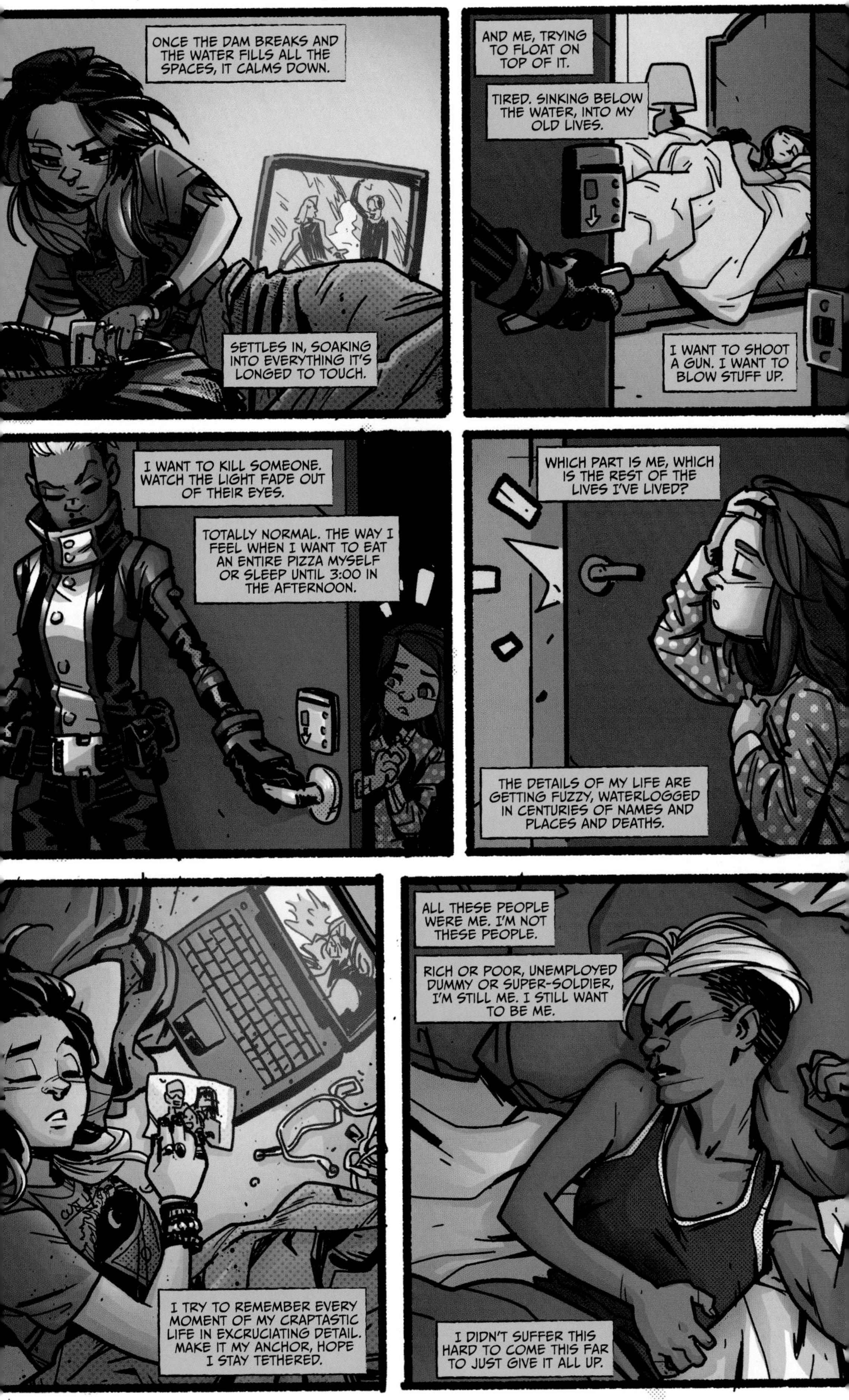
ONCE THE DAM BREAKS AND THE WATER FILLS ALL THE SPACES, IT CALMS DOWN.
SETTLES IN, SOAKING INTO EVERYTHING IT'S LONGED TO TOUCH.
AND ME, TRYING TO FLOAT ON TOP OF IT.
TIRED. SINKING BELOW THE WATER, INTO MY OLD LIVES.
I WANT TO SHOOT A GUN. I WANT TO BLOW STUFF UP.
I WANT TO KILL SOMEONE. WATCH THE LIGHT FADE OUT OF THEIR EYES.
TOTALLY NORMAL. THE WAY I FEEL WHEN I WANT TO EAT AN ENTIRE PIZZA MYSELF OR SLEEP UNTIL 3:00 IN THE AFTERNOON.
WHICH PART IS ME, WHICH IS THE REST OF THE LIVES I'VE LIVED?
THE DETAILS OF MY LIFE ARE GETTING FUZZY, WATERLOGGED IN CENTURIES OF NAMES AND PLACES AND DEATHS.
I TRY TO REMEMBER EVERY MOMENT OF MY CRAPTASTIC LIFE IN EXCRUCIATING DETAIL. MAKE IT MY ANCHOR, HOPE I STAY TETHERED.
ALL THESE PEOPLE WERE ME. I'M NOT THESE PEOPLE.
RICH OR POOR, UNEMPLOYED DUMMY OR SUPER-SOLDIER, I'M STILL ME. I STILL WANT TO BE ME.
I DIDN'T SUFFER THIS HARD TO COME THIS FAR TO JUST GIVE IT ALL UP.

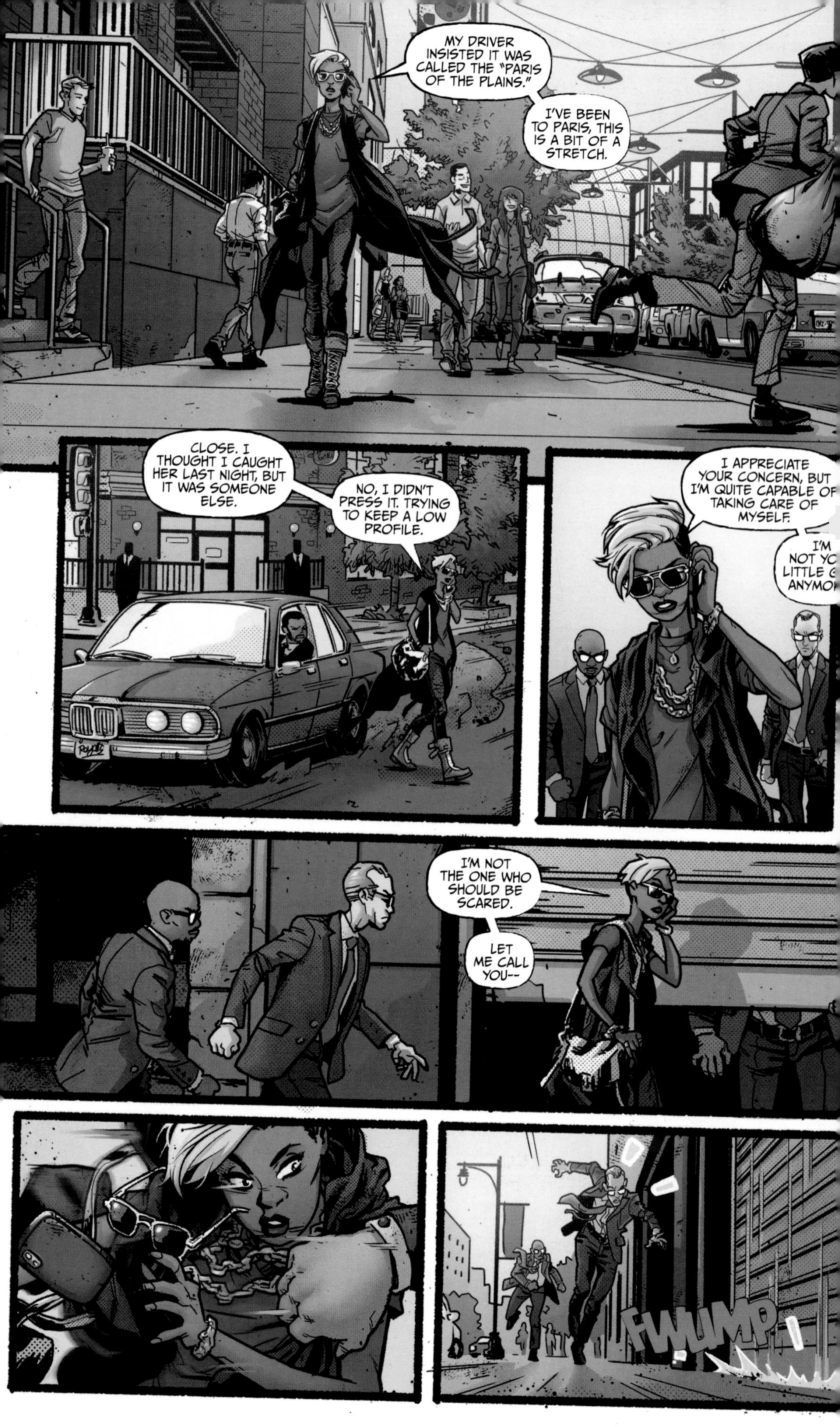
MY DRIVER INSISTED IT WAS CALLED THE "PARIS OF THE PLAINS."
I'VE BEEN TO PARIS, THIS IS A BIT OF A STRETCH.
CLOSE. I THOUGHT I CAUGHT HER LAST NIGHT, BUT IT WAS SOMEONE ELSE.
NO, I DIDN'T PRESS IT. TRYING TO KEEP A LOW PROFILE.
I APPRECIATE YOUR CONCERN, BUT I'M QUITE CAPABLE OF TAKING CARE OF MYSELF.
I'M NOT YO LITTLE G ANYMO
I'M NOT THE ONE WHO SHOULD BE SCARED.
LET ME CALL YOU--
FWUMP

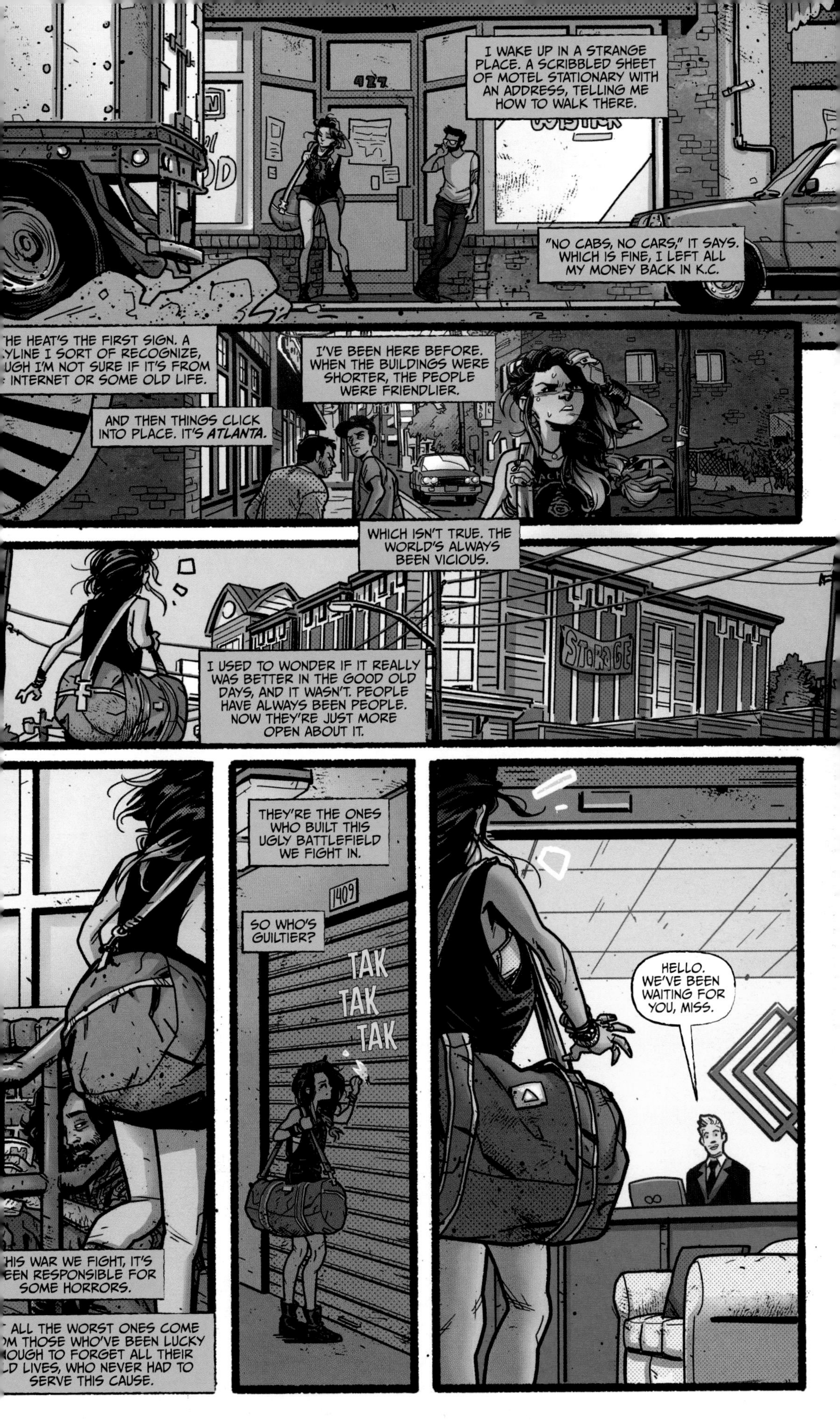
I WAKE UP IN A STRANGE PLACE. A SCRIBBLED SHEET OF MOTEL STATIONARY WITH AN ADDRESS, TELLING ME HOW TO WALK THERE.
427
"NO CABS, NO CARS," IT SAYS. WHICH IS FINE, I LEFT ALL MY MONEY BACK IN K.C.
HE HEAT'S THE FIRST SIGN. A YLINE I SORT OF RECOGNIZE, UGH I'M NOT SURE IF IT'S FROM INTERNET OR SOME OLD LIFE.
AND THEN THINGS CLICK INTO PLACE. IT'S *ATLANTA.*
I'VE BEEN HERE BEFORE. WHEN THE BUILDINGS WERE SHORTER, THE PEOPLE WERE FRIENDLIER.
WHICH ISN'T TRUE. THE WORLD'S ALWAYS BEEN VICIOUS.
STORAGE
I USED TO WONDER IF IT REALLY WAS BETTER IN THE GOOD OLD DAYS, AND IT WASN'T. PEOPLE HAVE ALWAYS BEEN PEOPLE. NOW THEY'RE JUST MORE OPEN ABOUT IT.
HIS WAR WE FIGHT, IT'S EEN RESPONSIBLE FOR SOME HORRORS.
ALL THE WORST ONES COME OM THOSE WHO'VE BEEN LUCKY OUGH TO FORGET ALL THEIR D LIVES, WHO NEVER HAD TO SERVE THIS CAUSE.
THEY'RE THE ONES WHO BUILT THIS UGLY BATTLEFIELD WE FIGHT IN.
1409
SO WHO'S GUILTIER?
TAK
TAK
TAK
HELLO. WE'VE BEEN WAITING FOR YOU, MISS.

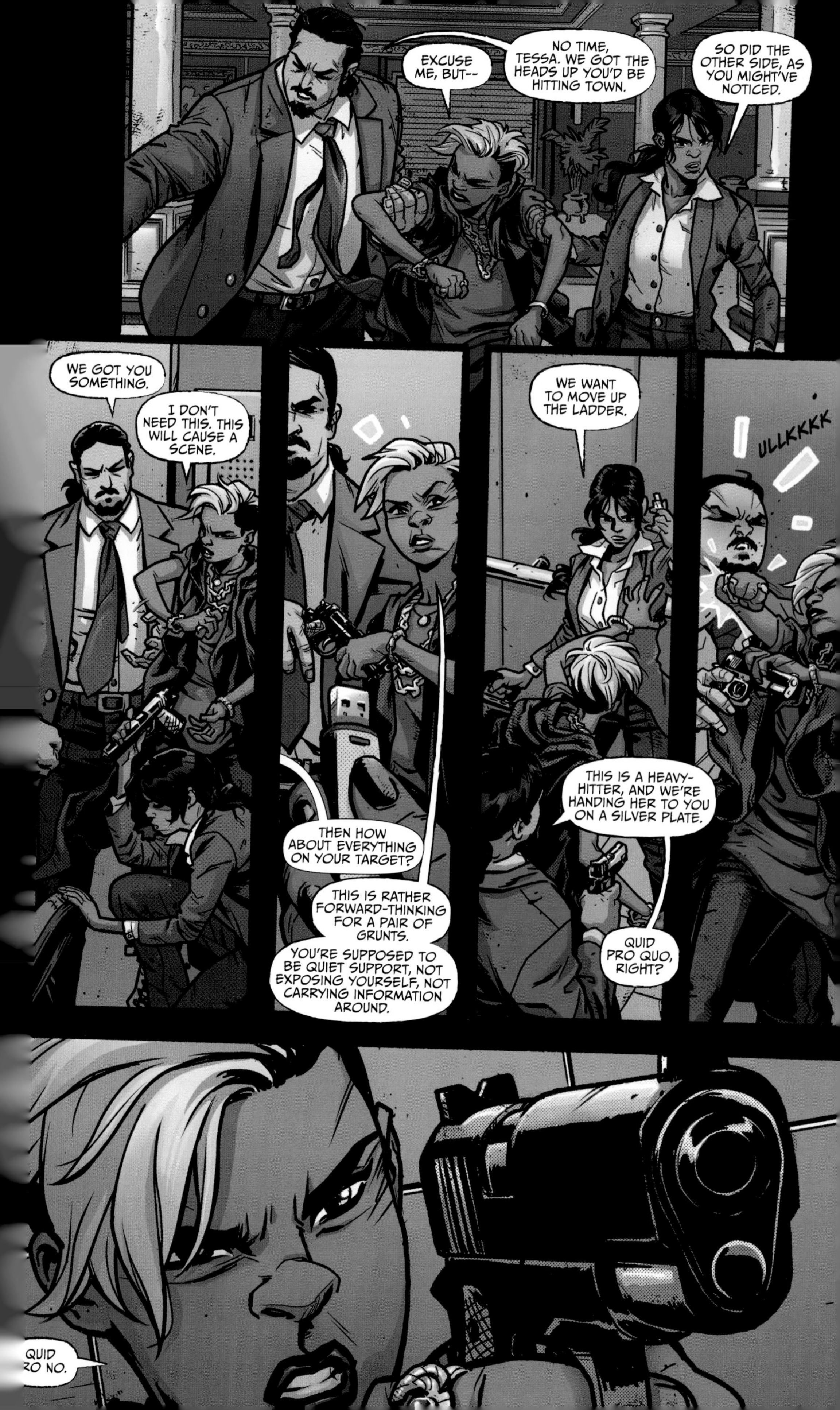
EXCUSE ME, BUT--
NO TIME, TESSA. WE GOT THE HEADS UP YOU'D BE HITTING TOWN.
SO DID THE OTHER SIDE, AS YOU MIGHT'VE NOTICED.
WE GOT YOU SOMETHING.
I DON'T NEED THIS. THIS WILL CAUSE A SCENE.
THEN HOW ABOUT EVERYTHING ON YOUR TARGET?
THIS IS RATHER FORWARD-THINKING FOR A PAIR OF GRUNTS.
YOU'RE SUPPOSED TO BE QUIET SUPPORT, NOT EXPOSING YOURSELF, NOT CARRYING INFORMATION AROUND.
WE WANT TO MOVE UP THE LADDER.
THIS IS A HEAVY-HITTER, AND WE'RE HANDING HER TO YOU ON A SILVER PLATE.
QUID PRO QUO, RIGHT?
ULLKKKK
QUID ZO NO.

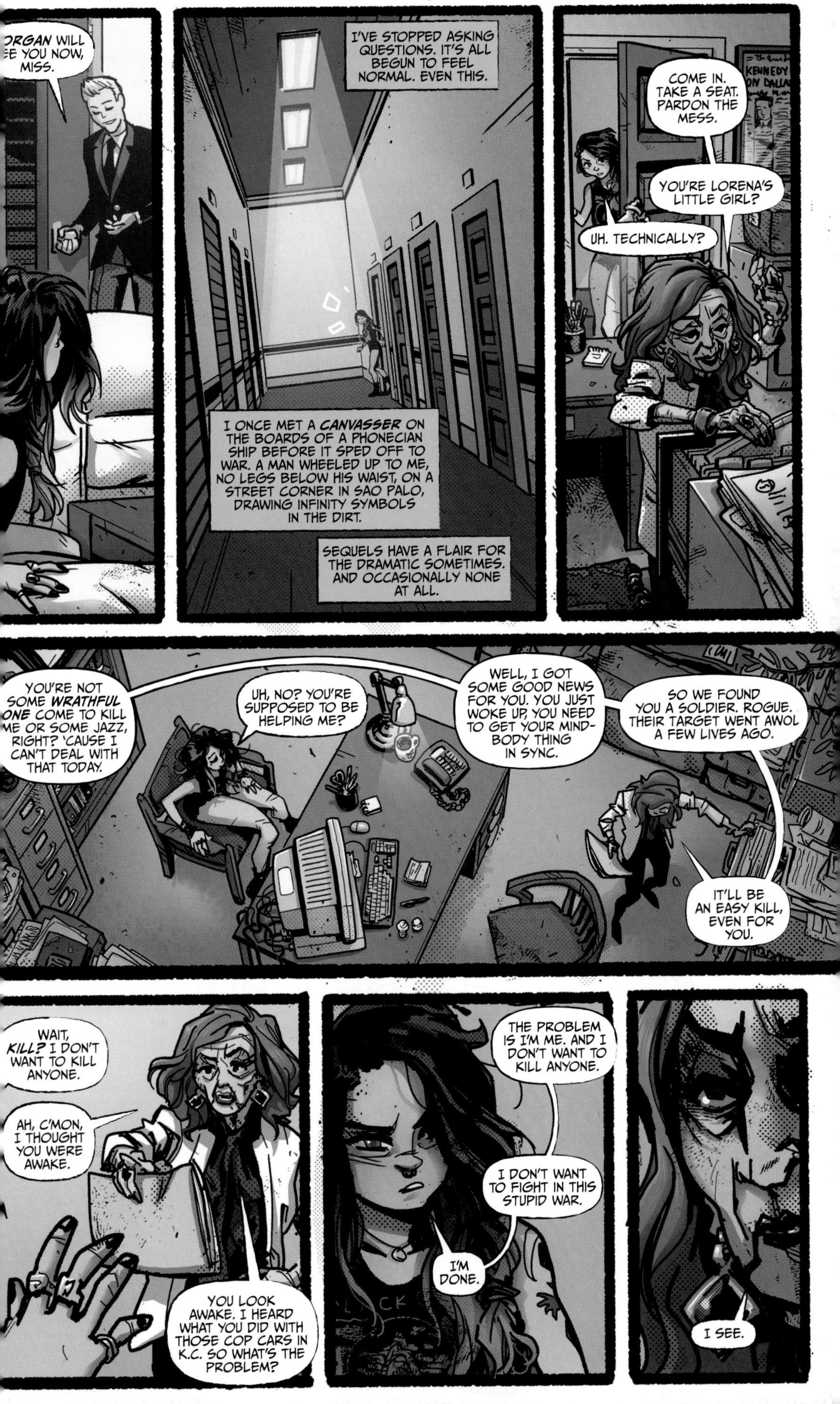
ORGAN WILL
EE YOU NOW,
MISS.
I'VE STOPPED ASKING QUESTIONS. IT'S ALL BEGUN TO FEEL NORMAL. EVEN THIS.
I ONCE MET A CANVASSER ON THE BOARDS OF A PHONECIAN SHIP BEFORE IT SPED OFF TO WAR. A MAN WHEELED UP TO ME, NO LEGS BELOW HIS WAIST, ON A STREET CORNER IN SAO PALO, DRAWING INFINITY SYMBOLS IN THE DIRT.
SEQUELS HAVE A FLAIR FOR THE DRAMATIC SOMETIMES. AND OCCASIONALLY NONE AT ALL.
COME IN. TAKE A SEAT. PARDON THE MESS.
YOU'RE LORENA'S LITTLE GIRL?
UH. TECHNICALLY?
YOU'RE NOT SOME WRATHFUL ONE COME TO KILL ME OR SOME JAZZ, RIGHT? 'CAUSE I CAN'T DEAL WITH THAT TODAY.
UH, NO? YOU'RE SUPPOSED TO BE HELPING ME?
WELL, I GOT SOME GOOD NEWS FOR YOU. YOU JUST WOKE UP, YOU NEED TO GET YOUR MIND-BODY THING IN SYNC.
SO WE FOUND YOU A SOLDIER. ROGUE. THEIR TARGET WENT AWOL A FEW LIVES AGO.
IT'LL BE AN EASY KILL, EVEN FOR YOU.
WAIT, KILL? I DON'T WANT TO KILL ANYONE.
AH, C'MON, I THOUGHT YOU WERE AWAKE.
YOU LOOK AWAKE. I HEARD WHAT YOU DID WITH THOSE COP CARS IN K.C. SO WHAT'S THE PROBLEM?
THE PROBLEM IS I'M ME. AND I DON'T WANT TO KILL ANYONE.
I DON'T WANT TO FIGHT IN THIS STUPID WAR.
I'M DONE.
I SEE.

"HA. HA HA. GOING DOWN."

"I'M GOING TO TELL YOU A STORY, YOUNG LADY.

"SIT STILL AND LISTEN. IT WON'T TAKE LONG.

"THERE WAS A QUEEN WHO BECAME LOST IN THE WOODS. FOR YEARS, DECADES. HER KINGDOM UNATTENDED TO.

"UNTIL ONE DAY SHE FOUND HER WAY OUT, BACK INTO THE WORLD SHE LEFT. AND IT LOOKED AS IF IT WAS DIFFERENT, MORE ENLIGHTENED, BETTER."

I SURRENDER.

"BUT THE WORLD SHE CAME BACK TO WAS EXACTLY AS SHE'D LEFT IT. ONLY HIDDEN BETTER.

"SO IS THAT A THREAT?

"DO WHAT WE SAY OR WE KILL EVERYONE YOU LOVE?"

"IT'S A REALITY, MALI. THERE ARE NO CONSCIENTIOUS OBJECTORS IN THIS FIGHT.

"YOU STILL HAVE A CHOICE. YOU CAN LEAVE, GO BACK HOME, PRETEND YOU'RE NOT WHO YOU ARE.

"BUT THAT LIFE ISN'T YOURS ANYMORE, YOU WERE BORROWING IT UNTIL YOU WOKE UP.

"YOU GO BACK AND EVERYTHING YOU CHERISHED ABOUT IT WILL DIE ALL AROUND YOU."

"I CAN PROT
THEM. I CAN
THEM ALIVE

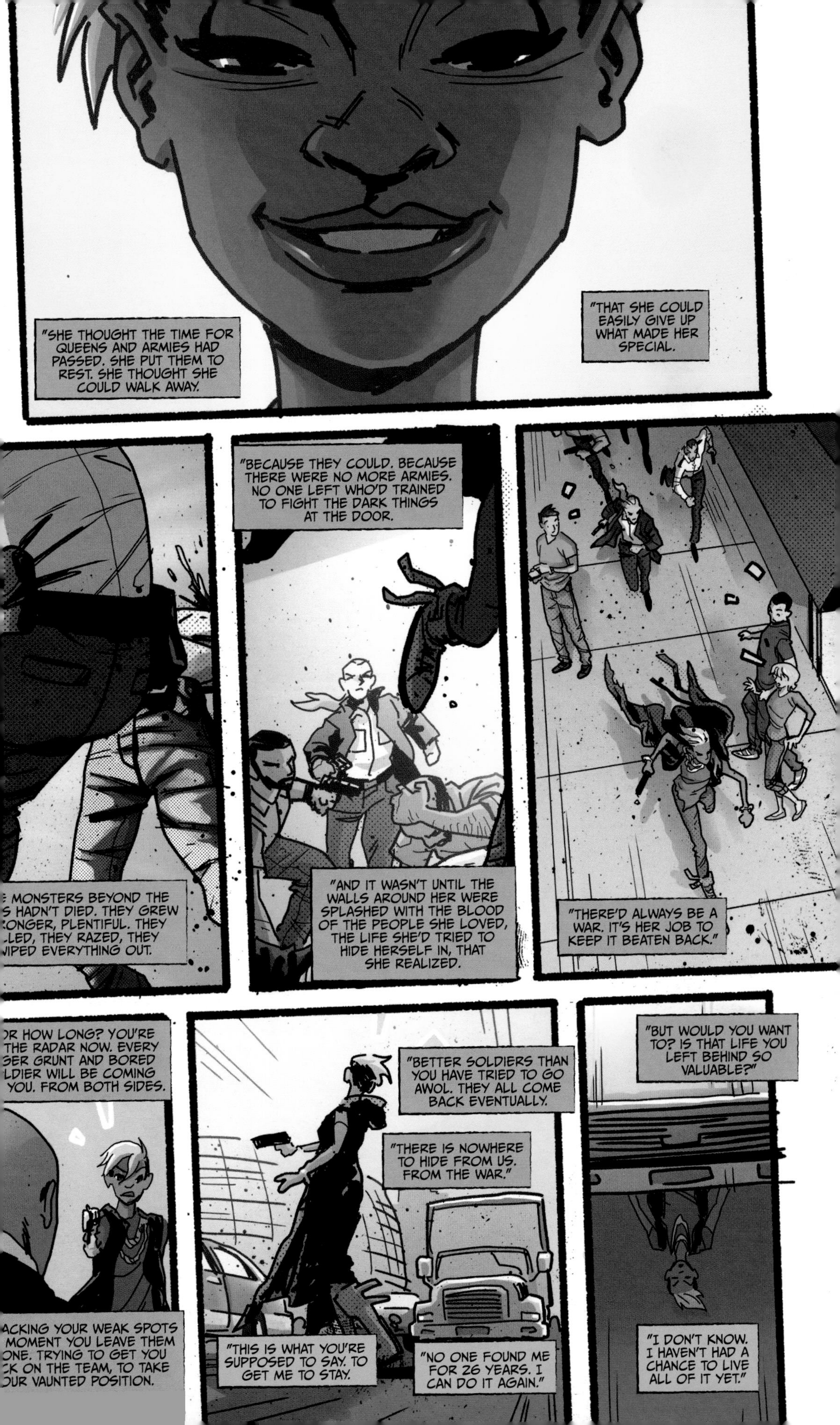
"SHE THOUGHT THE TIME FOR QUEENS AND ARMIES HAD PASSED. SHE PUT THEM TO REST. SHE THOUGHT SHE COULD WALK AWAY.
"THAT SHE COULD EASILY GIVE UP WHAT MADE HER SPECIAL.
"BECAUSE THEY COULD. BECAUSE THERE WERE NO MORE ARMIES. NO ONE LEFT WHO'D TRAINED TO FIGHT THE DARK THINGS AT THE DOOR.
E MONSTERS BEYOND THE S HADN'T DIED. THEY GREW RONGER, PLENTIFUL. THEY LLED, THEY RAZED, THEY WIPED EVERYTHING OUT.
"AND IT WASN'T UNTIL THE WALLS AROUND HER WERE SPLASHED WITH THE BLOOD OF THE PEOPLE SHE LOVED, THE LIFE SHE'D TRIED TO HIDE HERSELF IN, THAT SHE REALIZED.
"THERE'D ALWAYS BE A WAR. IT'S HER JOB TO KEEP IT BEATEN BACK."
OR HOW LONG? YOU'RE THE RADAR NOW. EVERY GER GRUNT AND BORED LDIER WILL BE COMING YOU. FROM BOTH SIDES.
ACKING YOUR WEAK SPOTS MOMENT YOU LEAVE THEM ONE. TRYING TO GET YOU CK ON THE TEAM, TO TAKE OUR VAUNTED POSITION.
"BETTER SOLDIERS THAN YOU HAVE TRIED TO GO AWOL. THEY ALL COME BACK EVENTUALLY.
"THERE IS NOWHERE TO HIDE FROM US. FROM THE WAR."
"THIS IS WHAT YOU'RE SUPPOSED TO SAY. TO GET ME TO STAY.
"NO ONE FOUND ME FOR 26 YEARS. I CAN DO IT AGAIN."
"BUT WOULD YOU WANT TO? IS THAT LIFE YOU LEFT BEHIND SO VALUABLE?"
"I DON'T KNOW. I HAVEN'T HAD A CHANCE TO LIVE ALL OF IT YET."

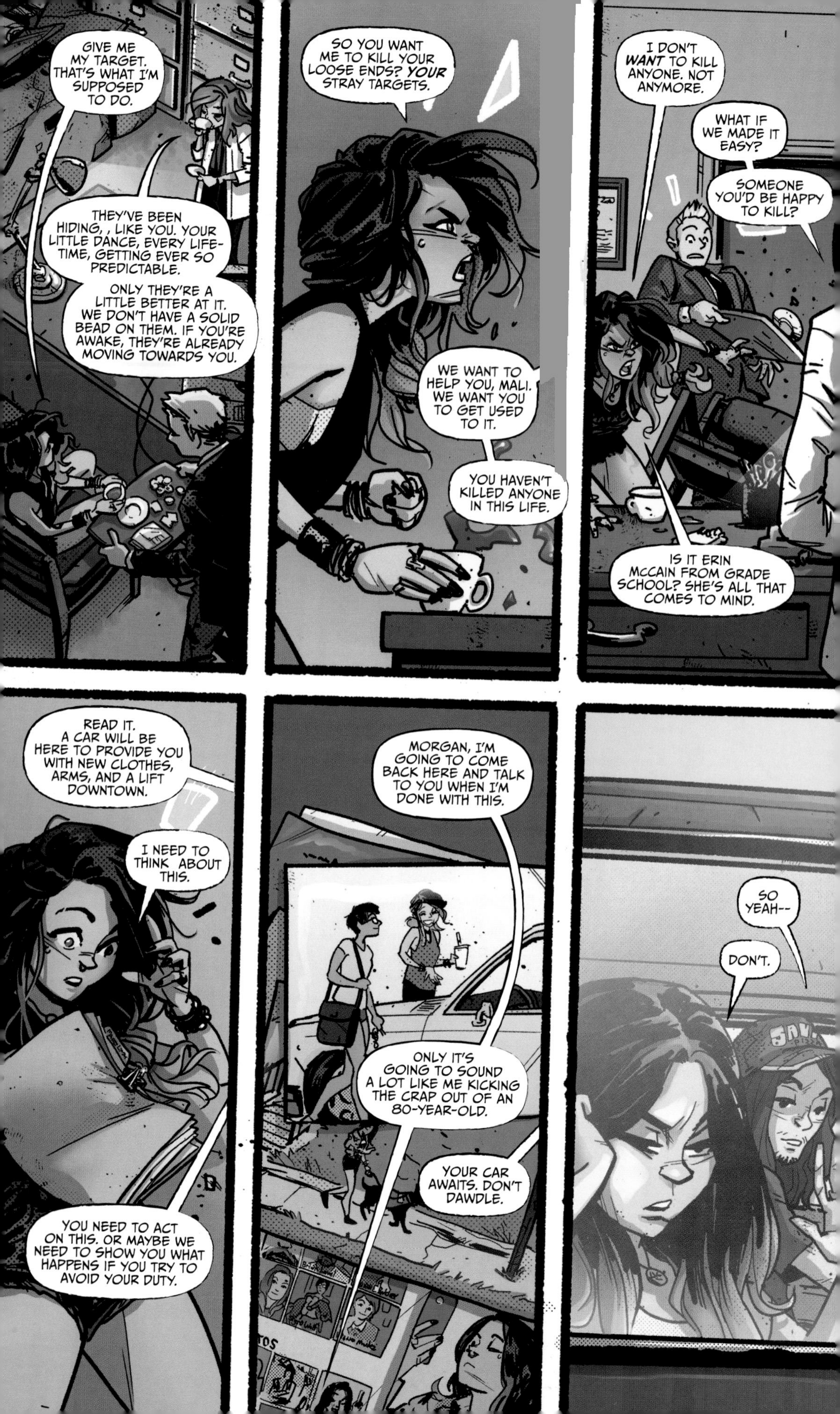
GIVE ME MY TARGET. THAT'S WHAT I'M SUPPOSED TO DO.
THEY'VE BEEN HIDING, , LIKE YOU. YOUR LITTLE DANCE, EVERY LIFE-TIME, GETTING EVER SO PREDICTABLE.
ONLY THEY'RE A LITTLE BETTER AT IT. WE DON'T HAVE A SOLID BEAD ON THEM. IF YOU'RE AWAKE, THEY'RE ALREADY MOVING TOWARDS YOU.
SO YOU WANT ME TO KILL YOUR LOOSE ENDS? YOUR STRAY TARGETS.
WE WANT TO HELP YOU, MALI. WE WANT YOU TO GET USED TO IT.
YOU HAVEN'T KILLED ANYONE IN THIS LIFE.
I DON'T WANT TO KILL ANYONE. NOT ANYMORE.
WHAT IF WE MADE IT EASY?
SOMEONE YOU'D BE HAPPY TO KILL?
IS IT ERIN McCAIN FROM GRADE SCHOOL? SHE'S ALL THAT COMES TO MIND.
READ IT. A CAR WILL BE HERE TO PROVIDE YOU WITH NEW CLOTHES, ARMS, AND A LIFT DOWNTOWN.
I NEED TO THINK ABOUT THIS.
YOU NEED TO ACT ON THIS. OR MAYBE WE NEED TO SHOW YOU WHAT HAPPENS IF YOU TRY TO AVOID YOUR DUTY.
MORGAN, I'M GOING TO COME BACK HERE AND TALK TO YOU WHEN I'M DONE WITH THIS.
ONLY IT'S GOING TO SOUND A LOT LIKE ME KICKING THE CRAP OUT OF AN 80-YEAR-OLD.
YOUR CAR AWAITS. DON'T DAWDLE.
SO YEAH--
DON'T.

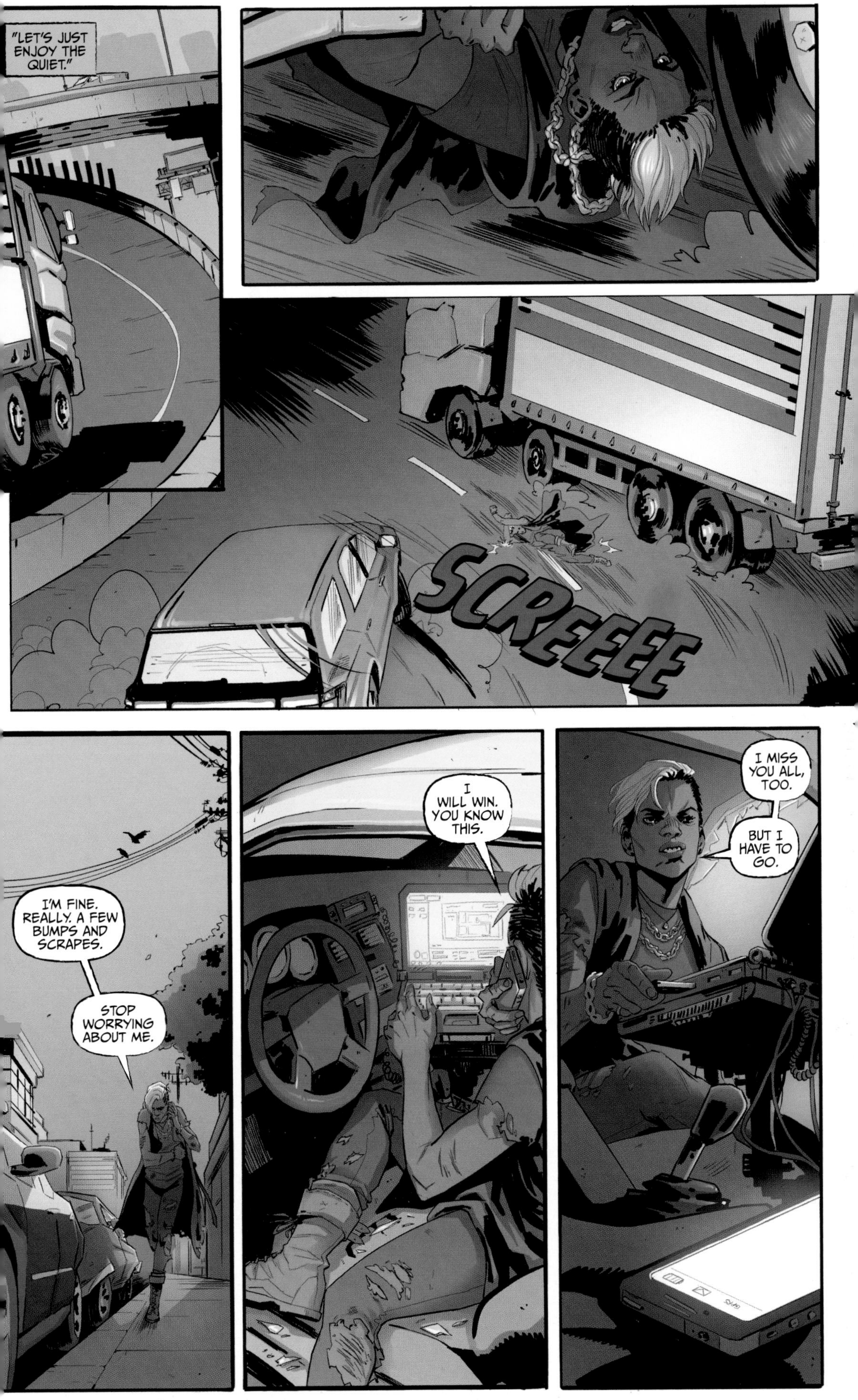
"LET'S JUST ENJOY THE QUIET."
SCREEEEE
I'M FINE. REALLY. A FEW BUMPS AND SCRAPES.
STOP WORRYING ABOUT ME.
I WILL WIN. YOU KNOW THIS.
I MISS YOU ALL, TOO.
BUT I HAVE TO GO.

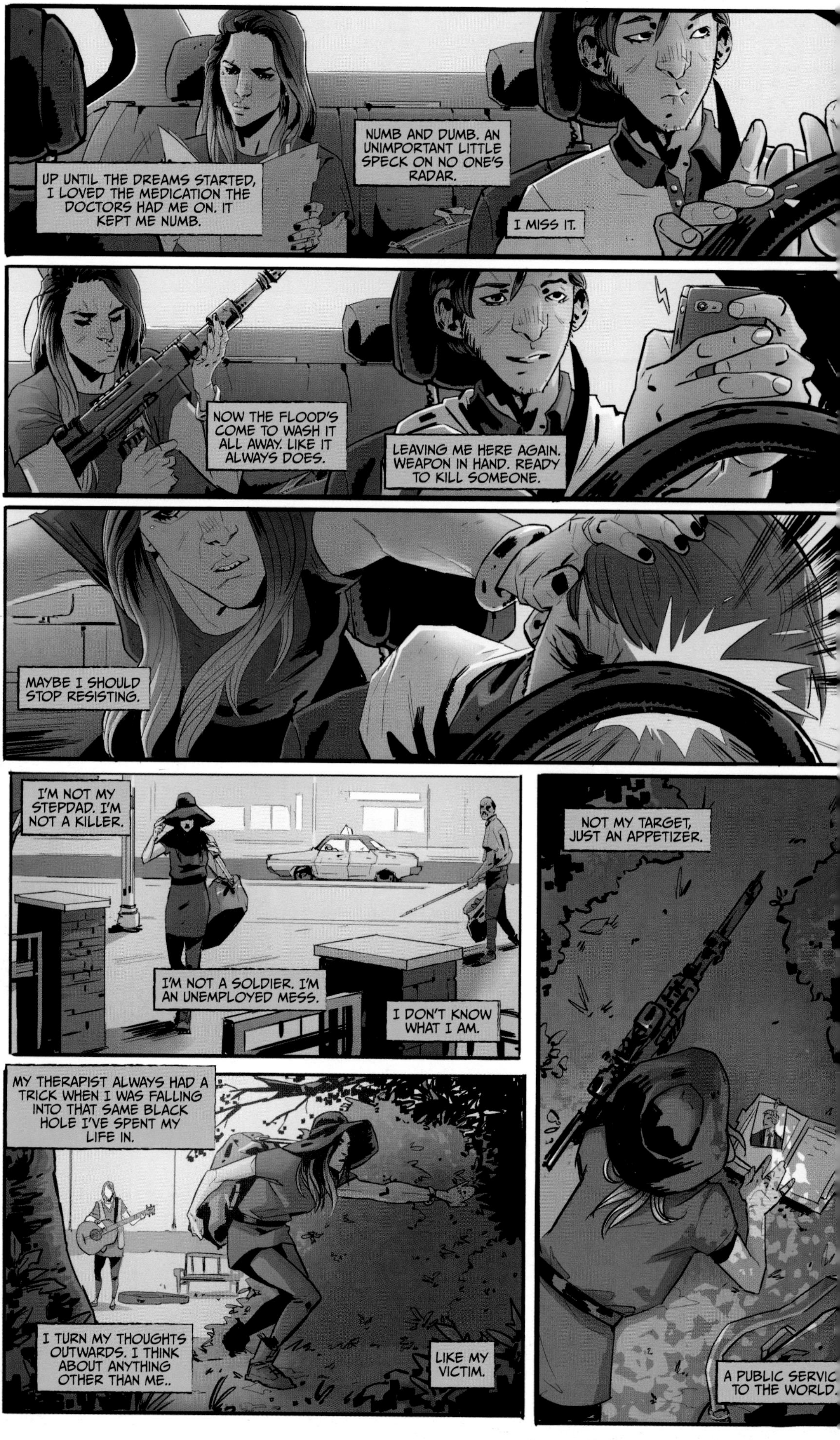
UP UNTIL THE DREAMS STARTED, I LOVED THE MEDICATION THE DOCTORS HAD ME ON. IT KEPT ME NUMB.
NUMB AND DUMB. AN UNIMPORTANT LITTLE SPECK ON NO ONE'S RADAR.
I MISS IT.
NOW THE FLOOD'S COME TO WASH IT ALL AWAY. LIKE IT ALWAYS DOES.
LEAVING ME HERE AGAIN. WEAPON IN HAND. READY TO KILL SOMEONE.
MAYBE I SHOULD STOP RESISTING.
I'M NOT MY STEPDAD. I'M NOT A KILLER.
I'M NOT A SOLDIER. I'M AN UNEMPLOYED MESS.
I DON'T KNOW WHAT I AM.
MY THERAPIST ALWAYS HAD A TRICK WHEN I WAS FALLING INTO THAT SAME BLACK HOLE I'VE SPENT MY LIFE IN.
I TURN MY THOUGHTS OUTWARDS. I THINK ABOUT ANYTHING OTHER THAN ME..
LIKE MY VICTIM.
NOT MY TARGET, JUST AN APPETIZER.
A PUBLIC SERVIC
TO THE WORLD.

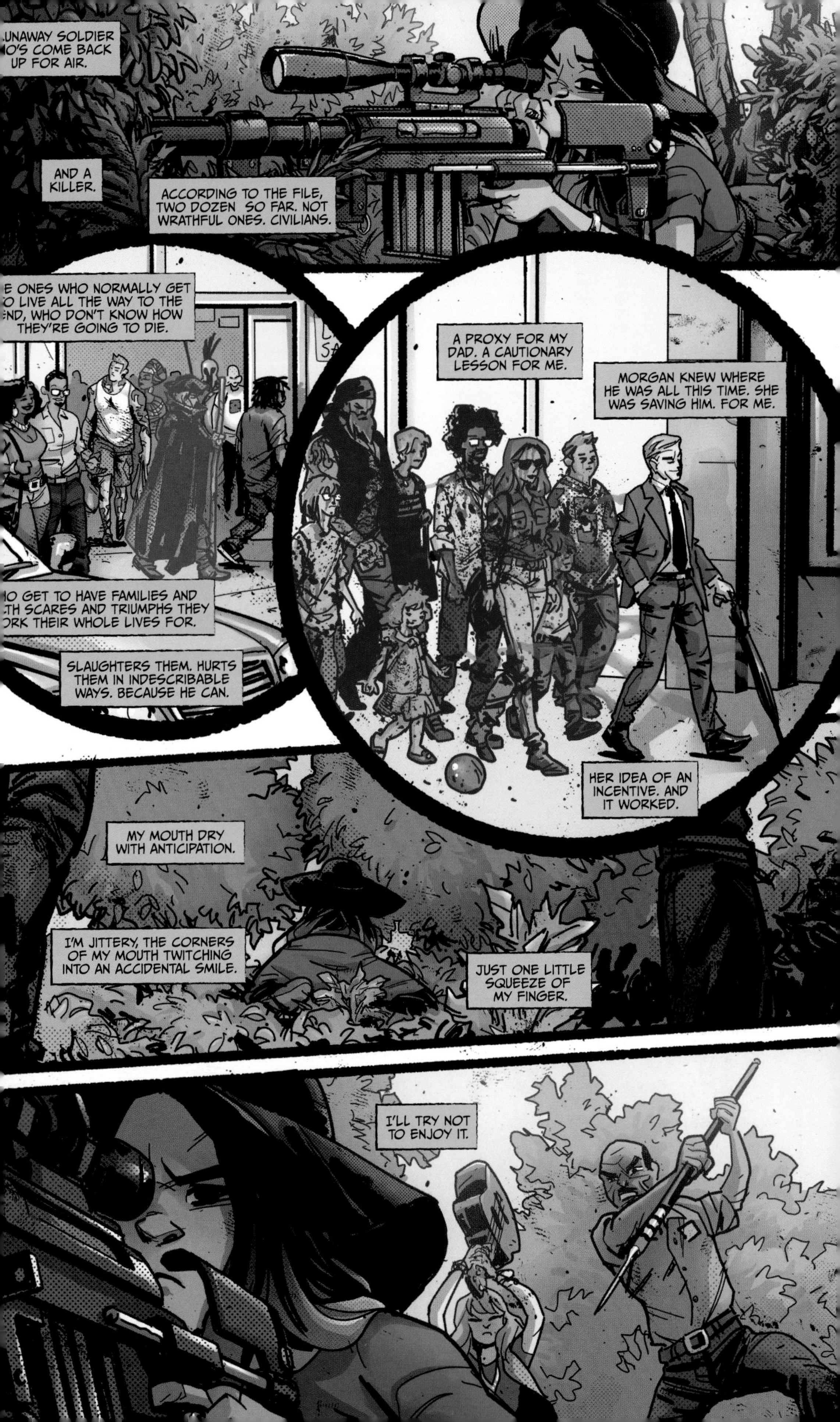

UNAWAY SOLDIER
O'S COME BACK
UP FOR AIR.
AND A KILLER.
ACCORDING TO THE FILE, TWO DOZEN SO FAR. NOT WRATHFUL ONES. CIVILIANS.
E ONES WHO NORMALLY GET
O LIVE ALL THE WAY TO THE
END, WHO DON'T KNOW HOW
THEY'RE GOING TO DIE.
O GET TO HAVE FAMILIES AND
TH SCARES AND TRIUMPHS THEY
ORK THEIR WHOLE LIVES FOR.
SLAUGHTERS THEM. HURTS THEM IN INDESCRIBABLE WAYS. BECAUSE HE CAN.
A PROXY FOR MY DAD. A CAUTIONARY LESSON FOR ME.
MORGAN KNEW WHERE HE WAS ALL THIS TIME. SHE WAS SAVING HIM. FOR ME.
HER IDEA OF AN INCENTIVE. AND IT WORKED.
MY MOUTH DRY WITH ANTICIPATION.
I'M JITTERY, THE CORNERS OF MY MOUTH TWITCHING INTO AN ACCIDENTAL SMILE.
JUST ONE LITTLE SQUEEZE OF MY FINGER.
I'LL TRY NOT TO ENJOY IT.

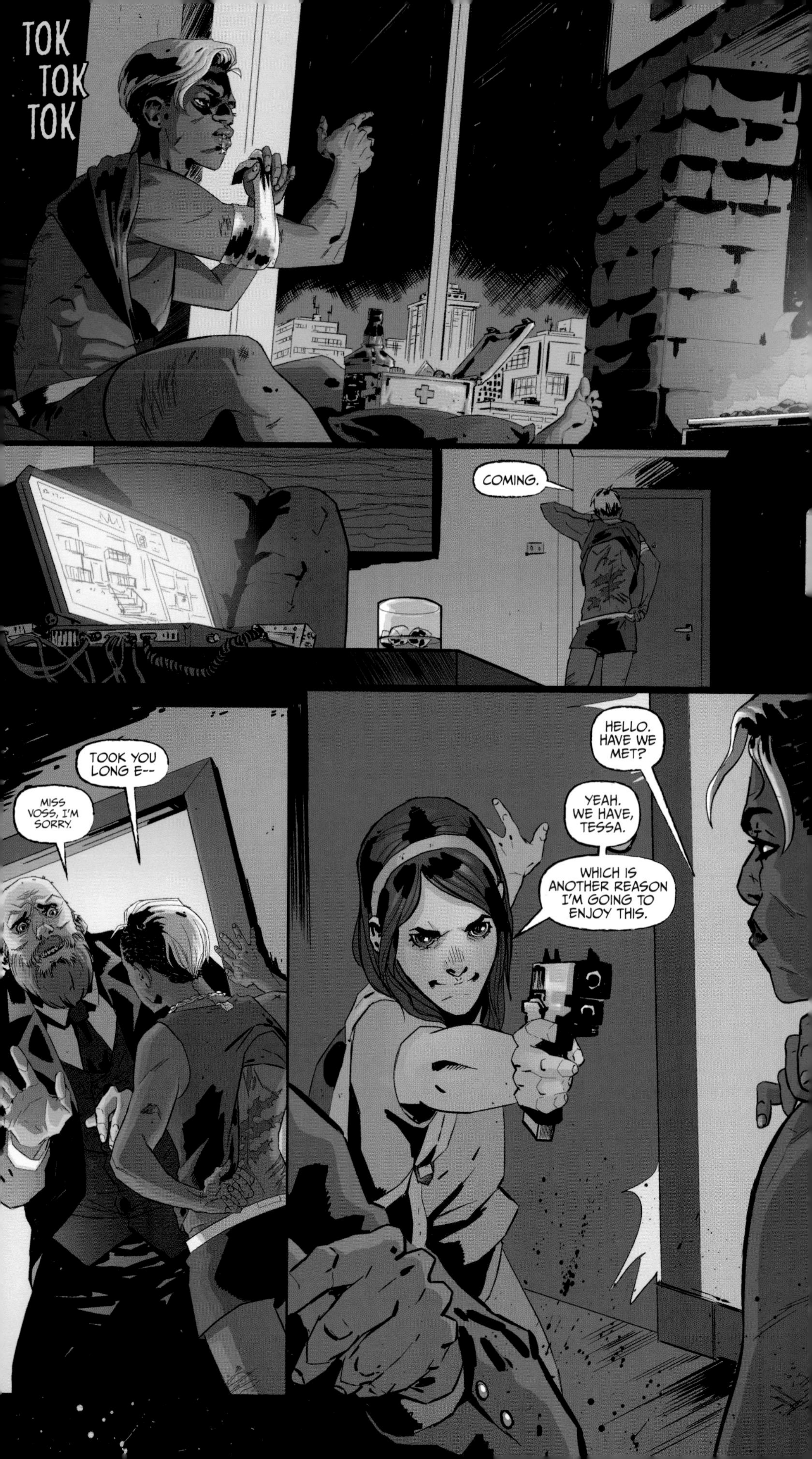
TOK
TOK
TOK
COMING.
TOOK YOU LONG E--
MISS VOSS, I'M SORRY.
HELLO. HAVE WE MET?
YEAH. WE HAVE, TESSA.
WHICH IS ANOTHER REASON I'M GOING TO ENJOY THIS.

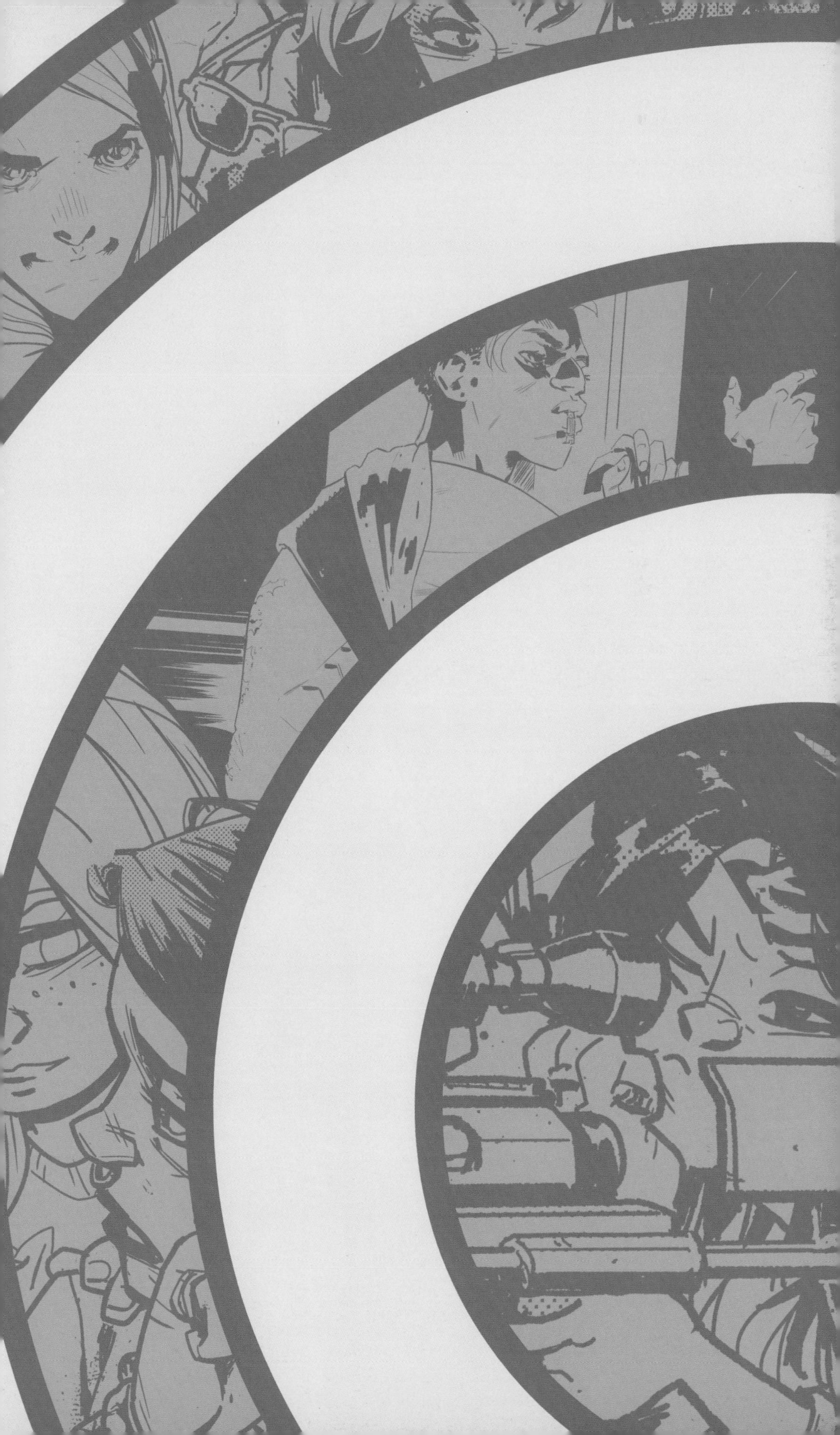

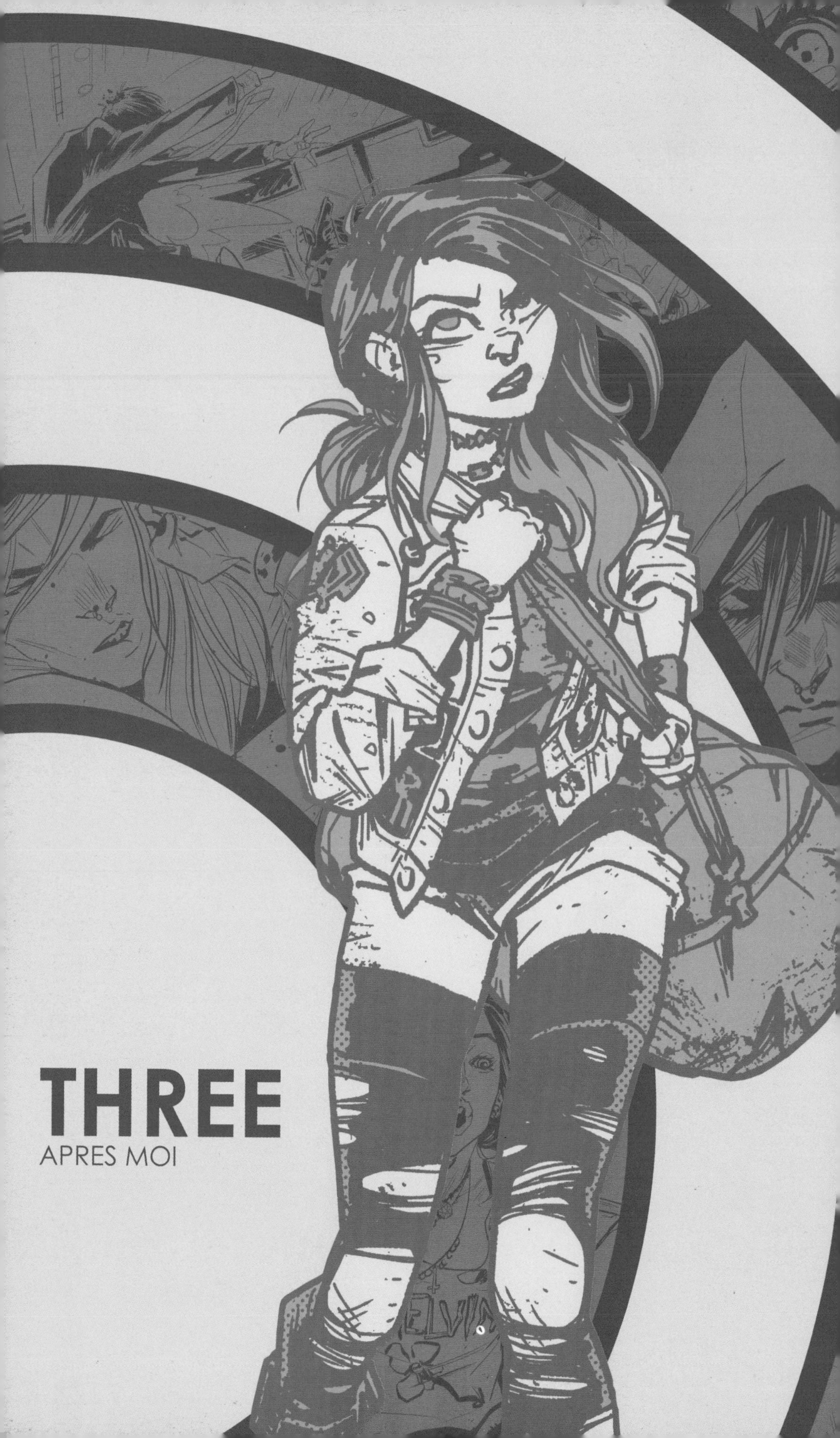

THREE
APRES MOI

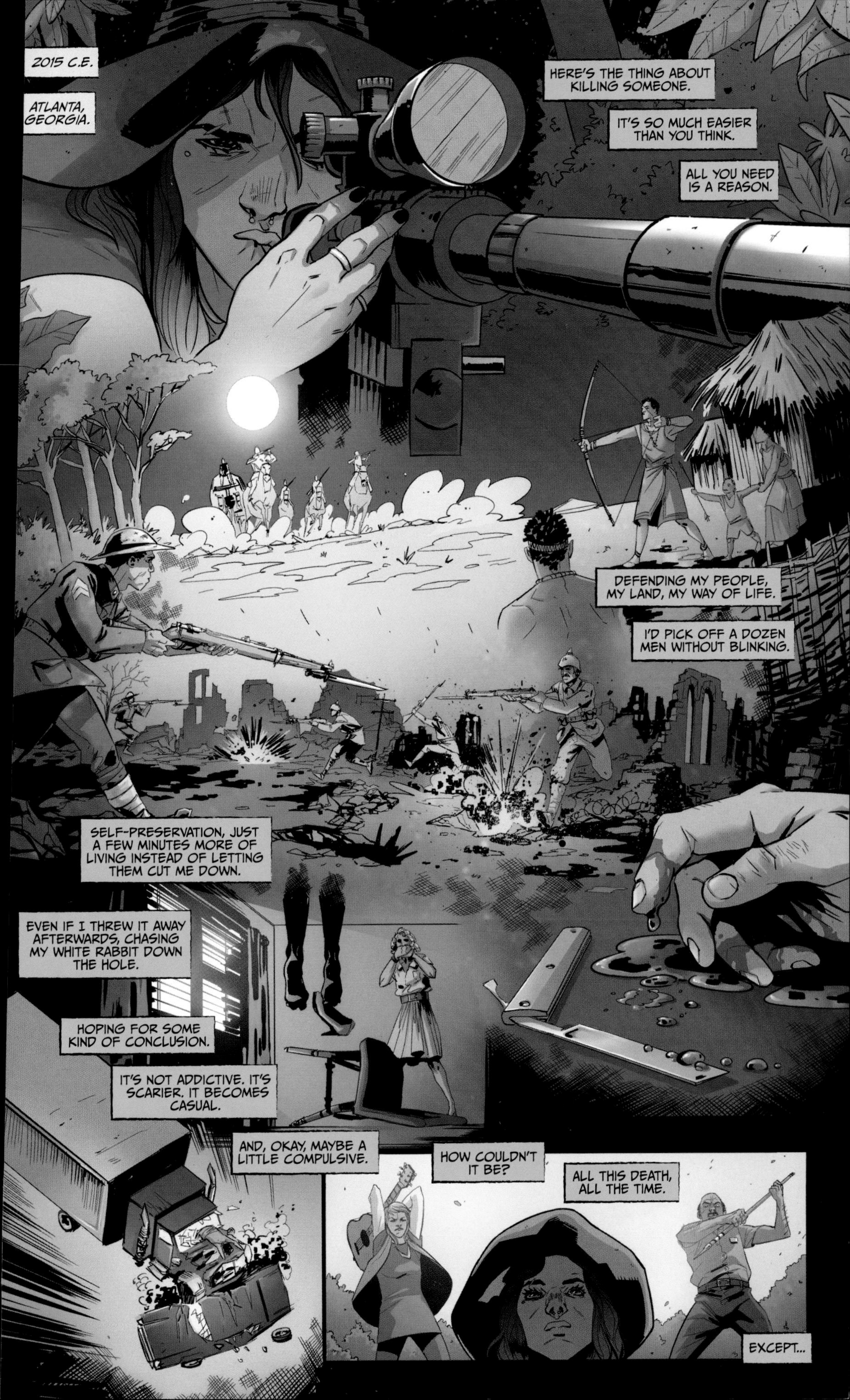
2015 C.E.
ATLANTA, GEORGIA.
HERE'S THE THING ABOUT KILLING SOMEONE.
IT'S SO MUCH EASIER THAN YOU THINK.
ALL YOU NEED IS A REASON.
DEFENDING MY PEOPLE, MY LAND, MY WAY OF LIFE.
I'D PICK OFF A DOZEN MEN WITHOUT BLINKING.
SELF-PRESERVATION, JUST A FEW MINUTES MORE OF LIVING INSTEAD OF LETTING THEM CUT ME DOWN.
EVEN IF I THREW IT AWAY AFTERWARDS, CHASING MY WHITE RABBIT DOWN THE HOLE.
HOPING FOR SOME KIND OF CONCLUSION.
IT'S NOT ADDICTIVE. IT'S SCARIER. IT BECOMES CASUAL.
AND, OKAY, MAYBE A LITTLE COMPULSIVE.
HOW COULDN'T IT BE?
ALL THIS DEATH, ALL THE TIME.
EXCEPT...

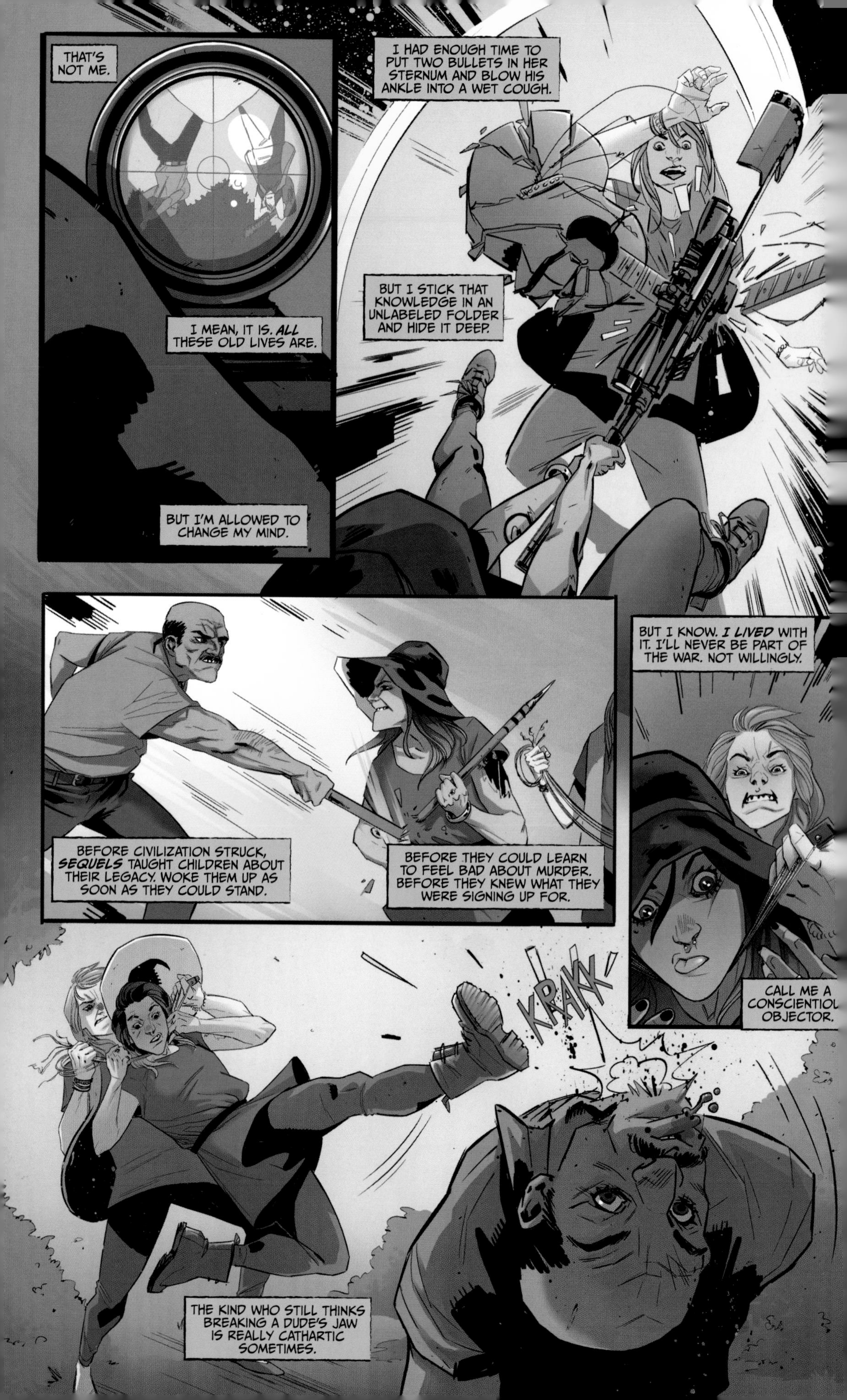
THAT'S NOT ME.
I MEAN, IT IS. *ALL* THESE OLD LIVES ARE.
BUT I'M ALLOWED TO CHANGE MY MIND.
I HAD ENOUGH TIME TO PUT TWO BULLETS IN HER STERNUM AND BLOW HIS ANKLE INTO A WET COUGH.
BUT I STICK THAT KNOWLEDGE IN AN UNLABELED FOLDER AND HIDE IT DEEP.
BEFORE CIVILIZATION STRUCK, *SEQUELS* TAUGHT CHILDREN ABOUT THEIR LEGACY. WOKE THEM UP AS SOON AS THEY COULD STAND.
BEFORE THEY COULD LEARN TO FEEL BAD ABOUT MURDER. BEFORE THEY KNEW WHAT THEY WERE SIGNING UP FOR.
BUT I KNOW. *I LIVED* WITH IT. I'LL NEVER BE PART OF THE WAR. NOT WILLINGLY.
CALL ME A CONSCIENTIOU OBJECTOR.
KRAKK'
THE KIND WHO STILL THINKS BREAKING A DUDE'S JAW IS REALLY CATHARTIC SOMETIMES.

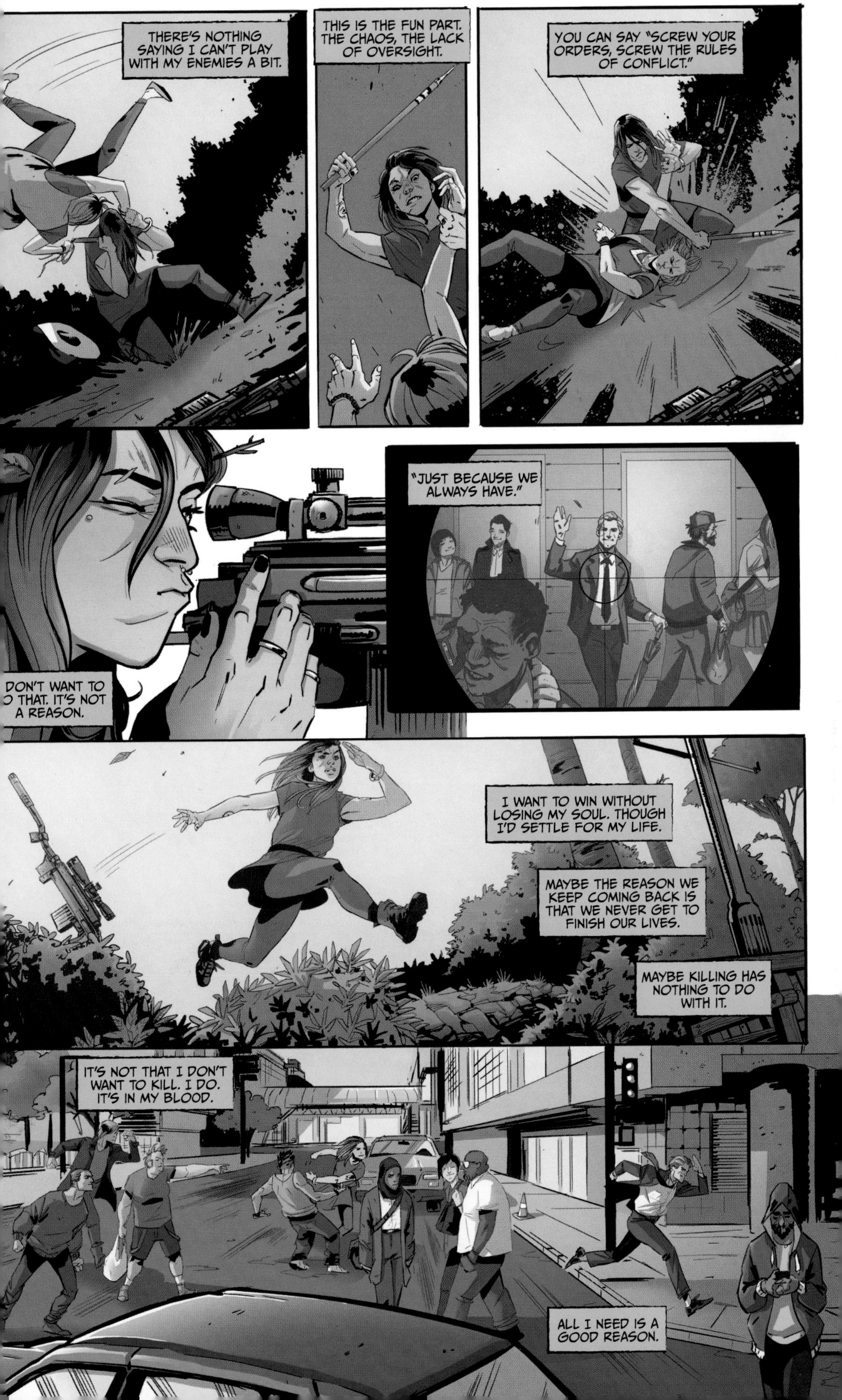
THERE'S NOTHING SAYING I CAN'T PLAY WITH MY ENEMIES A BIT.
THIS IS THE FUN PART. THE CHAOS, THE LACK OF OVERSIGHT.
YOU CAN SAY "SCREW YOUR ORDERS, SCREW THE RULES OF CONFLICT."
"JUST BECAUSE WE ALWAYS HAVE."
DON'T WANT TO O THAT. IT'S NOT A REASON.
I WANT TO WIN WITHOUT LOSING MY SOUL. THOUGH I'D SETTLE FOR MY LIFE.
MAYBE THE REASON WE KEEP COMING BACK IS THAT WE NEVER GET TO FINISH OUR LIVES.
MAYBE KILLING HAS NOTHING TO DO WITH IT.
IT'S NOT THAT I DON'T WANT TO KILL. I DO. IT'S IN MY BLOOD.
ALL I NEED IS A GOOD REASON.

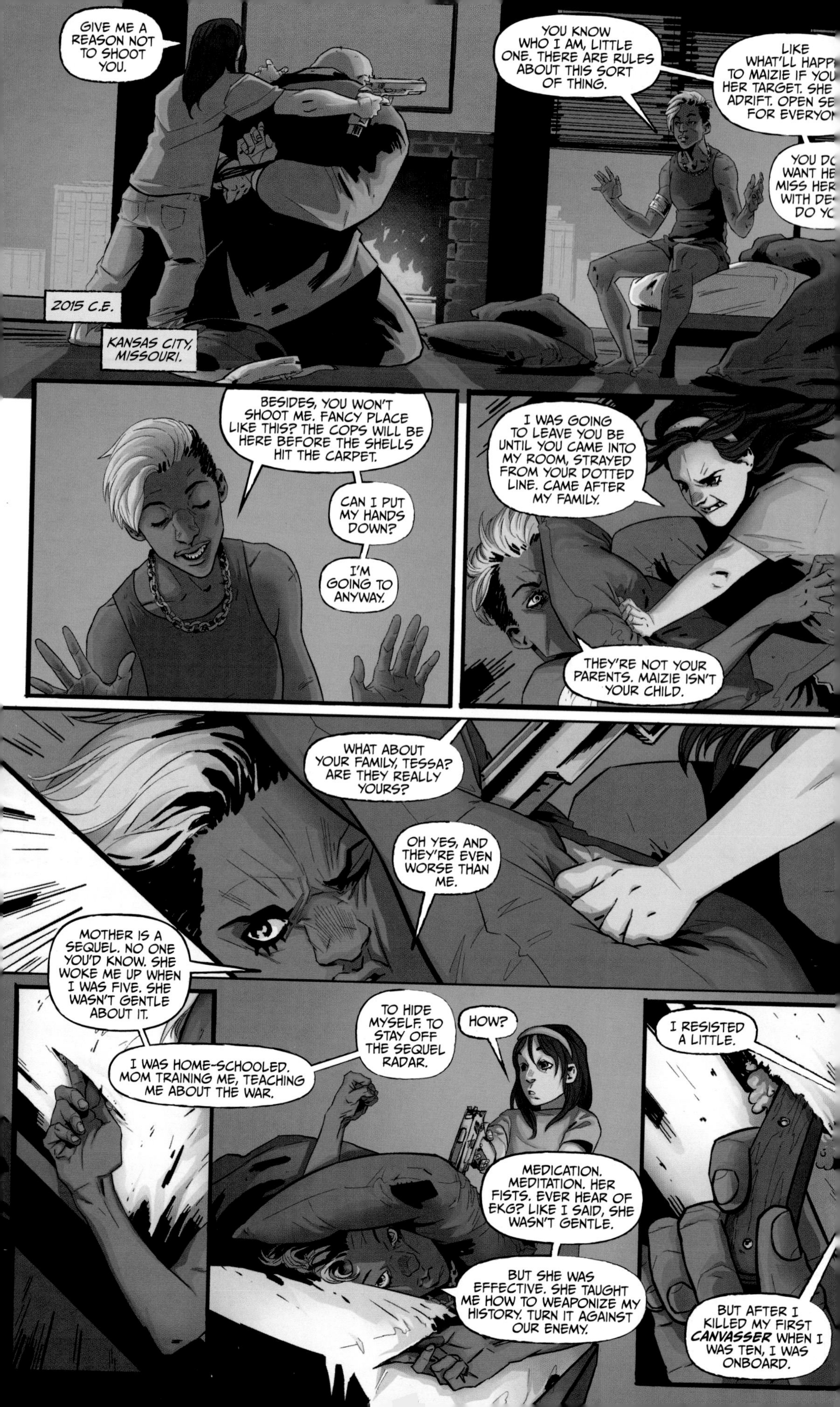
GIVE ME A REASON NOT TO SHOOT YOU.
YOU KNOW WHO I AM, LITTLE ONE. THERE ARE RULES ABOUT THIS SORT OF THING.
LIKE WHAT'LL HAPP TO MAIZIE IF YOU HER TARGET. SHE ADRIFT. OPEN SE FOR EVERYO
YOU DO WANT HE MISS HER WITH DE DO YO
2015 C.E.
KANSAS CITY, MISSOURI.
BESIDES, YOU WON'T SHOOT ME. FANCY PLACE LIKE THIS? THE COPS WILL BE HERE BEFORE THE SHELLS HIT THE CARPET.
CAN I PUT MY HANDS DOWN?
I'M GOING TO ANYWAY.
I WAS GOING TO LEAVE YOU BE UNTIL YOU CAME INTO MY ROOM, STRAYED FROM YOUR DOTTED LINE. CAME AFTER MY FAMILY.
THEY'RE NOT YOUR PARENTS. MAIZIE ISN'T YOUR CHILD.
WHAT ABOUT YOUR FAMILY, TESSA? ARE THEY REALLY YOURS?
OH YES, AND THEY'RE EVEN WORSE THAN ME.
MOTHER IS A SEQUEL. NO ONE YOU'D KNOW. SHE WOKE ME UP WHEN I WAS FIVE. SHE WASN'T GENTLE ABOUT IT.
I WAS HOME-SCHOOLED. MOM TRAINING ME, TEACHING ME ABOUT THE WAR.
TO HIDE MYSELF. TO STAY OFF THE SEQUEL RADAR.
HOW?
MEDICATION. MEDITATION. HER FISTS. EVER HEAR OF EKG? LIKE I SAID, SHE WASN'T GENTLE.
BUT SHE WAS EFFECTIVE. SHE TAUGHT ME HOW TO WEAPONIZE MY HISTORY. TURN IT AGAINST OUR ENEMY.
I RESISTED A LITTLE.
BUT AFTER I KILLED MY FIRST CANVASSER WHEN I WAS TEN, I WAS ONBOARD.

I CAN PUT TWO IN YOUR BRAIN BEFORE YOU GET THE BLADE UNFOLDED.

I'M FASTER THAN I USED TO BE, TESSA.

AND WHO ARE YOU, ANYHOW?

YOU OUGHT TO KNOW BY NOW.

YOU KILLED ME TWICE.

NO!

THAT'S HILARIOUS. WHO WERE YOU?

ISN'T IT FUNNY? HOW WE END UP HERE? LIKE THIS?

HYSTERICAL.

ON YOUR BELLY.

MALI'S GONE FAR AWAY. SHE'S NOT FIGHTING. NOT YOU. NOT ANYONE.

SHE CAN HIDE, TOO. GO BACK TO JO'BERG. TELL YOUR INSANE MOTHER YOU LOVE HER. FIND A NEW TARGET.

YOU HAVE FIVE SECONDS TO--

...ENA DAISY! ...P HIDING AND ...ER ME NOW, ...O LADY! WE'RE ...NG TO MISS ...R FLIGHT!

I'LL SCREAM. LOUD ENOUGH TO BRING HER IN HERE, TO BURY YOU IN THE JUVENILE CORRECTIONS SYSTEM UNTIL YOU'RE 18.

YOU GO HOME. MAYBE I'LL COME VISIT WHEN I'M DONE WITH YOUR DARLING DAUGHTER.

THIRD TIME'S A CHARM.

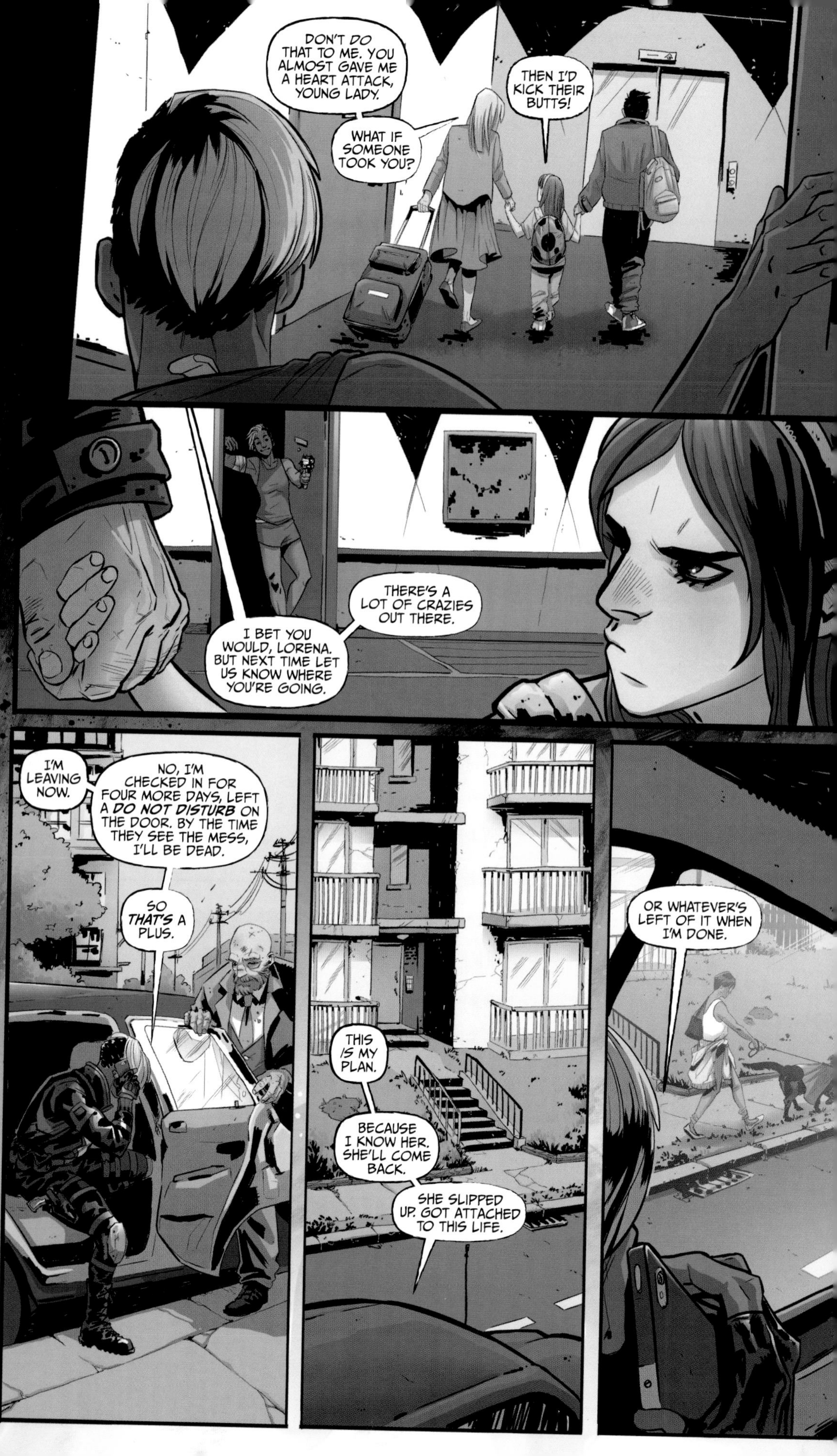
DON'T DO THAT TO ME. YOU ALMOST GAVE ME A HEART ATTACK, YOUNG LADY.
WHAT IF SOMEONE TOOK YOU?
THEN I'D KICK THEIR BUTTS!
I BET YOU WOULD, LORENA. BUT NEXT TIME LET US KNOW WHERE YOU'RE GOING.
THERE'S A LOT OF CRAZIES OUT THERE.
I'M LEAVING NOW.
NO, I'M CHECKED IN FOR FOUR MORE DAYS, LEFT A DO NOT DISTURB ON THE DOOR. BY THE TIME THEY SEE THE MESS, I'LL BE DEAD.
SO THAT'S A PLUS.
THIS IS MY PLAN.
BECAUSE I KNOW HER. SHE'LL COME BACK.
SHE SLIPPED UP. GOT ATTACHED TO THIS LIFE.
OR WHATEVER'S LEFT OF IT WHEN I'M DONE.

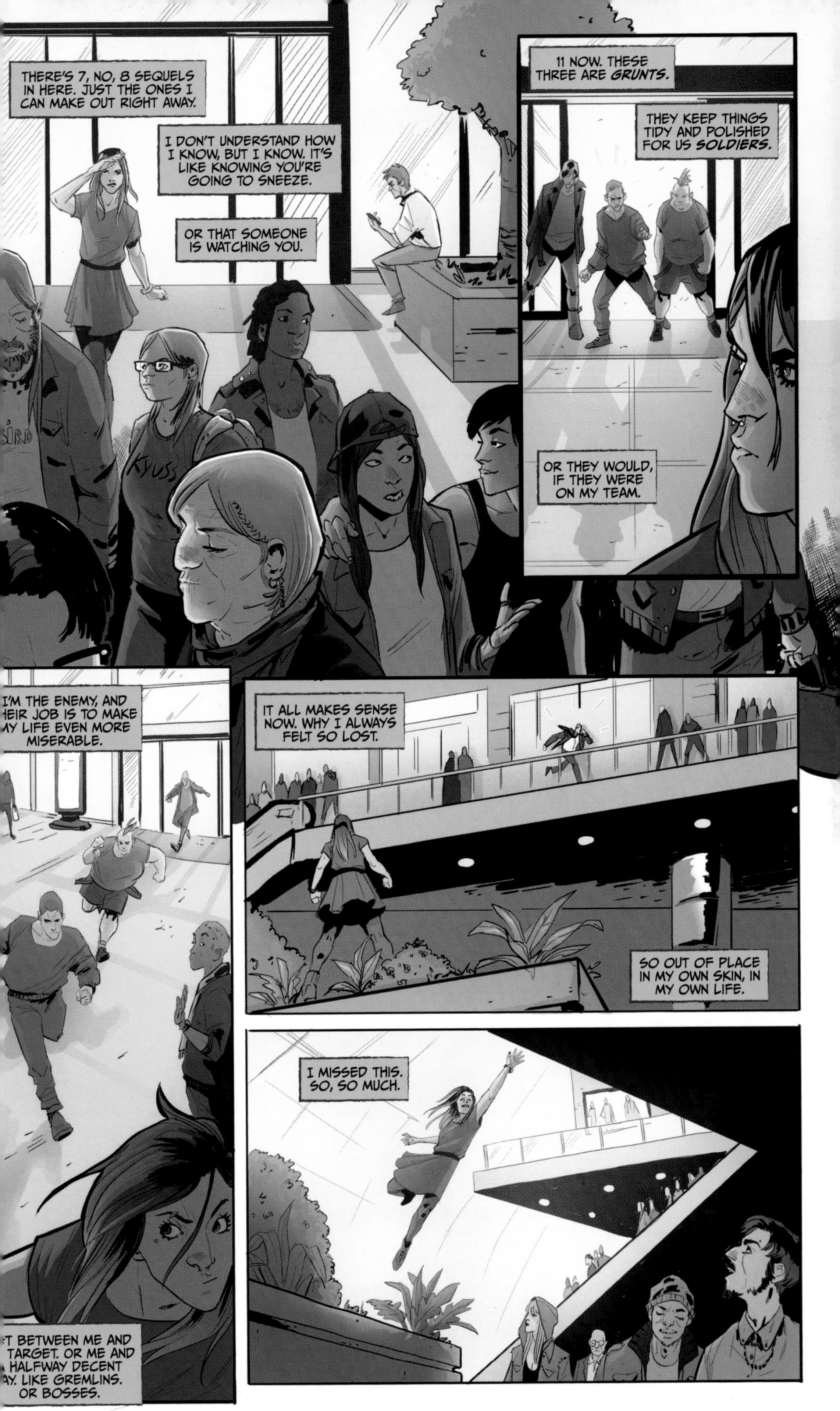

THERE'S 7, NO, 8 SEQUELS IN HERE. JUST THE ONES I CAN MAKE OUT RIGHT AWAY.
I DON'T UNDERSTAND HOW I KNOW, BUT I KNOW. IT'S LIKE KNOWING YOU'RE GOING TO SNEEZE.
OR THAT SOMEONE IS WATCHING YOU.
11 NOW. THESE THREE ARE *GRUNTS*.
THEY KEEP THINGS TIDY AND POLISHED FOR US *SOLDIERS*.
OR THEY WOULD, IF THEY WERE ON MY TEAM.
I'M THE ENEMY, AND HEIR JOB IS TO MAKE MY LIFE EVEN MORE MISERABLE.
T BETWEEN ME AND TARGET. OR ME AND HALFWAY DECENT AY. LIKE GREMLINS. OR BOSSES.
IT ALL MAKES SENSE NOW. WHY I ALWAYS FELT SO LOST.
SO OUT OF PLACE IN MY OWN SKIN, IN MY OWN LIFE.
I MISSED THIS. SO, SO MUCH.

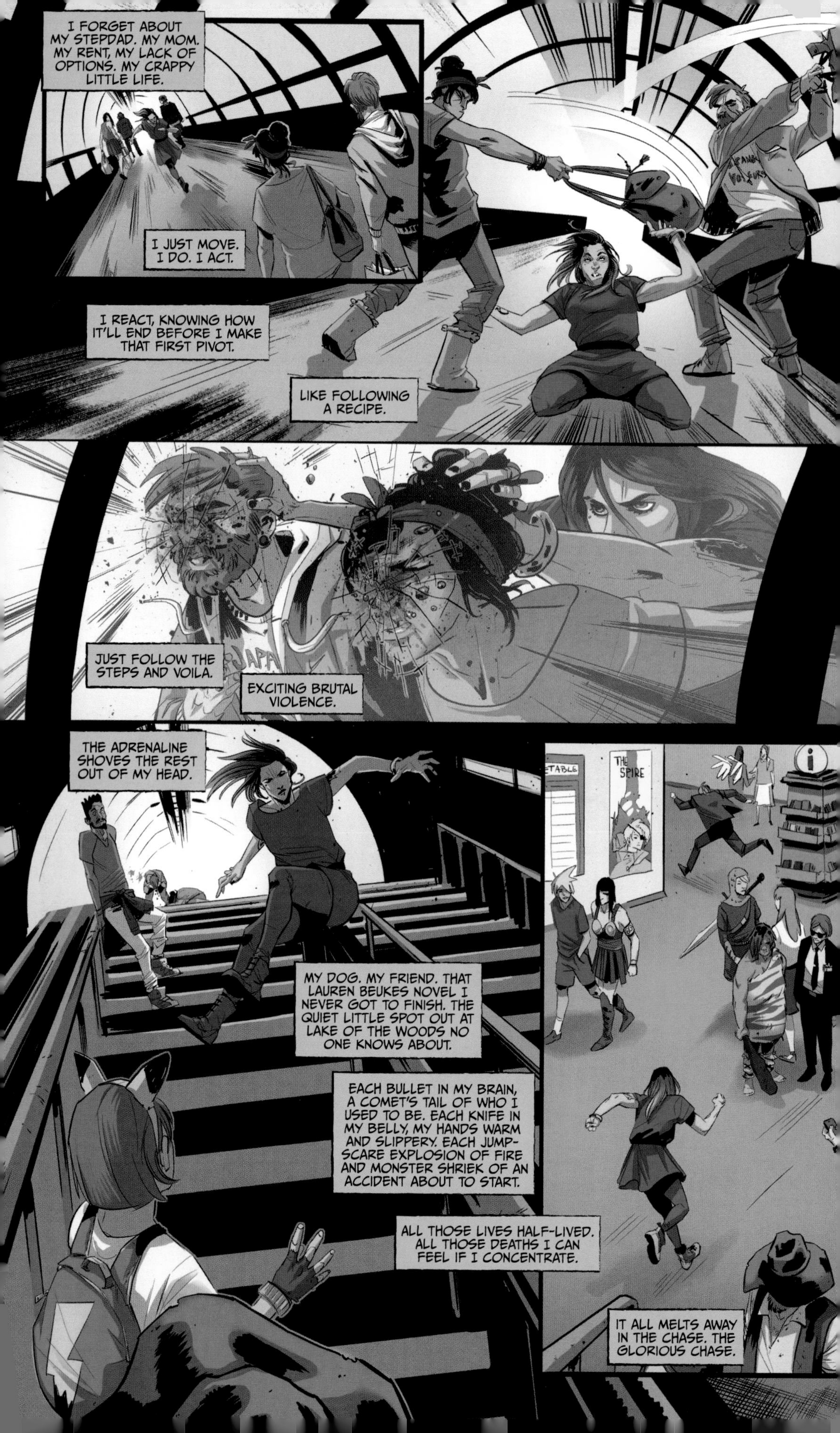
I FORGET ABOUT MY STEPDAD. MY MOM. MY RENT, MY LACK OF OPTIONS. MY CRAPPY LITTLE LIFE.
I JUST MOVE. I DO. I ACT.
I REACT, KNOWING HOW IT'LL END BEFORE I MAKE THAT FIRST PIVOT.
LIKE FOLLOWING A RECIPE.
JUST FOLLOW THE STEPS AND VOILA.
EXCITING BRUTAL VIOLENCE.
THE ADRENALINE SHOVES THE REST OUT OF MY HEAD.
MY DOG. MY FRIEND. THAT LAUREN BEUKES NOVEL I NEVER GOT TO FINISH. THE QUIET LITTLE SPOT OUT AT LAKE OF THE WOODS NO ONE KNOWS ABOUT.
EACH BULLET IN MY BRAIN, A COMET'S TAIL OF WHO I USED TO BE. EACH KNIFE IN MY BELLY, MY HANDS WARM AND SLIPPERY. EACH JUMP-SCARE EXPLOSION OF FIRE AND MONSTER SHRIEK OF AN ACCIDENT ABOUT TO START.
ALL THOSE LIVES HALF-LIVED. ALL THOSE DEATHS I CAN FEEL IF I CONCENTRATE.
THE SPIRE
IT ALL MELTS AWAY IN THE CHASE. THE GLORIOUS CHASE.

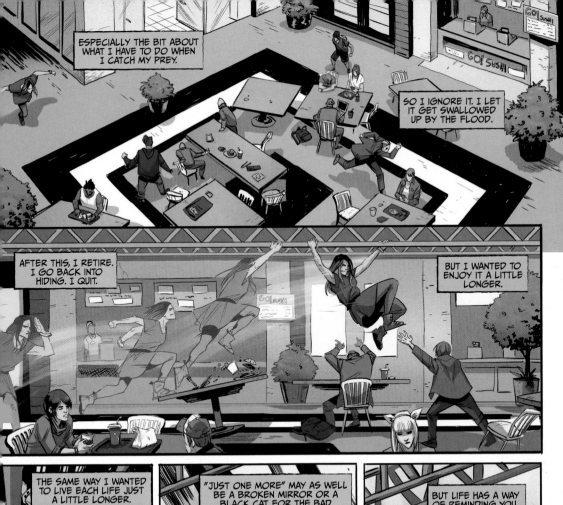

ESPECIALLY THE BIT ABOUT WHAT I HAVE TO DO WHEN I CATCH MY PREY.

SO I IGNORE IT. I LET IT GET SWALLOWED UP BY THE FLOOD.

AFTER THIS, I RETIRE. I GO BACK INTO HIDING. I QUIT.

BUT I WANTED TO ENJOY IT A LITTLE LONGER.

THE SAME WAY I WANTED TO LIVE EACH LIFE JUST A LITTLE LONGER.

E MORE SUNSET, ONE MORE MOVIE, ONE MORE DRINK.

"JUST ONE MORE" MAY AS WELL BE A BROKEN MIRROR OR A BLACK CAT FOR THE BAD LUCK IT BRINGS WITH IT.

I TRIED PUSHING THAT OUT OF MY HEAD, TOO.

BUT LIFE HAS A WAY OF REMINDING YOU...

NO MATTER WHAT, YOU'RE GONNA LOSE EVENTUALLY.

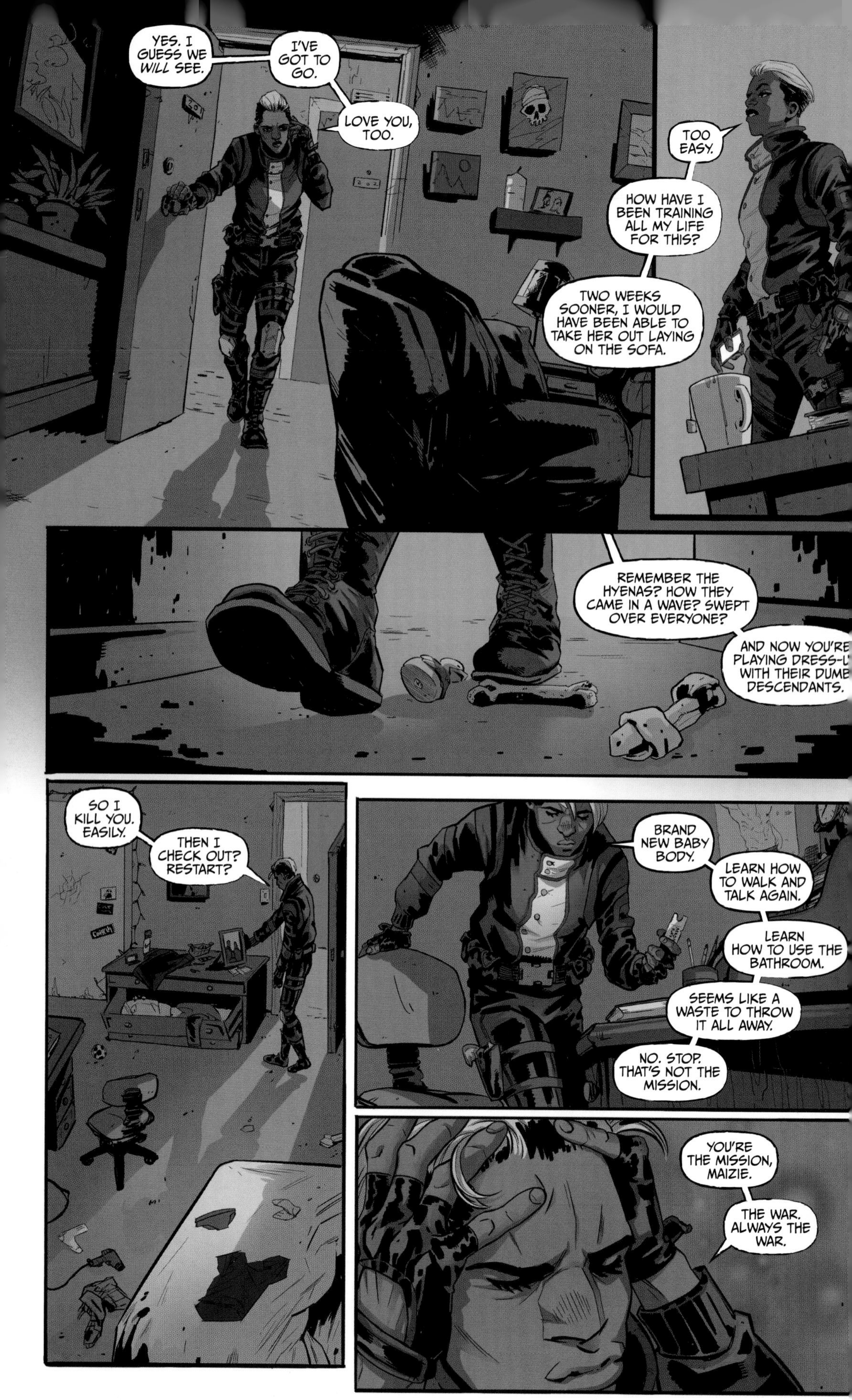
YES. I GUESS WE WILL SEE.
I'VE GOT TO GO.
LOVE YOU, TOO.
TOO EASY.
HOW HAVE I BEEN TRAINING ALL MY LIFE FOR THIS?
TWO WEEKS SOONER, I WOULD HAVE BEEN ABLE TO TAKE HER OUT LAYING ON THE SOFA.
REMEMBER THE HYENAS? HOW THEY CAME IN A WAVE? SWEPT OVER EVERYONE?
AND NOW YOU'RE PLAYING DRESS-U WITH THEIR DUMB DESCENDANTS.
SO I KILL YOU. EASILY.
THEN I CHECK OUT? RESTART?
BRAND NEW BABY BODY.
LEARN HOW TO WALK AND TALK AGAIN.
LEARN HOW TO USE THE BATHROOM.
SEEMS LIKE A WASTE TO THROW IT ALL AWAY.
NO. STOP. THAT'S NOT THE MISSION.
YOU'RE THE MISSION, MAIZIE.
THE WAR. ALWAYS THE WAR.

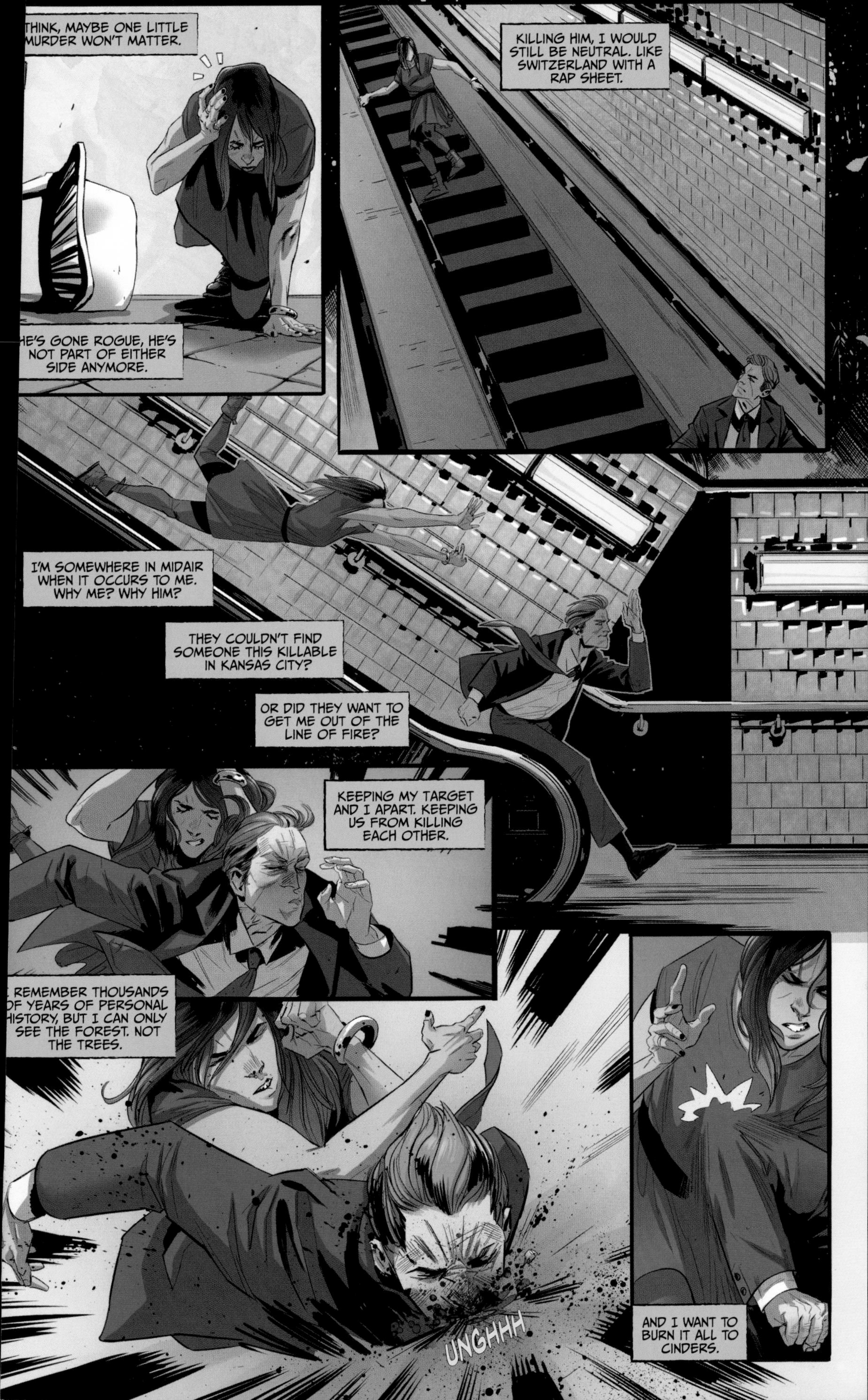
THINK, MAYBE ONE LITTLE MURDER WON'T MATTER.
HE'S GONE ROGUE, HE'S NOT PART OF EITHER SIDE ANYMORE.
KILLING HIM, I WOULD STILL BE NEUTRAL. LIKE SWITZERLAND WITH A RAP SHEET.
I'M SOMEWHERE IN MIDAIR WHEN IT OCCURS TO ME. WHY ME? WHY HIM?
THEY COULDN'T FIND SOMEONE THIS KILLABLE IN KANSAS CITY?
OR DID THEY WANT TO GET ME OUT OF THE LINE OF FIRE?
KEEPING MY TARGET AND I APART. KEEPING US FROM KILLING EACH OTHER.
REMEMBER THOUSANDS OF YEARS OF PERSONAL HISTORY, BUT I CAN ONLY SEE THE FOREST. NOT THE TREES.
UNGHHH
AND I WANT TO BURN IT ALL TO CINDERS.

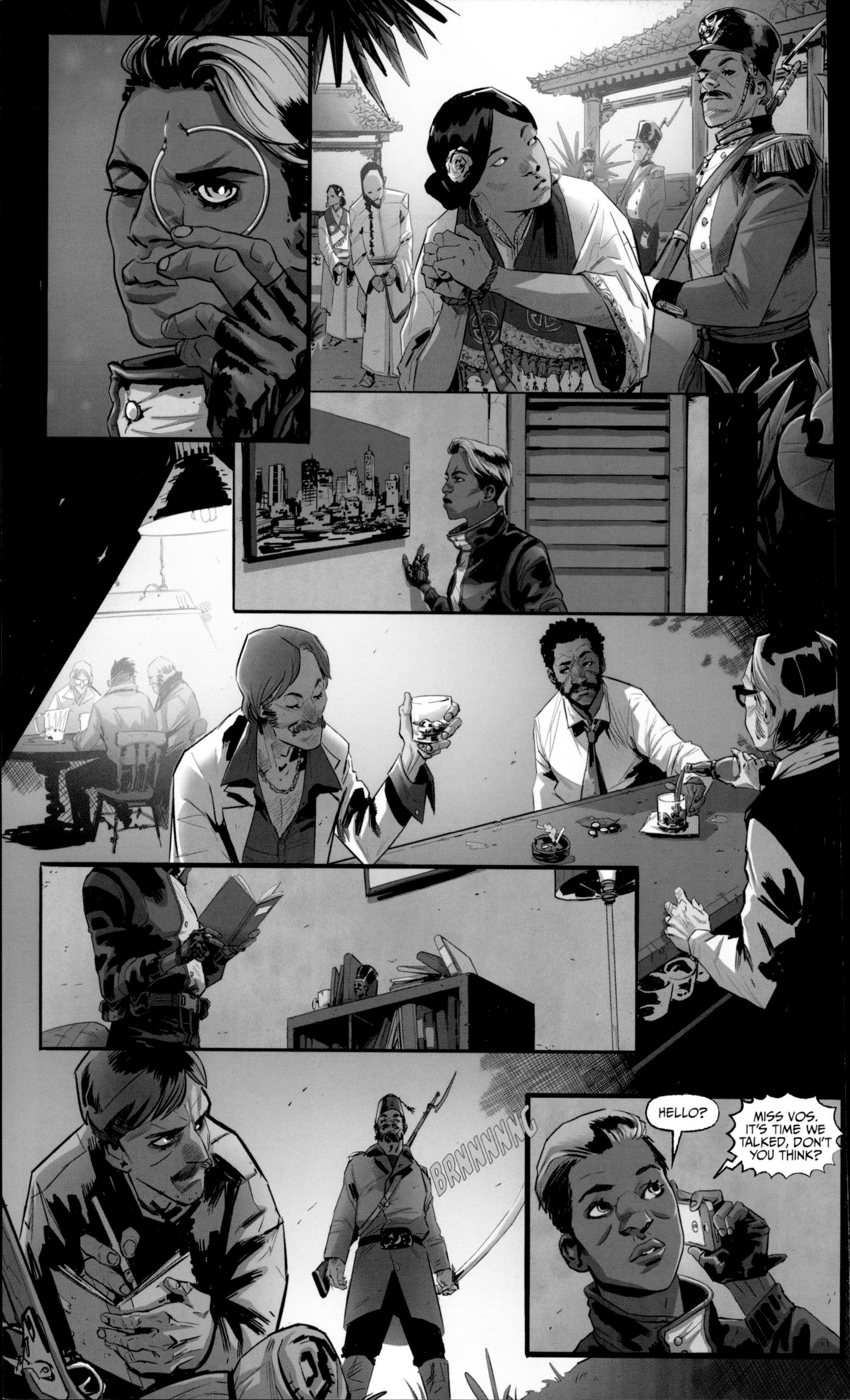
BRNNNNNG
HELLO?
MISS VOS. IT'S TIME WE TALKED, DON'T YOU THINK?

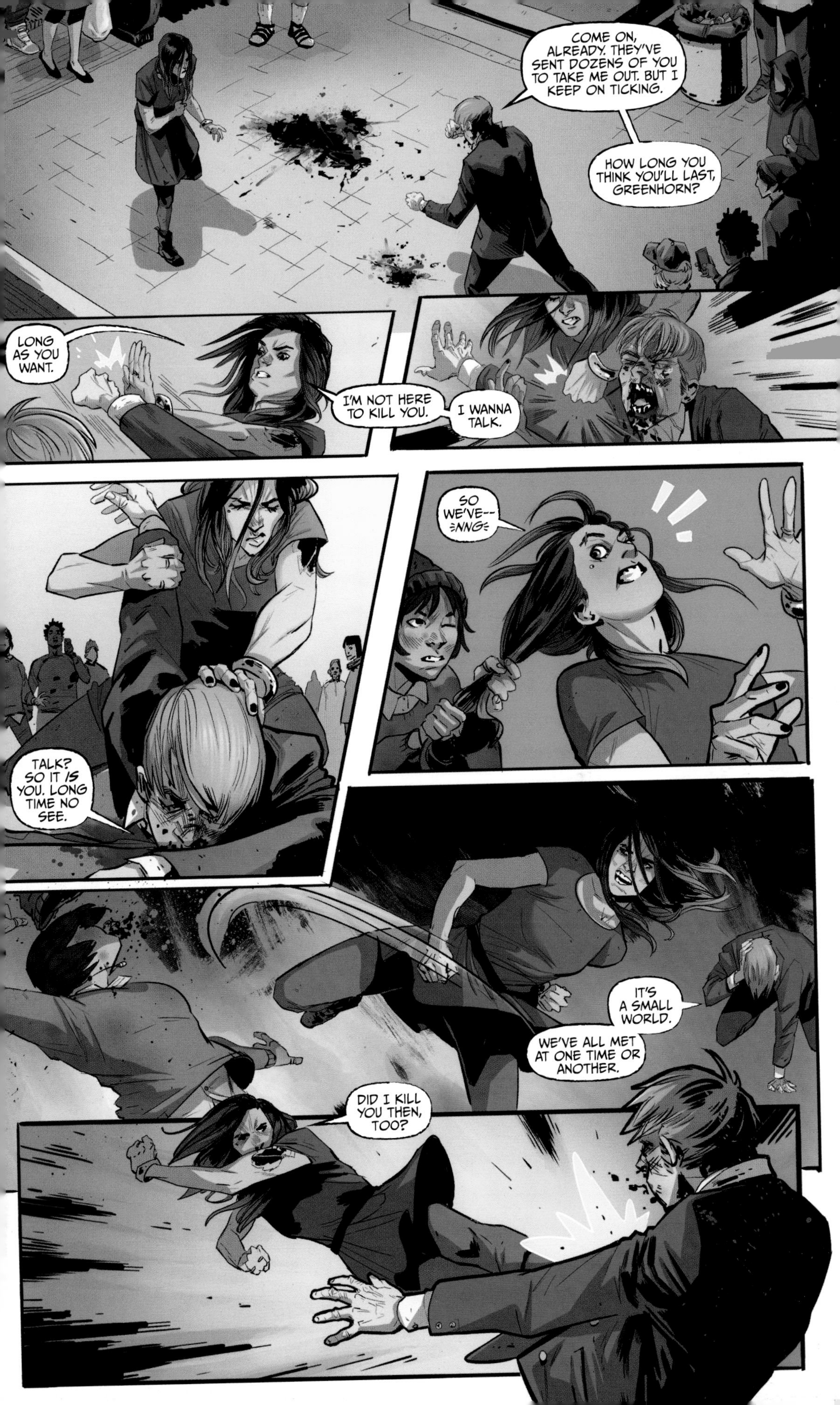
COME ON, ALREADY. THEY'VE SENT DOZENS OF YOU TO TAKE ME OUT. BUT I KEEP ON TICKING.
HOW LONG YOU THINK YOU'LL LAST, GREENHORN?
LONG AS YOU WANT.
I'M NOT HERE TO KILL YOU.
I WANNA TALK.
TALK? SO IT *IS* YOU. LONG TIME NO SEE.
SO WE'VE-- NNG
IT'S A SMALL WORLD.
WE'VE ALL MET AT ONE TIME OR ANOTHER.
DID I KILL YOU THEN, TOO?

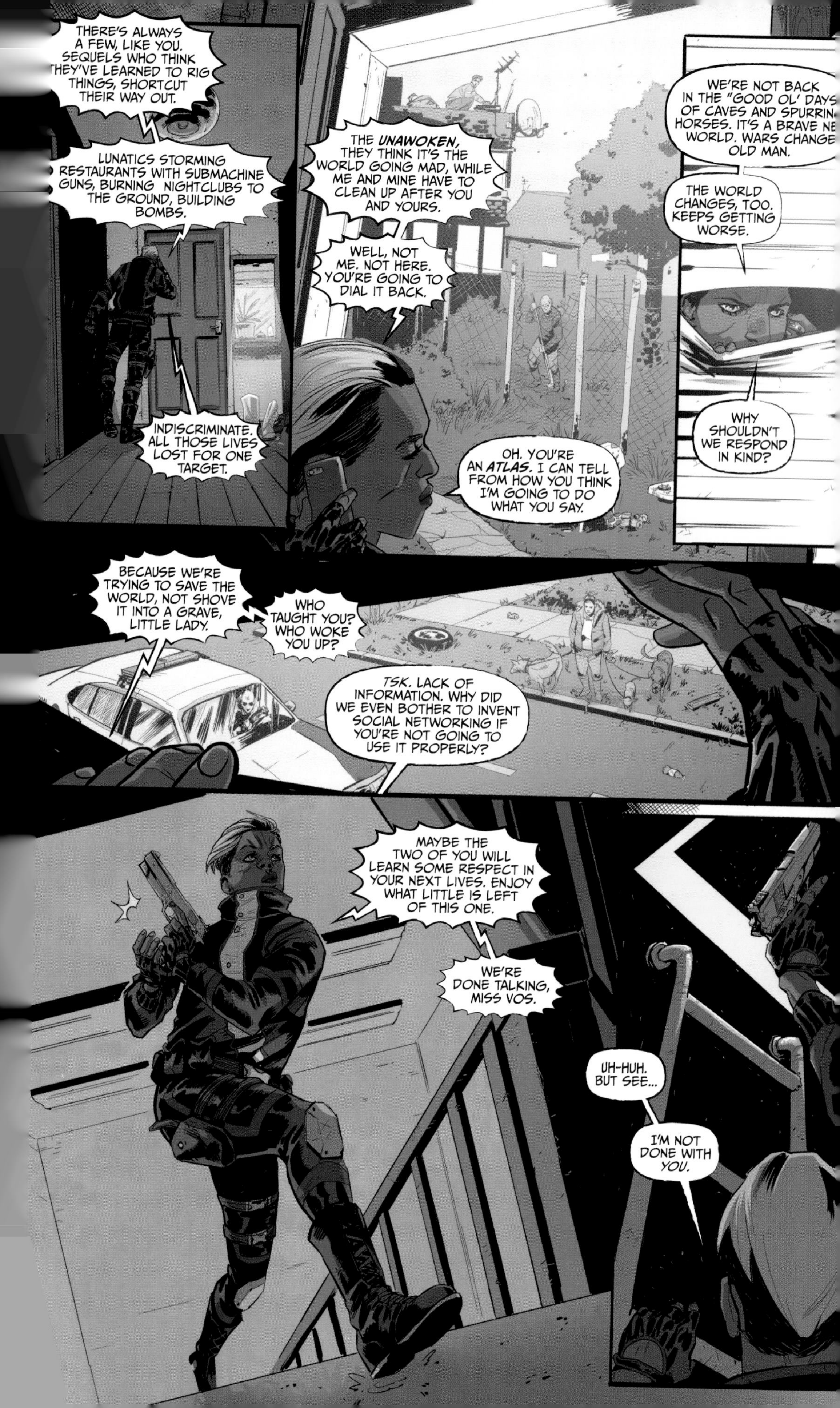
THERE'S ALWAYS A FEW, LIKE YOU. SEQUELS WHO THINK THEY'VE LEARNED TO RIG THINGS, SHORTCUT THEIR WAY OUT.
LUNATICS STORMING RESTAURANTS WITH SUBMACHINE GUNS, BURNING NIGHTCLUBS TO THE GROUND, BUILDING BOMBS.
INDISCRIMINATE. ALL THOSE LIVES LOST FOR ONE TARGET.
THE *UNAWOKEN,* THEY THINK IT'S THE WORLD GOING MAD, WHILE ME AND MINE HAVE TO CLEAN UP AFTER YOU AND YOURS.
WELL, NOT ME. NOT HERE. YOU'RE GOING TO DIAL IT BACK.
OH. YOU'RE AN *ATLAS.* I CAN TELL FROM HOW YOU THINK I'M GOING TO DO WHAT YOU SAY.
WE'RE NOT BACK IN THE "GOOD OL' DAYS" OF CAVES AND SPURRING HORSES. IT'S A BRAVE NEW WORLD. WARS CHANGE, OLD MAN.
THE WORLD CHANGES, TOO. KEEPS GETTING WORSE.
WHY SHOULDN'T WE RESPOND IN KIND?
BECAUSE WE'RE TRYING TO SAVE THE WORLD, NOT SHOVE IT INTO A GRAVE, LITTLE LADY.
WHO TAUGHT YOU? WHO WOKE YOU UP?
TSK. LACK OF INFORMATION. WHY DID WE EVEN BOTHER TO INVENT SOCIAL NETWORKING IF YOU'RE NOT GOING TO USE IT PROPERLY?
MAYBE THE TWO OF YOU WILL LEARN SOME RESPECT IN YOUR NEXT LIVES. ENJOY WHAT LITTLE IS LEFT OF THIS ONE.
WE'RE DONE TALKING, MISS VOS.
UH-HUH. BUT SEE...
I'M NOT DONE WITH *YOU.*

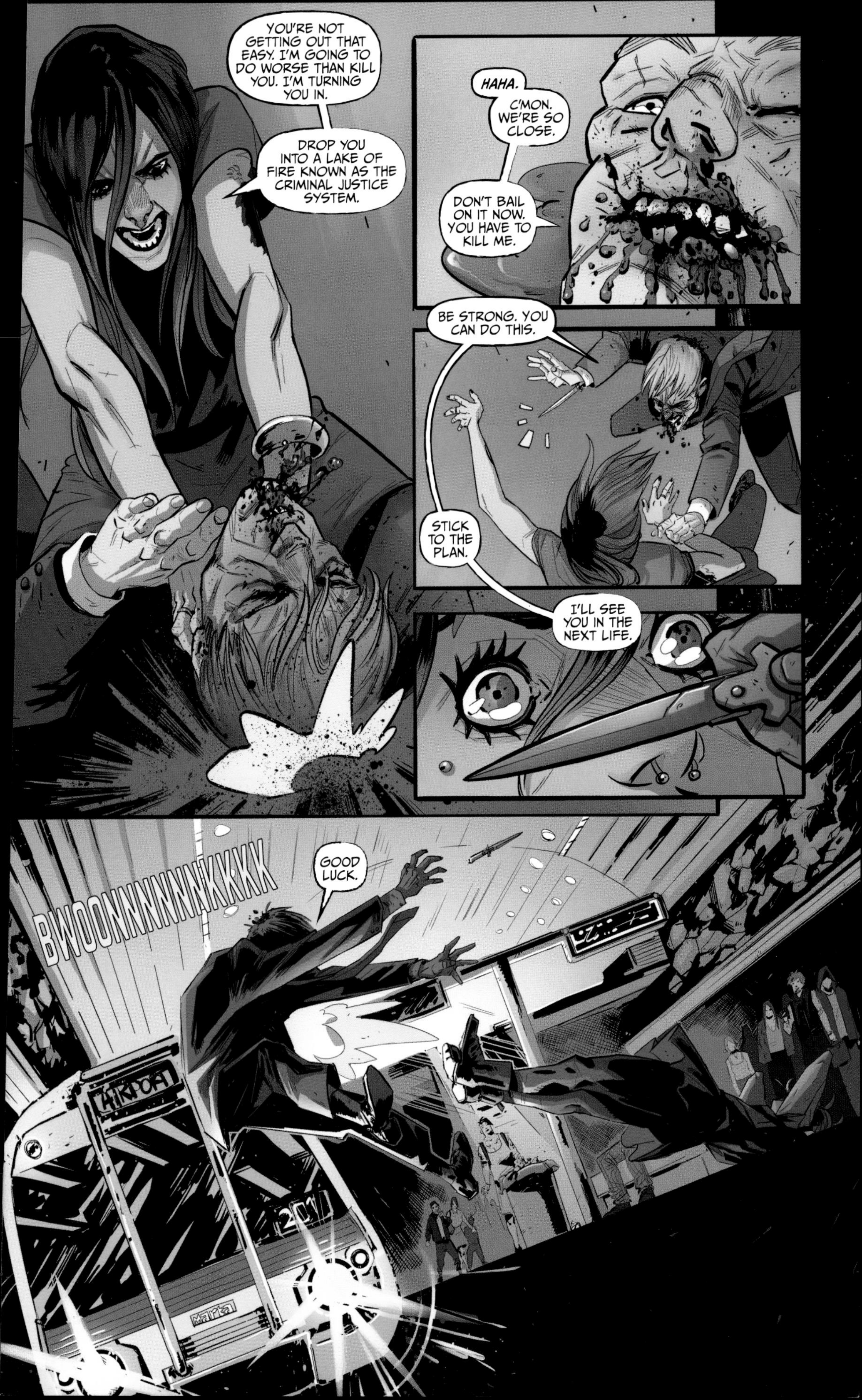
YOU'RE NOT GETTING OUT THAT EASY. I'M GOING TO DO WORSE THAN KILL YOU. I'M TURNING YOU IN.
DROP YOU INTO A LAKE OF FIRE KNOWN AS THE CRIMINAL JUSTICE SYSTEM.
HAHA.
C'MON. WE'RE SO CLOSE.
DON'T BAIL ON IT NOW. YOU HAVE TO KILL ME.
BE STRONG. YOU CAN DO THIS.
STICK TO THE PLAN.
I'LL SEE YOU IN THE NEXT LIFE.
BWOONNNNNNNKKKKK
GOOD LUCK.
AIRPORT
201
MARTA

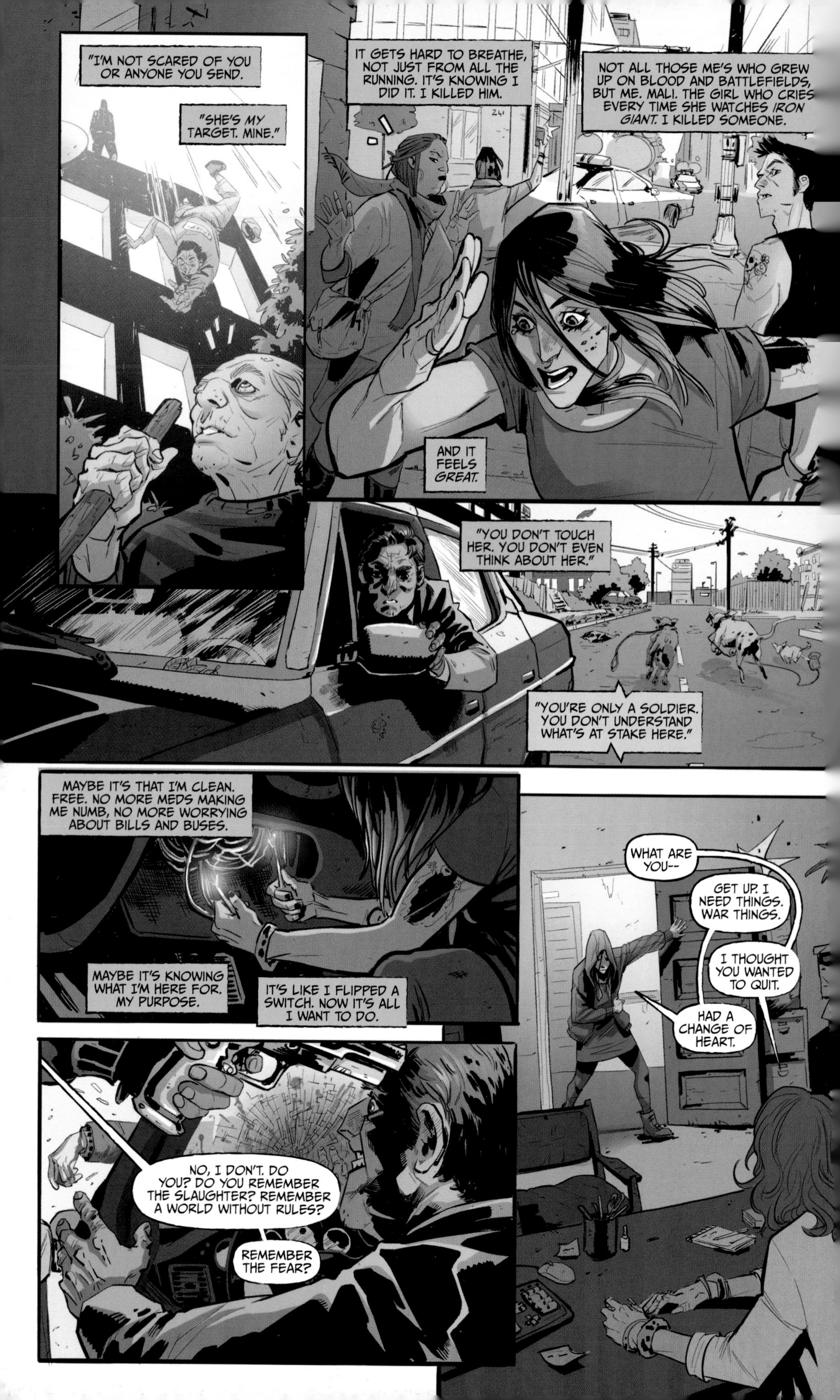

"I'M NOT SCARED OF YOU OR ANYONE YOU SEND.
"SHE'S MY TARGET. MINE."
IT GETS HARD TO BREATHE, NOT JUST FROM ALL THE RUNNING. IT'S KNOWING I DID IT. I KILLED HIM.
NOT ALL THOSE ME'S WHO GREW UP ON BLOOD AND BATTLEFIELDS, BUT ME. MALI. THE GIRL WHO CRIES EVERY TIME SHE WATCHES *IRON GIANT*. I KILLED SOMEONE.
AND IT FEELS *GREAT*.
"YOU DON'T TOUCH HER. YOU DON'T EVEN THINK ABOUT HER."
"YOU'RE ONLY A SOLDIER. YOU DON'T UNDERSTAND WHAT'S AT STAKE HERE."
MAYBE IT'S THAT I'M CLEAN. FREE. NO MORE MEDS MAKING ME NUMB, NO MORE WORRYING ABOUT BILLS AND BUSES.
MAYBE IT'S KNOWING WHAT I'M HERE FOR. MY PURPOSE.
IT'S LIKE I FLIPPED A SWITCH. NOW IT'S ALL I WANT TO DO.
NO, I DON'T. DO YOU? DO YOU REMEMBER THE SLAUGHTER? REMEMBER A WORLD WITHOUT RULES?
REMEMBER THE FEAR?
WHAT ARE YOU--
GET UP. I NEED THINGS. WAR THINGS.
I THOUGHT YOU WANTED TO QUIT.
HAD A CHANGE OF HEART.

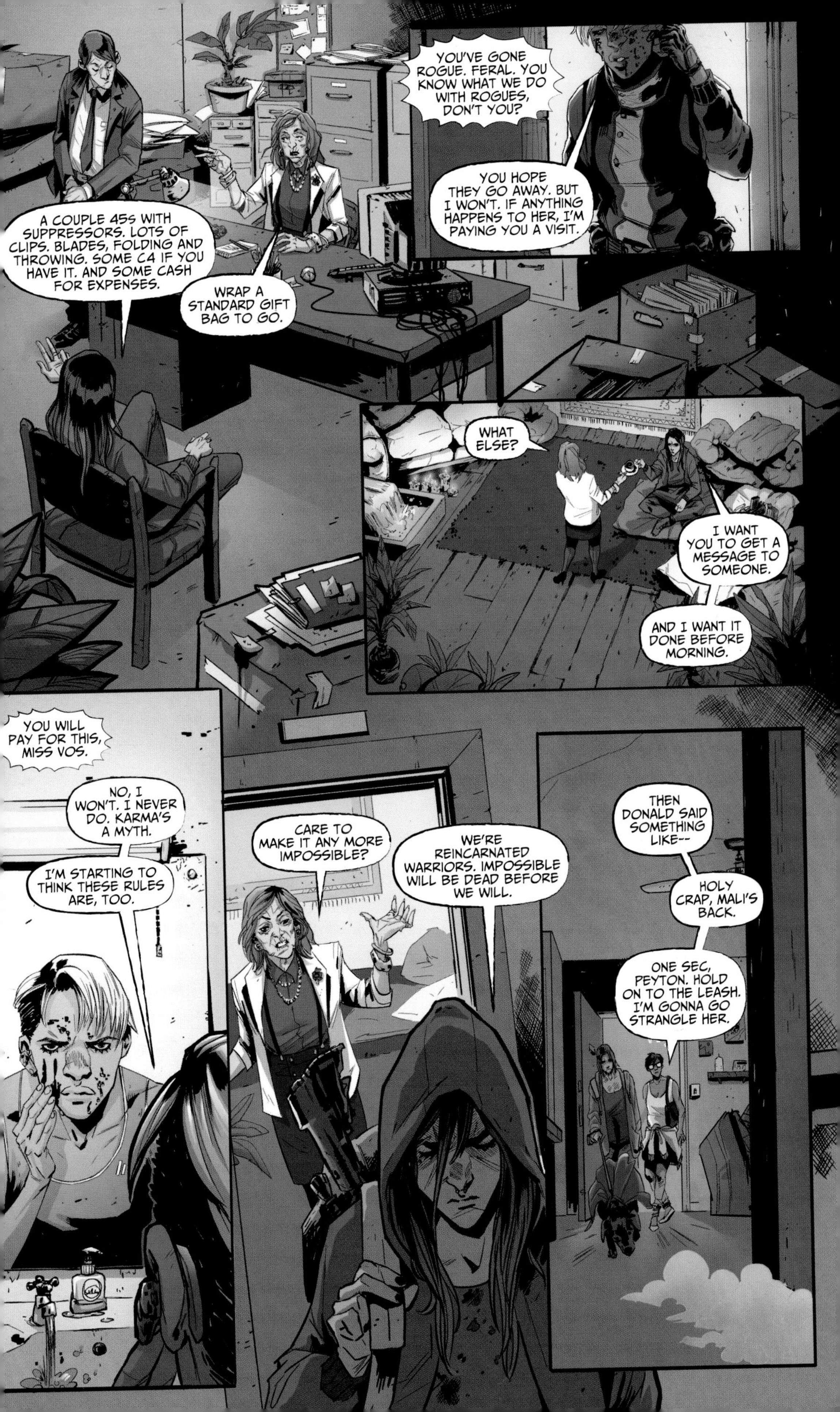
A COUPLE 45s WITH SUPPRESSORS. LOTS OF CLIPS. BLADES, FOLDING AND THROWING. SOME C4 IF YOU HAVE IT. AND SOME CASH FOR EXPENSES.
WRAP A STANDARD GIFT BAG TO GO.
YOU'VE GONE ROGUE. FERAL. YOU KNOW WHAT WE DO WITH ROGUES, DON'T YOU?
YOU HOPE THEY GO AWAY. BUT I WON'T. IF ANYTHING HAPPENS TO HER, I'M PAYING YOU A VISIT.
WHAT ELSE?
I WANT YOU TO GET A MESSAGE TO SOMEONE.
AND I WANT IT DONE BEFORE MORNING.
YOU WILL PAY FOR THIS, MISS VOS.
NO, I WON'T. I NEVER DO. KARMA'S A MYTH.
I'M STARTING TO THINK THESE RULES ARE, TOO.
CARE TO MAKE IT ANY MORE IMPOSSIBLE?
WE'RE REINCARNATED WARRIORS. IMPOSSIBLE WILL BE DEAD BEFORE WE WILL.
THEN DONALD SAID SOMETHING LIKE--
HOLY CRAP, MALI'S BACK.
ONE SEC, PEYTON. HOLD ON TO THE LEASH. I'M GONNA GO STRANGLE HER.

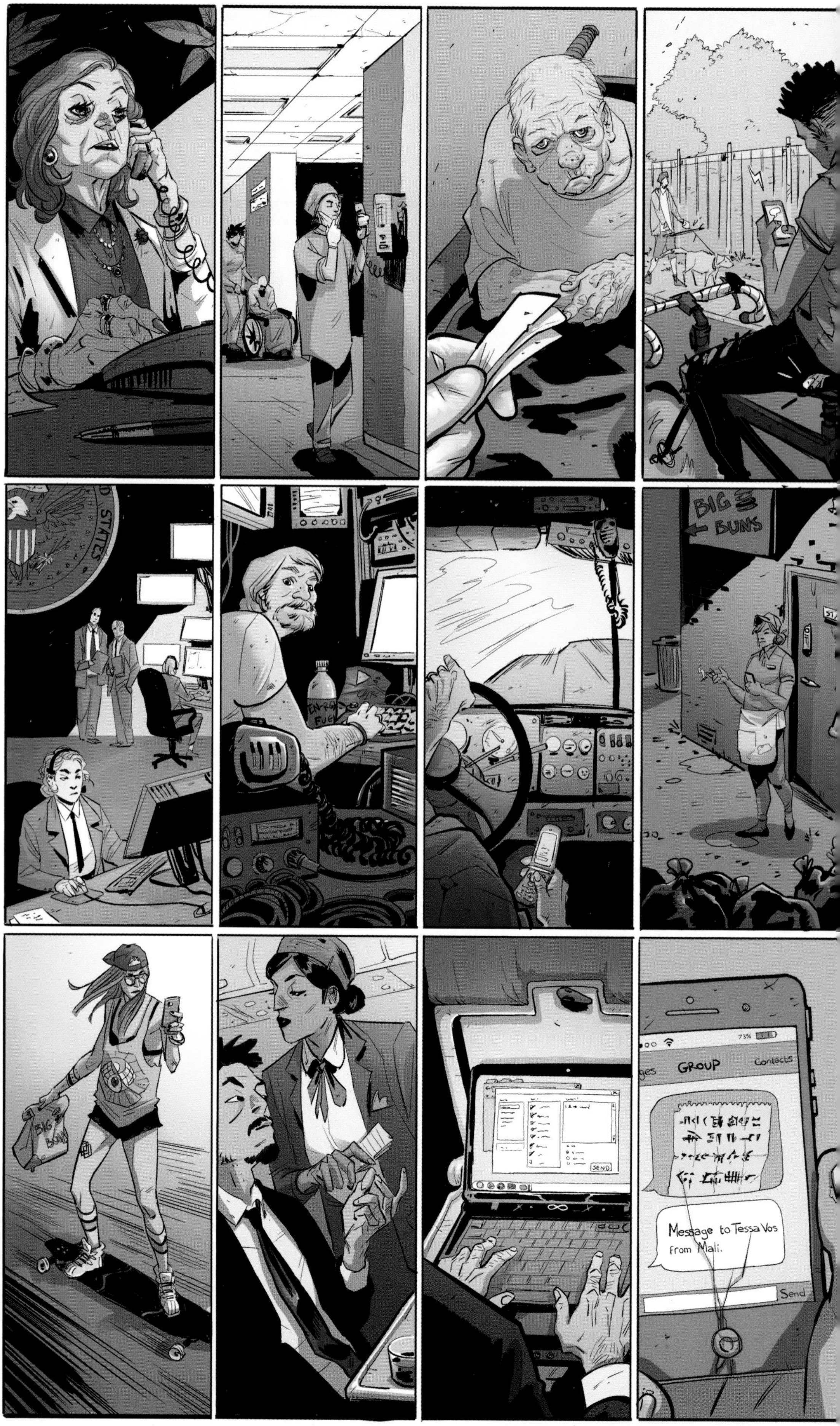
STATES
BIG BUNS
BIG BUNS
SEND
73%
GROUP
Contacts
Message to Tessa Vos from Mali.
Send

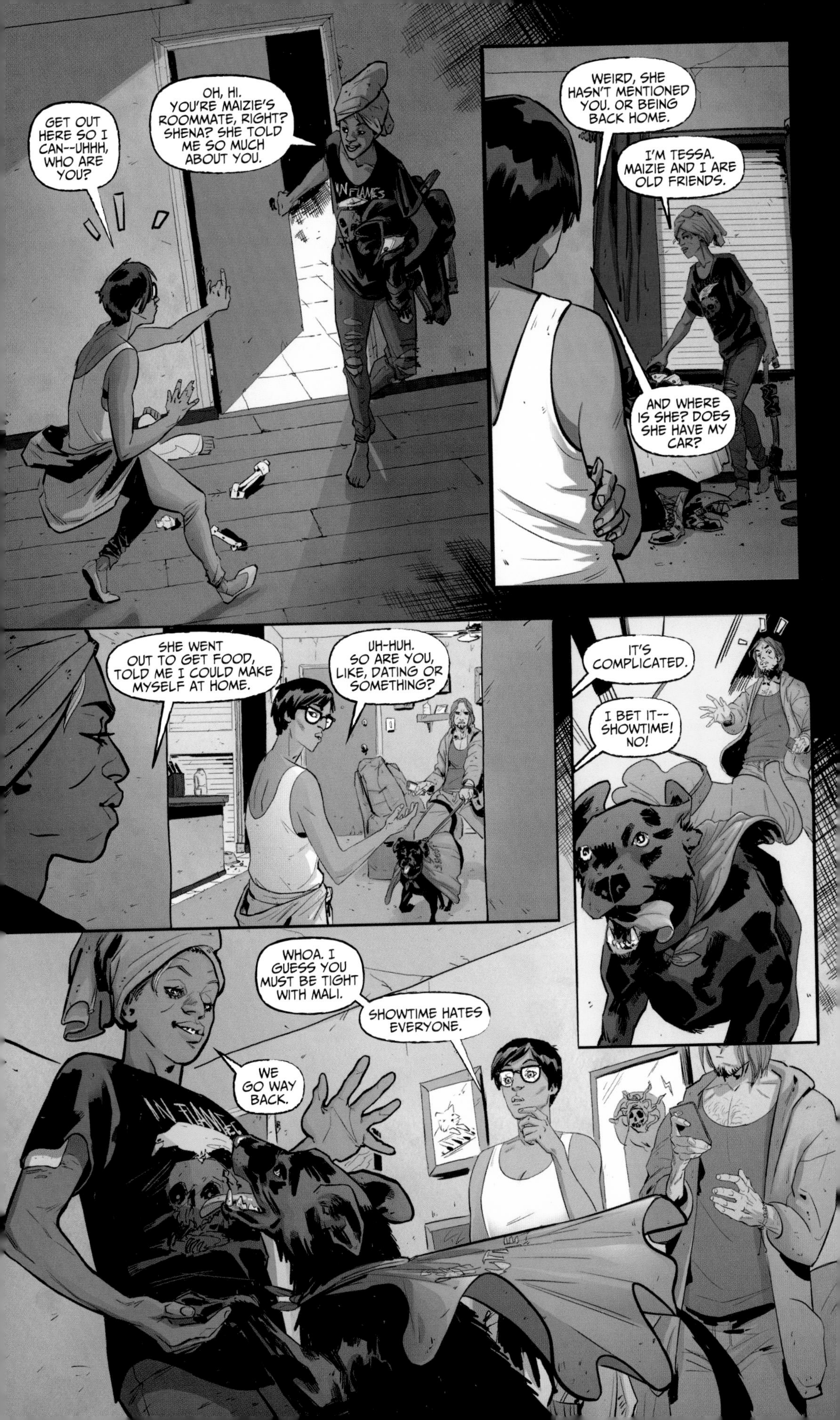

GET OUT HERE SO I CAN--UHHH, WHO ARE YOU?
OH, HI. YOU'RE MAIZIE'S ROOMMATE, RIGHT? SHENA? SHE TOLD ME SO MUCH ABOUT YOU.
WEIRD, SHE HASN'T MENTIONED YOU. OR BEING BACK HOME.
I'M TESSA. MAIZIE AND I ARE OLD FRIENDS.
AND WHERE IS SHE? DOES SHE HAVE MY CAR?
SHE WENT OUT TO GET FOOD, TOLD ME I COULD MAKE MYSELF AT HOME.
UH-HUH. SO ARE YOU, LIKE, DATING OR SOMETHING?
IT'S COMPLICATED.
I BET IT--SHOWTIME! NO!
WHOA. I GUESS YOU MUST BE TIGHT WITH MALI.
SHOWTIME HATES EVERYONE.
WE GO WAY BACK.

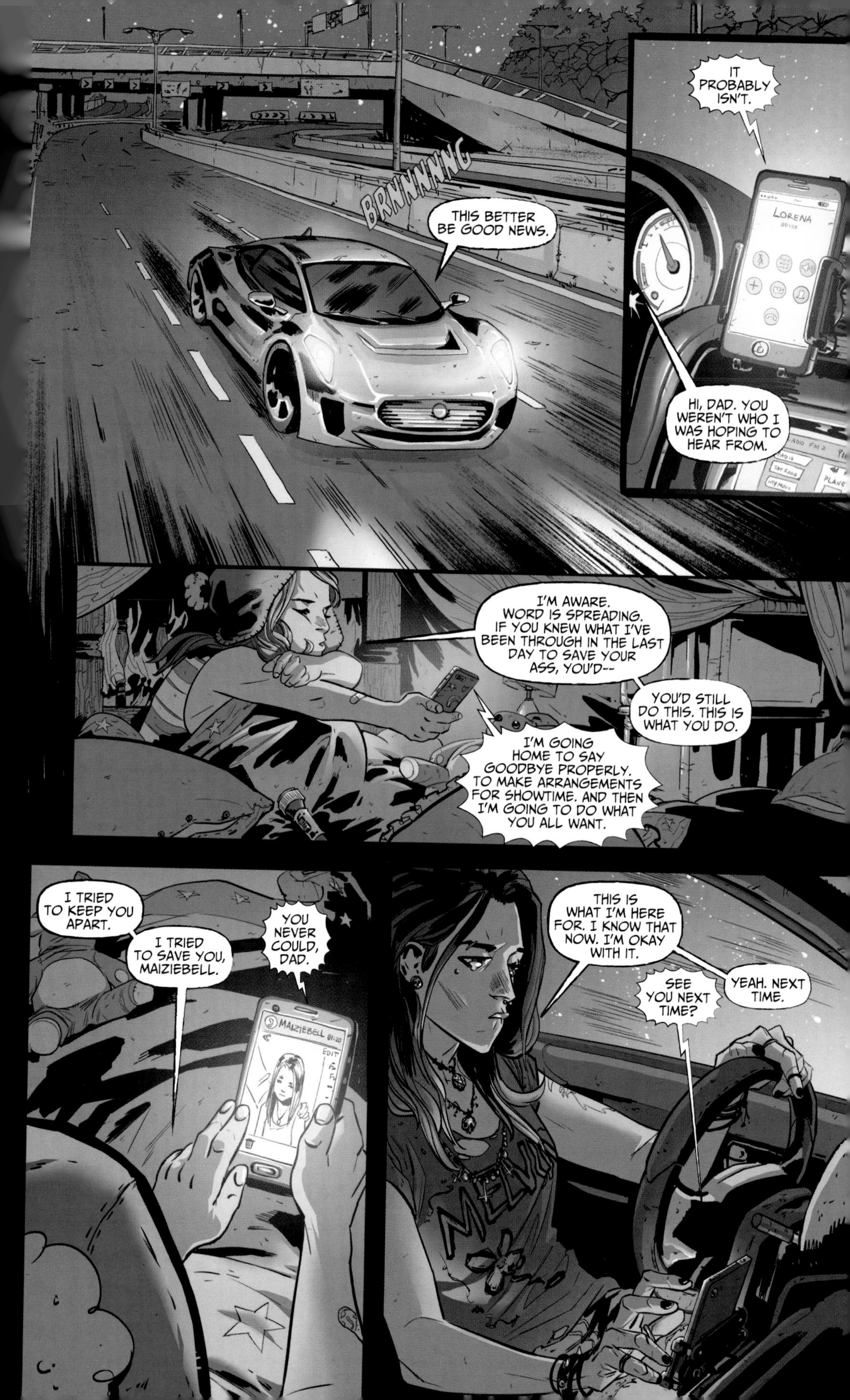
BRNNNNNG
THIS BETTER BE GOOD NEWS.
IT PROBABLY ISN'T.
LORENA
HI, DAD. YOU WEREN'T WHO I WAS HOPING TO HEAR FROM.
I'M AWARE. WORD IS SPREADING. IF YOU KNEW WHAT I'VE BEEN THROUGH IN THE LAST DAY TO SAVE YOUR ASS, YOU'D--
YOU'D STILL DO THIS. THIS IS WHAT YOU DO.
I'M GOING HOME TO SAY GOODBYE PROPERLY. TO MAKE ARRANGEMENTS FOR SHOWTIME. AND THEN I'M GOING TO DO WHAT YOU ALL WANT.
I TRIED TO KEEP YOU APART.
I TRIED TO SAVE YOU, MAIZIEBELL.
YOU NEVER COULD, DAD.
MAIZIEBELL 01:20
EDIT
THIS IS WHAT I'M HERE FOR. I KNOW THAT NOW. I'M OKAY WITH IT.
SEE YOU NEXT TIME?
YEAH. NEXT TIME.

INTERESTING ACCENT. IS THAT... AUSTRALIAN?

SOUTH AFRICAN.

HOW EXACTLY DO YOU KNOW MALI, THEN? THAT'S A LONG WAY FROM OMAHA.

WE MET ON THE INTERNET.

OH MY GOD, YOU NERDS.

THAT'S ADORABLE.

WELL, I BETTER GO LAY DOWN. JET LAG AND ALL.

STICK AROUND, TESSA.

PEYTON, WHAT ARE YOU LOOKING FOR?

THIS.

KZZZZKK

TESSA VOS, RIGHT?

I'VE GOT A MESSAGE.

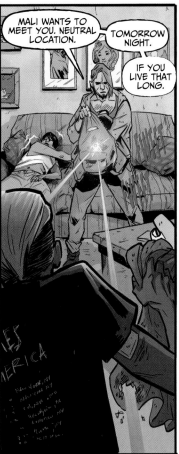

MALI WANTS TO MEET YOU. NEUTRAL LOCATION.

TOMORROW NIGHT.

IF YOU LIVE THAT LONG.

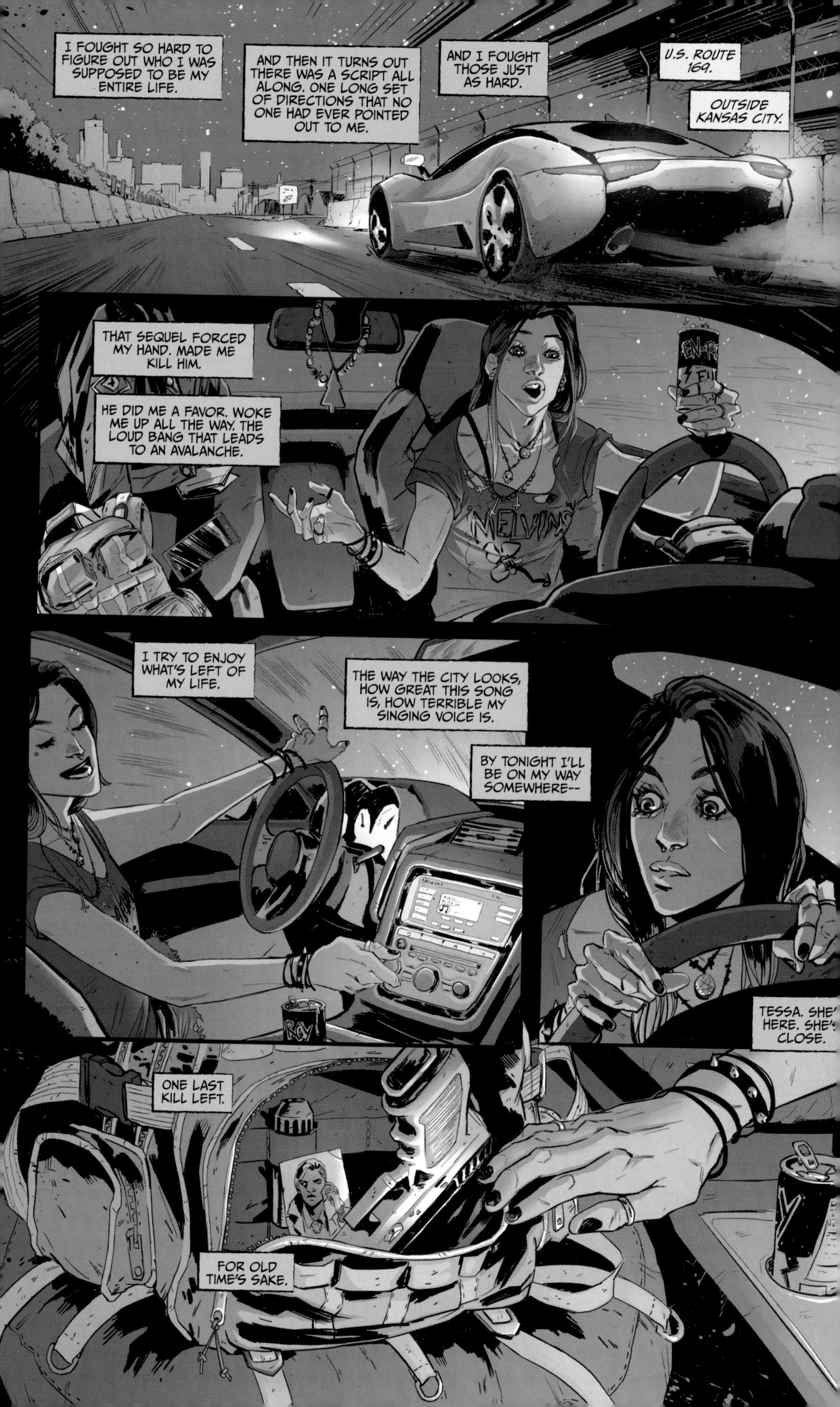
I FOUGHT SO HARD TO FIGURE OUT WHO I WAS SUPPOSED TO BE MY ENTIRE LIFE.
AND THEN IT TURNS OUT THERE WAS A SCRIPT ALL ALONG. ONE LONG SET OF DIRECTIONS THAT NO ONE HAD EVER POINTED OUT TO ME.
AND I FOUGHT THOSE JUST AS HARD.
U.S. ROUTE 169.
OUTSIDE KANSAS CITY.
THAT SEQUEL FORCED MY HAND. MADE ME KILL HIM.
HE DID ME A FAVOR. WOKE ME UP ALL THE WAY. THE LOUD BANG THAT LEADS TO AN AVALANCHE.
MELVINS
I TRY TO ENJOY WHAT'S LEFT OF MY LIFE.
THE WAY THE CITY LOOKS, HOW GREAT THIS SONG IS, HOW TERRIBLE MY SINGING VOICE IS.
BY TONIGHT I'LL BE ON MY WAY SOMEWHERE--
TESSA. SHE'S HERE. SHE'S CLOSE.
ONE LAST KILL LEFT.
FOR OLD TIME'S SAKE.

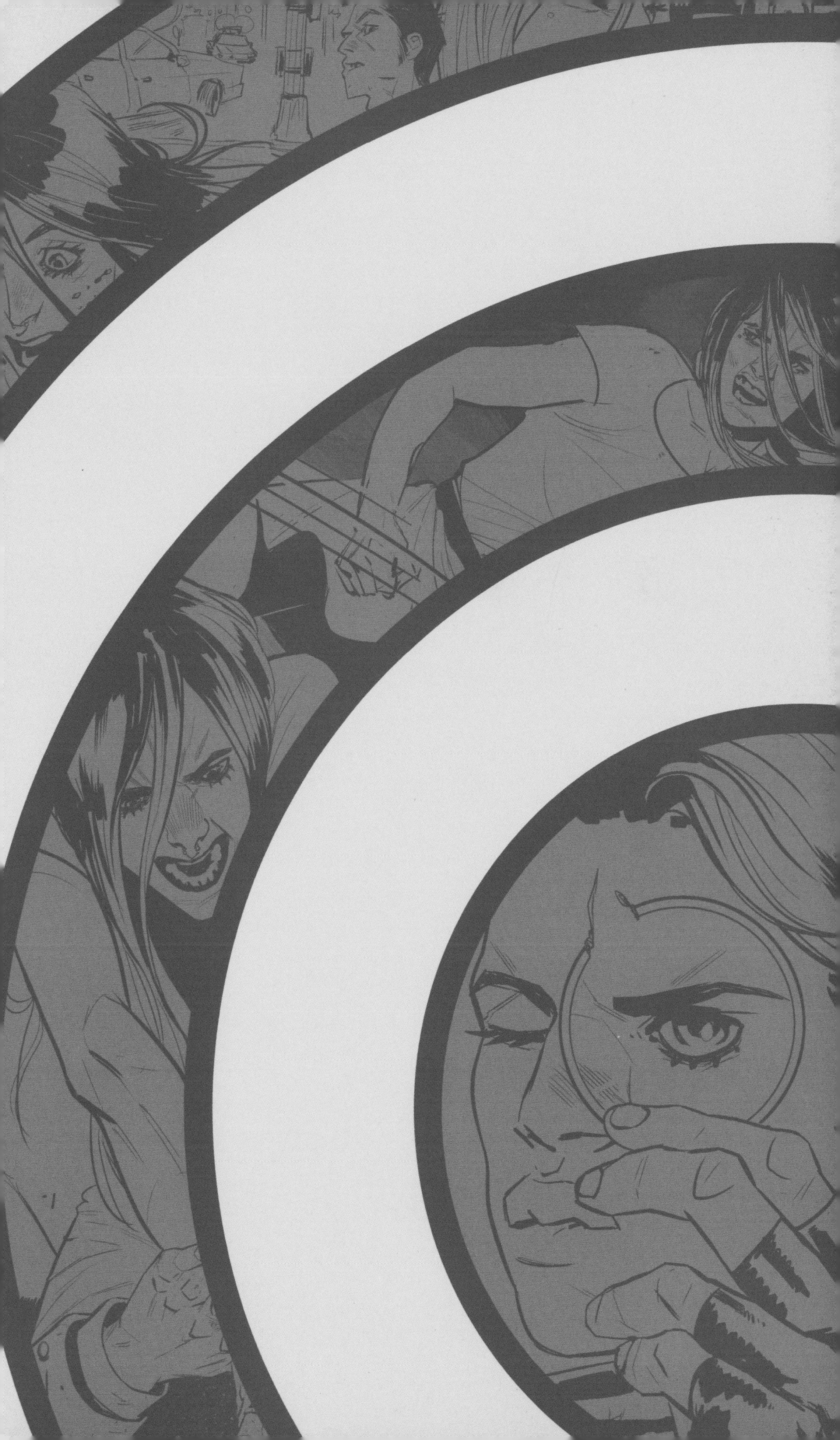

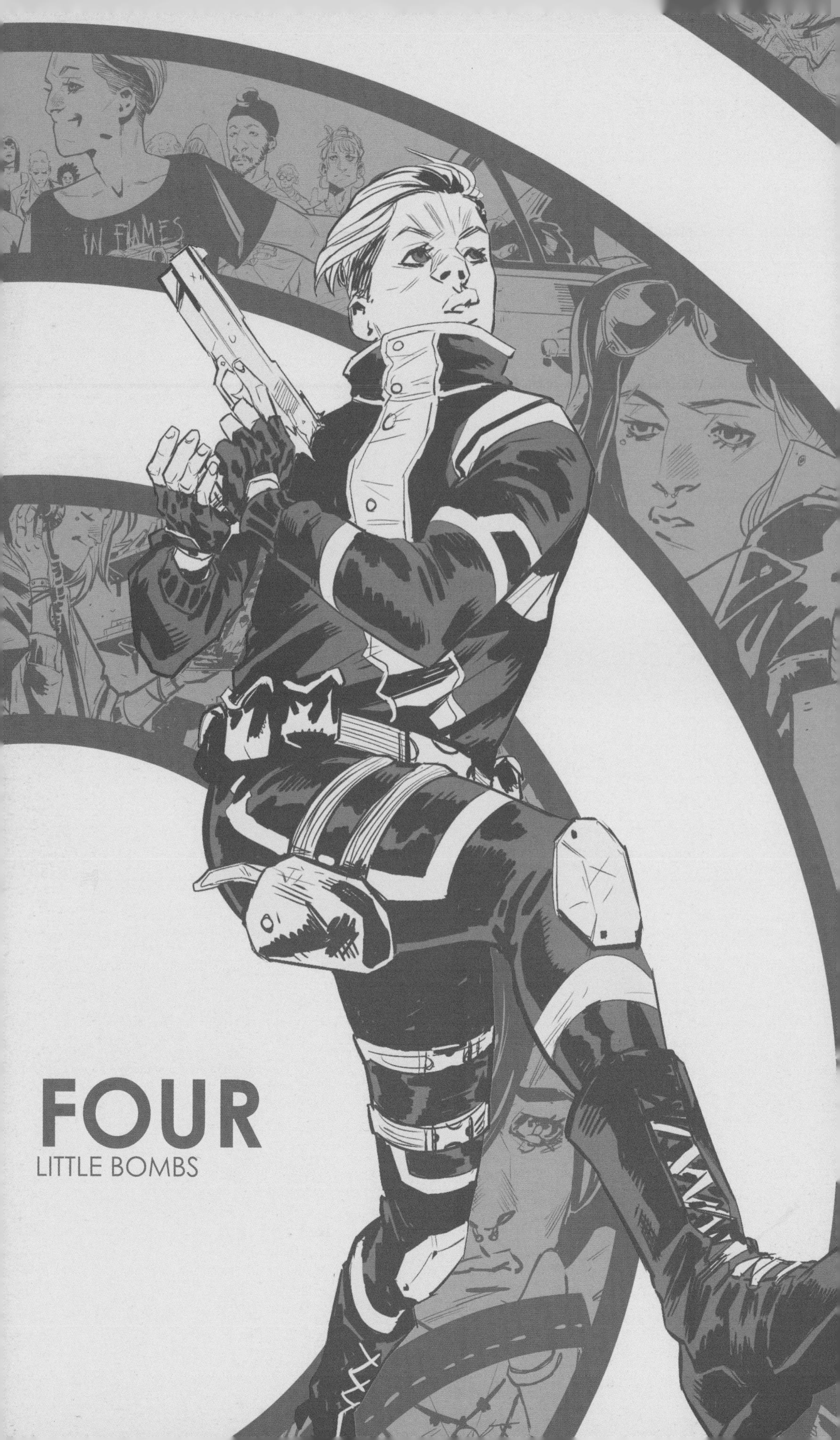
IN FLAMES

FOUR
LITTLE BOMBS

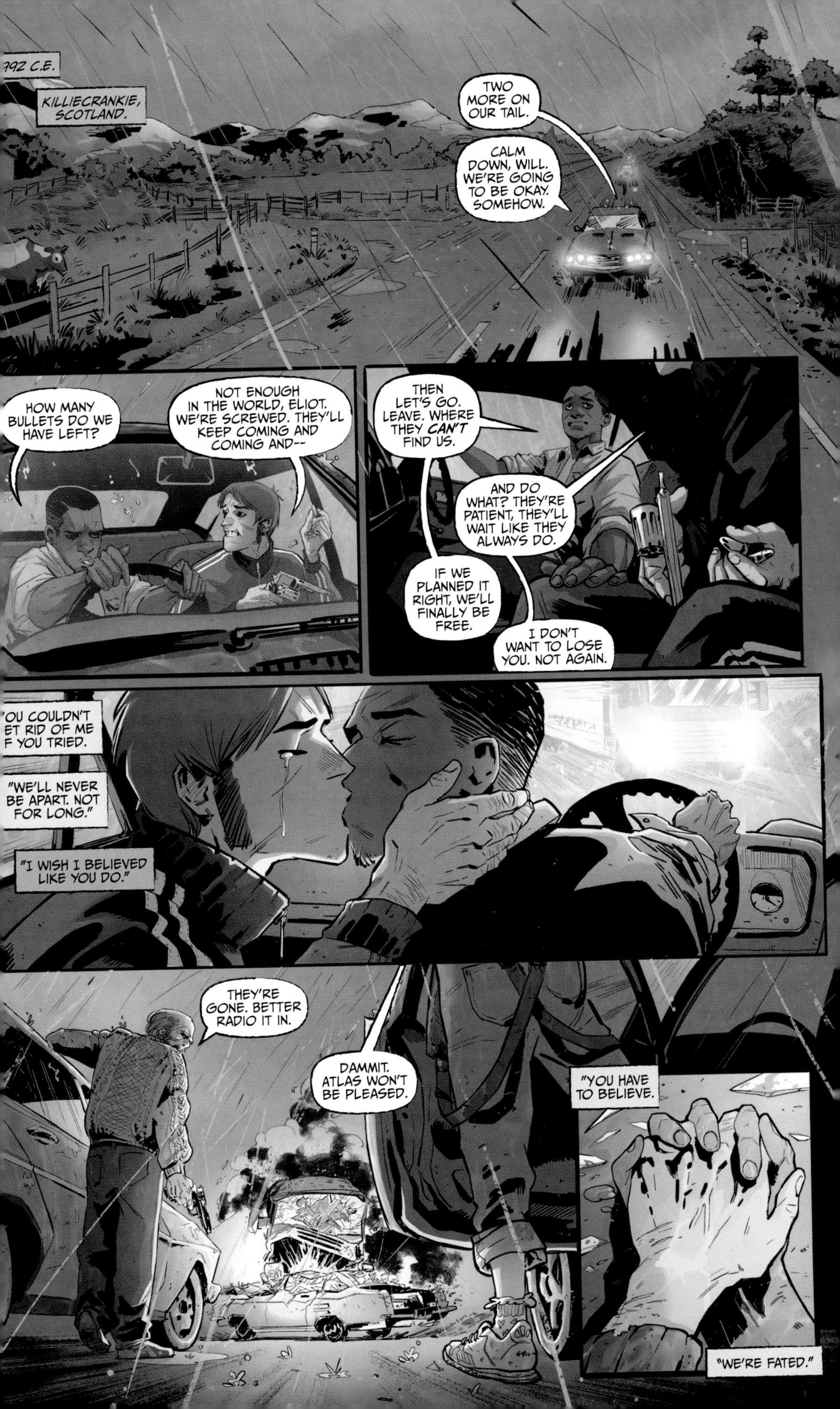
792 C.E.
KILLIECRANKIE, SCOTLAND.
TWO MORE ON OUR TAIL.
CALM DOWN, WILL. WE'RE GOING TO BE OKAY. SOMEHOW.
HOW MANY BULLETS DO WE HAVE LEFT?
NOT ENOUGH IN THE WORLD, ELIOT. WE'RE SCREWED. THEY'LL KEEP COMING AND COMING AND--
THEN LET'S GO. LEAVE. WHERE THEY *CAN'T* FIND US.
AND DO WHAT? THEY'RE PATIENT, THEY'LL WAIT LIKE THEY ALWAYS DO.
IF WE PLANNED IT RIGHT, WE'LL FINALLY BE FREE.
I DON'T WANT TO LOSE YOU. NOT AGAIN.
OU COULDN'T ET RID OF ME F YOU TRIED.
"WE'LL NEVER BE APART. NOT FOR LONG."
"I WISH I BELIEVED LIKE YOU DO."
THEY'RE GONE. BETTER RADIO IT IN.
DAMMIT. ATLAS WON'T BE PLEASED.
"YOU HAVE TO BELIEVE.
"WE'RE FATED."

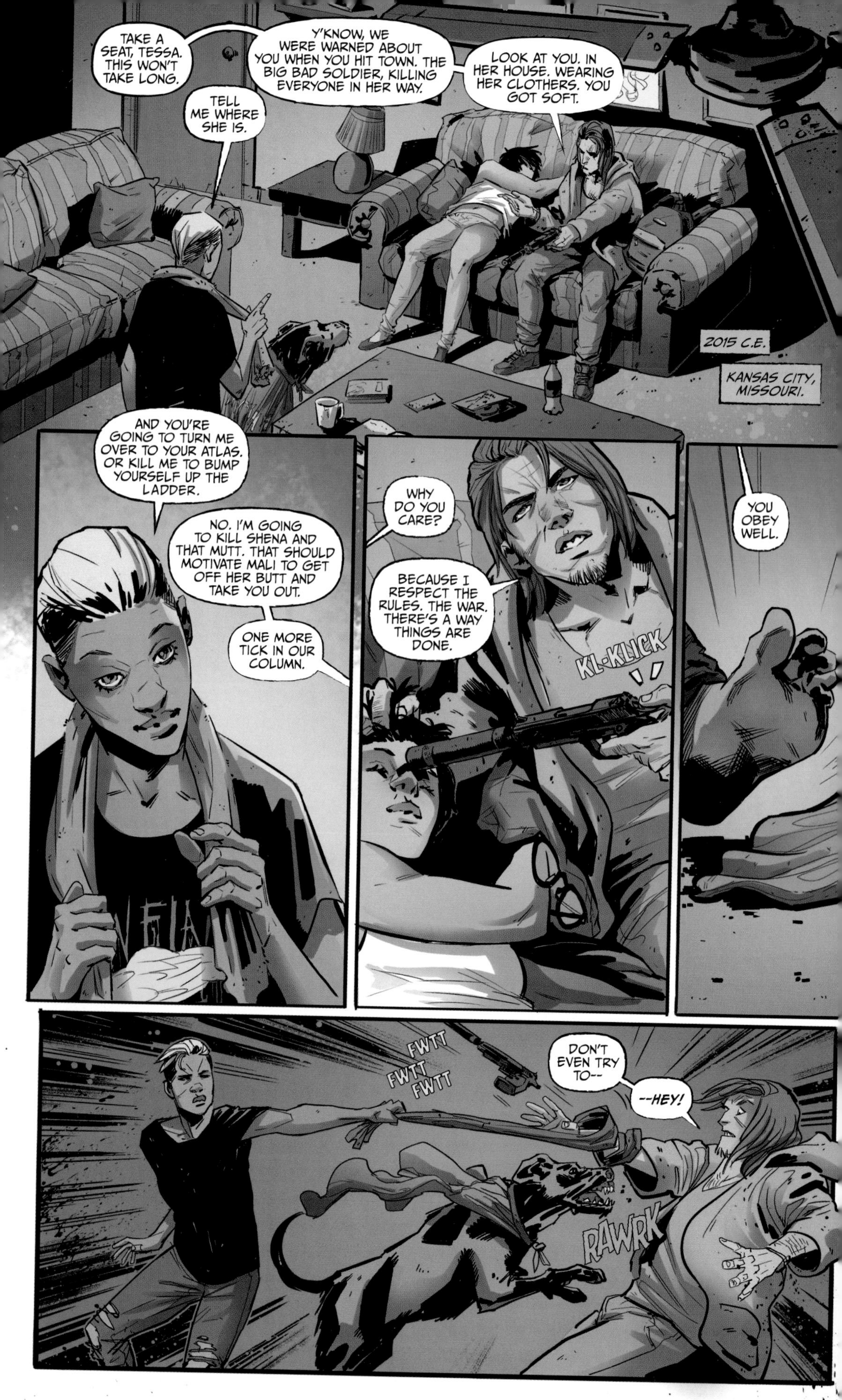
TAKE A SEAT, TESSA. THIS WON'T TAKE LONG.
Y'KNOW, WE WERE WARNED ABOUT YOU WHEN YOU HIT TOWN. THE BIG BAD SOLDIER, KILLING EVERYONE IN HER WAY.
TELL ME WHERE SHE IS.
LOOK AT YOU. IN HER HOUSE. WEARING HER CLOTHERS. YOU GOT SOFT.
2015 C.E.
KANSAS CITY, MISSOURI.
AND YOU'RE GOING TO TURN ME OVER TO YOUR ATLAS. OR KILL ME TO BUMP YOURSELF UP THE LADDER.
NO. I'M GOING TO KILL SHENA AND THAT MUTT. THAT SHOULD MOTIVATE MALI TO GET OFF HER BUTT AND TAKE YOU OUT.
ONE MORE TICK IN OUR COLUMN.
WHY DO YOU CARE?
BECAUSE I RESPECT THE RULES. THE WAR. THERE'S A WAY THINGS ARE DONE.
KL-KLICK
YOU OBEY WELL.
FWTT
FWTT
FWTT
DON'T EVEN TRY TO--
--HEY!
RAWRK

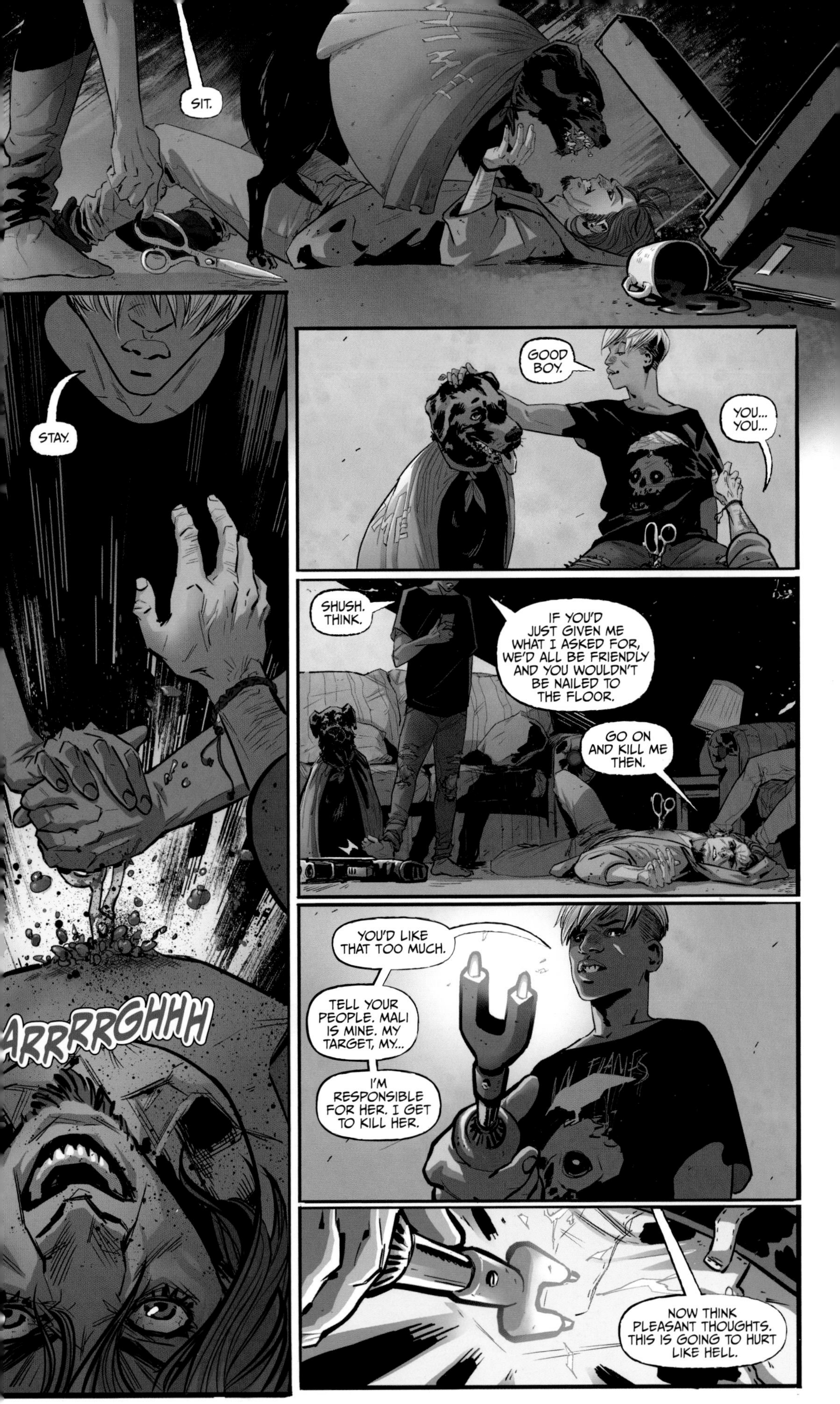
SIT.
STAY.
ARRRRGHHH
GOOD BOY.
YOU... YOU...
SHUSH. THINK.
IF YOU'D JUST GIVEN ME WHAT I ASKED FOR, WE'D ALL BE FRIENDLY AND YOU WOULDN'T BE NAILED TO THE FLOOR.
GO ON AND KILL ME THEN.
YOU'D LIKE THAT TOO MUCH.
TELL YOUR PEOPLE. MALI IS MINE. MY TARGET, MY...
I'M RESPONSIBLE FOR HER. I GET TO KILL HER.
NOW THINK PLEASANT THOUGHTS. THIS IS GOING TO HURT LIKE HELL.

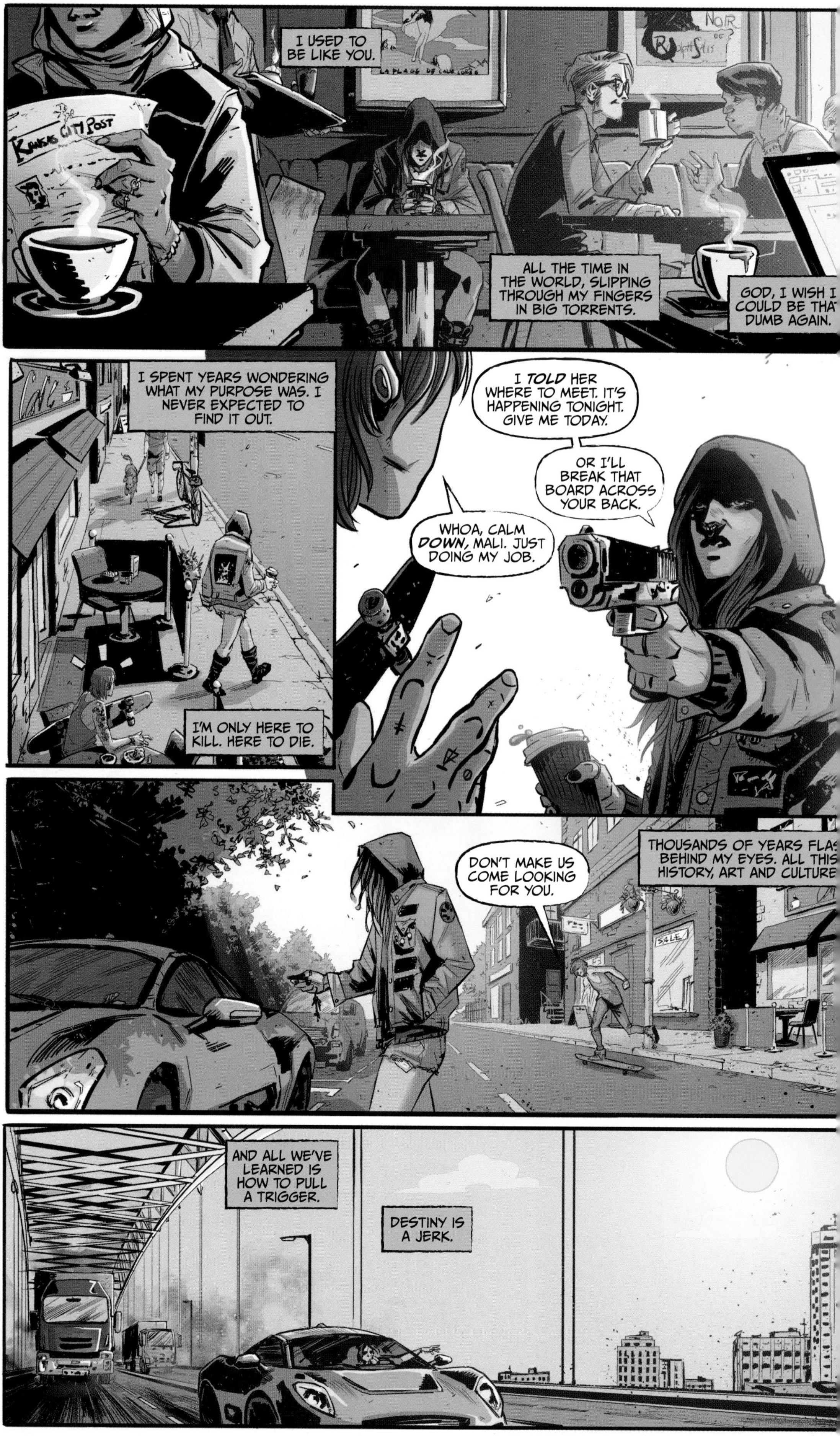
I USED TO BE LIKE YOU.
KANSAS CITY POST
ALL THE TIME IN THE WORLD, SLIPPING THROUGH MY FINGERS IN BIG TORRENTS.
GOD, I WISH I COULD BE THAT DUMB AGAIN.
I SPENT YEARS WONDERING WHAT MY PURPOSE WAS. I NEVER EXPECTED TO FIND IT OUT.
I'M ONLY HERE TO KILL. HERE TO DIE.
I *TOLD* HER WHERE TO MEET. IT'S HAPPENING TONIGHT. GIVE ME TODAY.
OR I'LL BREAK THAT BOARD ACROSS YOUR BACK.
WHOA, CALM *DOWN,* MALI. JUST DOING MY JOB.
DON'T MAKE US COME LOOKING FOR YOU.
THOUSANDS OF YEARS FLAS BEHIND MY EYES. ALL THIS HISTORY, ART AND CULTURE
SALE
AND ALL WE'VE LEARNED IS HOW TO PULL A TRIGGER.
DESTINY IS A JERK.

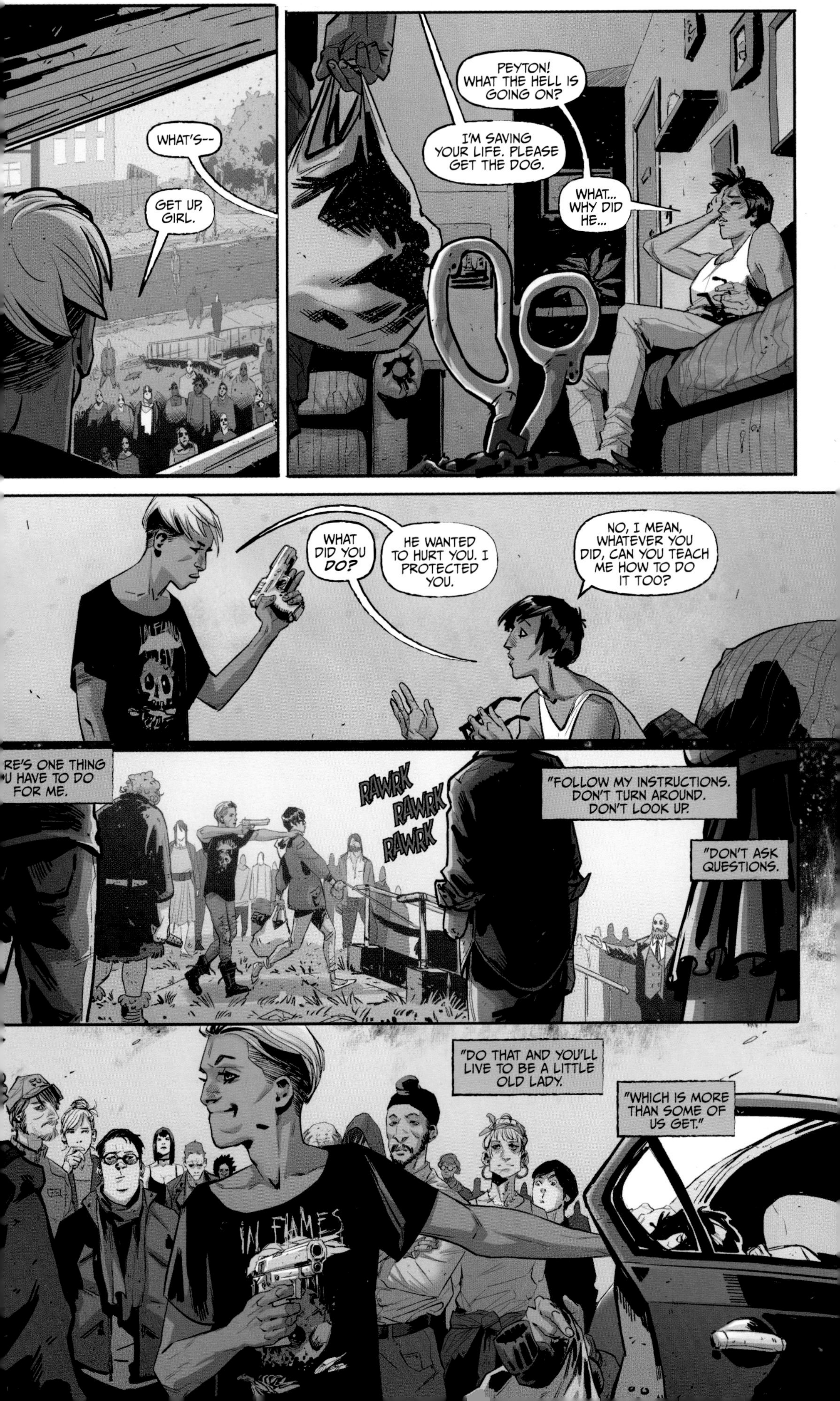
WHAT'S--
GET UP, GIRL.
PEYTON! WHAT THE HELL IS GOING ON?
I'M SAVING YOUR LIFE. PLEASE GET THE DOG.
WHAT... WHY DID HE...
WHAT DID YOU DO?
HE WANTED TO HURT YOU. I PROTECTED YOU.
NO, I MEAN, WHATEVER YOU DID, CAN YOU TEACH ME HOW TO DO IT TOO?
RE'S ONE THING
U HAVE TO DO FOR ME.
RAWRK
RAWRK
RAWRK
"FOLLOW MY INSTRUCTIONS. DON'T TURN AROUND. DON'T LOOK UP.
"DON'T ASK QUESTIONS.
"DO THAT AND YOU'LL LIVE TO BE A LITTLE OLD LADY.
"WHICH IS MORE THAN SOME OF US GET."

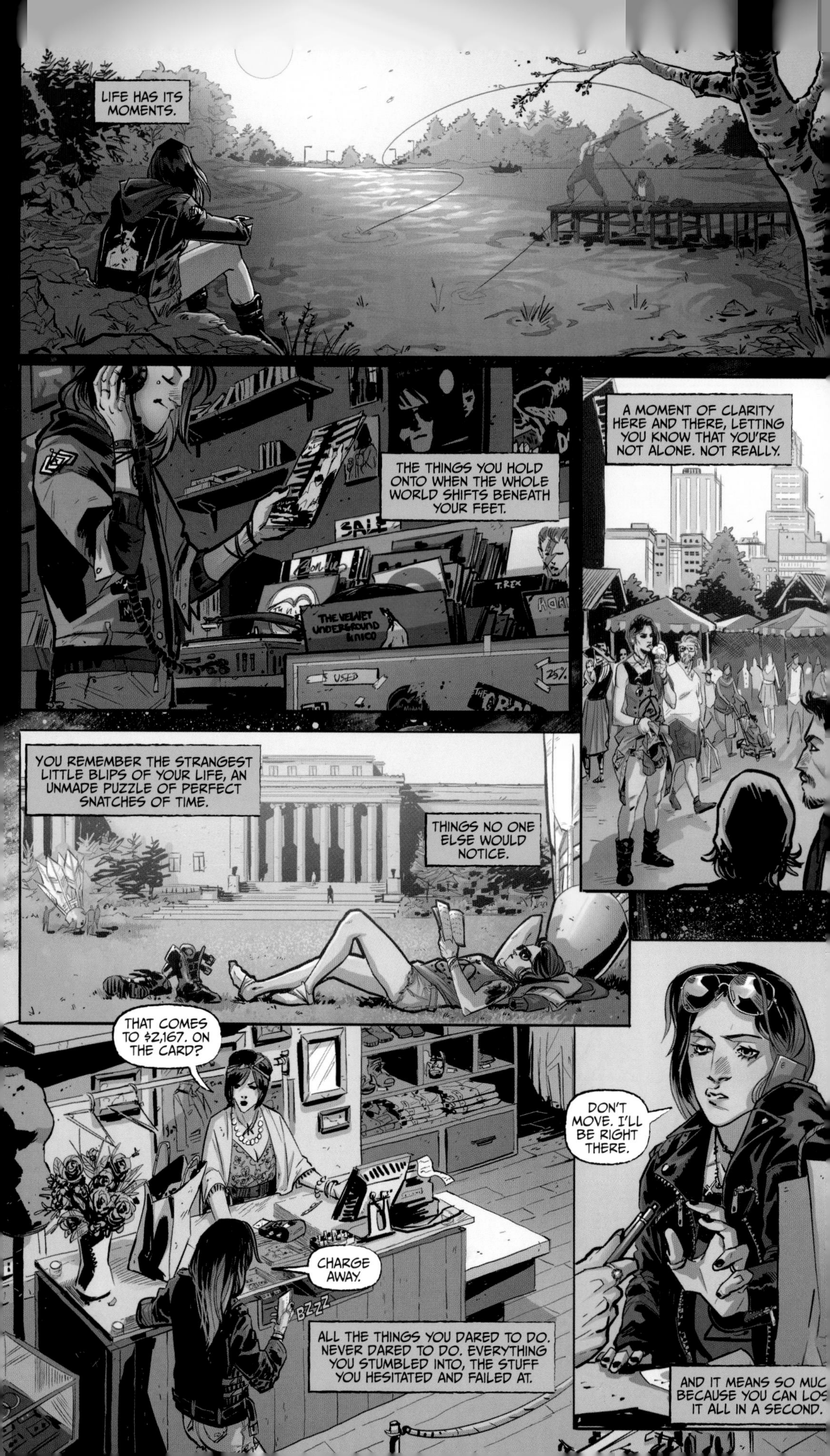
LIFE HAS ITS MOMENTS.
THE THINGS YOU HOLD ONTO WHEN THE WHOLE WORLD SHIFTS BENEATH YOUR FEET.
SALE
T. REX
THE VELVET UNDERGROUND & NICO
USED
25%
A MOMENT OF CLARITY HERE AND THERE, LETTING YOU KNOW THAT YOU'RE NOT ALONE. NOT REALLY.
YOU REMEMBER THE STRANGEST LITTLE BLIPS OF YOUR LIFE, AN UNMADE PUZZLE OF PERFECT SNATCHES OF TIME.
THINGS NO ONE ELSE WOULD NOTICE.
THAT COMES TO $2,167. ON THE CARD?
CHARGE AWAY.
BZZZ
ALL THE THINGS YOU DARED TO DO. NEVER DARED TO DO. EVERYTHING YOU STUMBLED INTO, THE STUFF YOU HESITATED AND FAILED AT.
DON'T MOVE. I'LL BE RIGHT THERE.
AND IT MEANS SO MUC
BECAUSE YOU CAN LOS
IT ALL IN A SECOND.

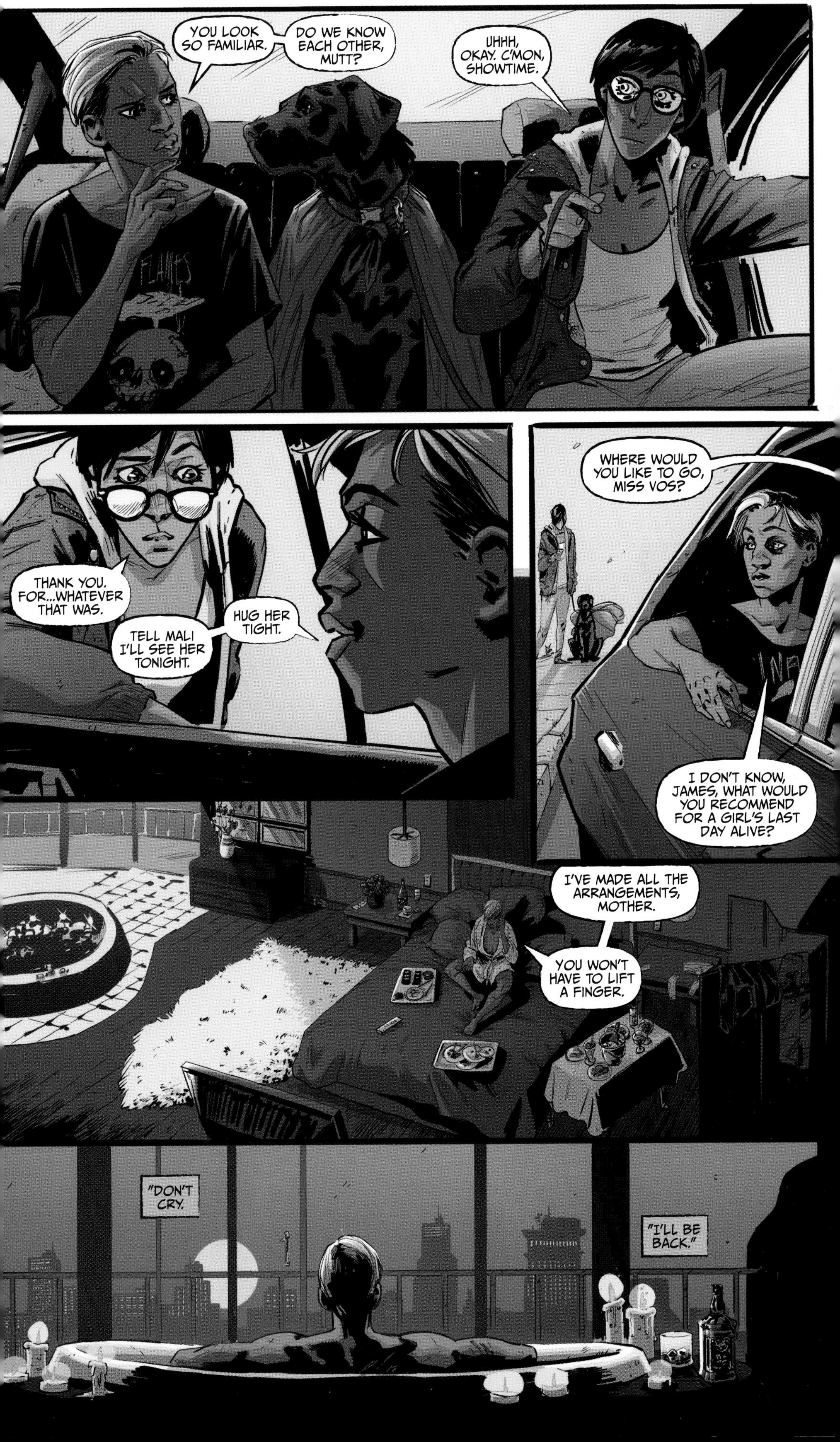

YOU LOOK SO FAMILIAR.
DO WE KNOW EACH OTHER, MUTT?
UHHH, OKAY. C'MON, SHOWTIME.
THANK YOU. FOR...WHATEVER THAT WAS.
HUG HER TIGHT.
TELL MALI I'LL SEE HER TONIGHT.
WHERE WOULD YOU LIKE TO GO, MISS VOS?
I DON'T KNOW, JAMES, WHAT WOULD YOU RECOMMEND FOR A GIRL'S LAST DAY ALIVE?
I'VE MADE ALL THE ARRANGEMENTS, MOTHER.
YOU WON'T HAVE TO LIFT A FINGER.
"DON'T CRY.
"I'LL BE BACK."

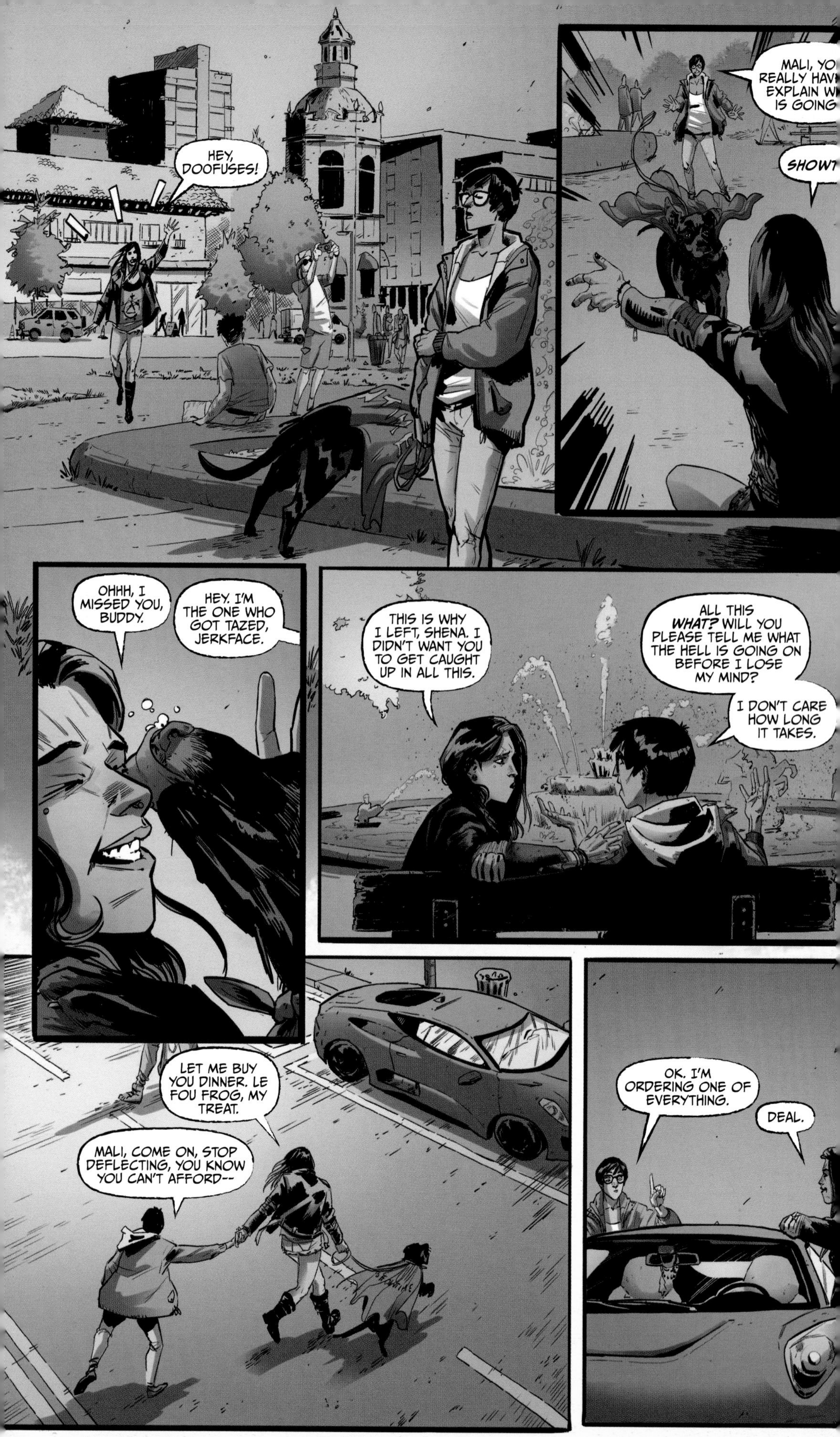

HEY, DOOFUSES!
MALI, YO REALLY HAV EXPLAIN W IS GOING
SHOWT
OHHH, I MISSED YOU, BUDDY.
HEY. I'M THE ONE WHO GOT TAZED, JERKFACE.
THIS IS WHY I LEFT, SHENA. I DIDN'T WANT YOU TO GET CAUGHT UP IN ALL THIS.
ALL THIS *WHAT?* WILL YOU PLEASE TELL ME WHAT THE HELL IS GOING ON BEFORE I LOSE MY MIND?
I DON'T CARE HOW LONG IT TAKES.
LET ME BUY YOU DINNER. LE FOU FROG, MY TREAT.
MALI, COME ON, STOP DEFLECTING, YOU KNOW YOU CAN'T AFFORD--
OK. I'M ORDERING ONE OF EVERYTHING.
DEAL.

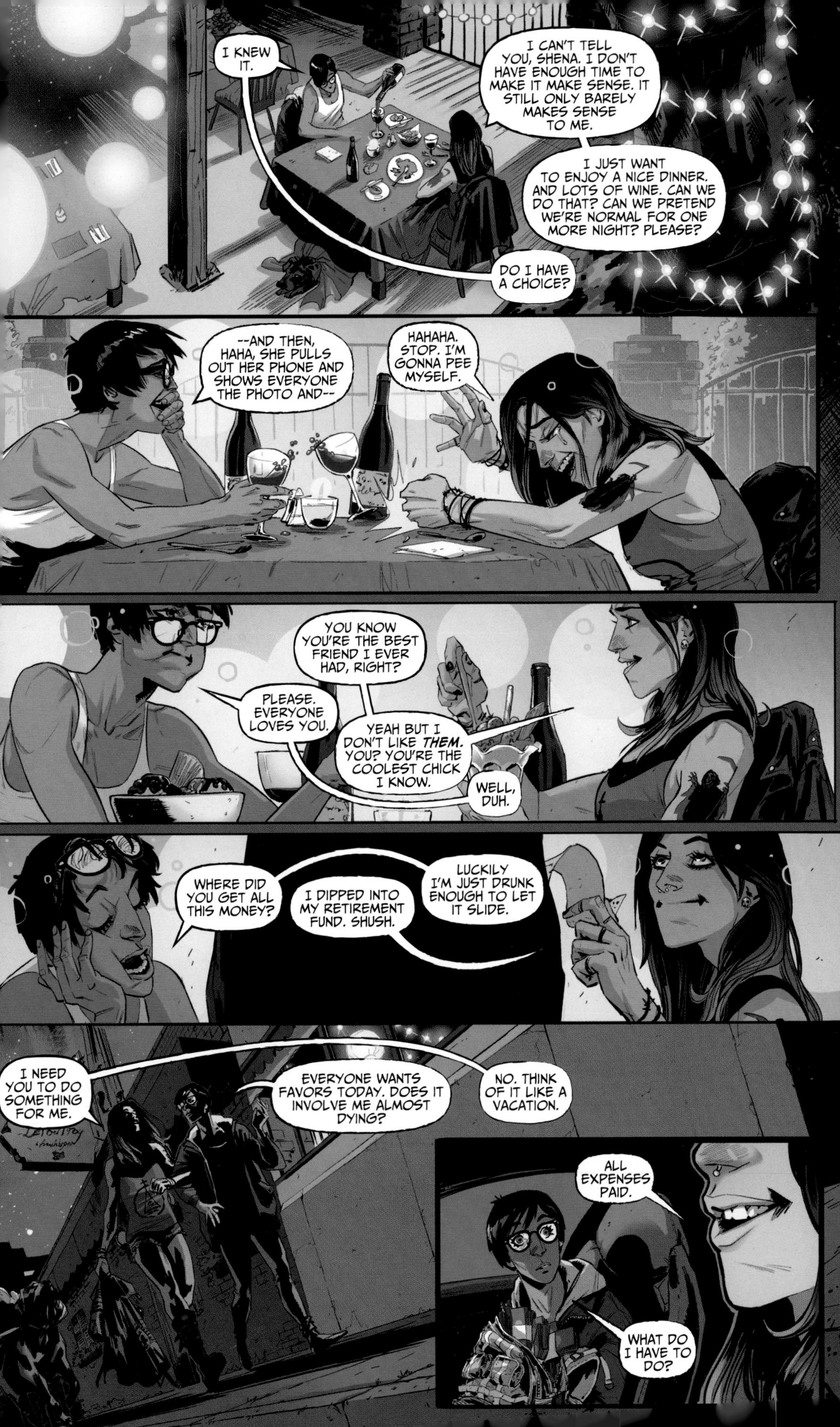
I KNEW IT.
I CAN'T TELL YOU, SHENA. I DON'T HAVE ENOUGH TIME TO MAKE IT MAKE SENSE. IT STILL ONLY BARELY MAKES SENSE TO ME.
I JUST WANT TO ENJOY A NICE DINNER. AND LOTS OF WINE. CAN WE DO THAT? CAN WE PRETEND WE'RE NORMAL FOR ONE MORE NIGHT? PLEASE?
DO I HAVE A CHOICE?
--AND THEN, HAHA, SHE PULLS OUT HER PHONE AND SHOWS EVERYONE THE PHOTO AND--
HAHAHA. STOP. I'M GONNA PEE MYSELF.
YOU KNOW YOU'RE THE BEST FRIEND I EVER HAD, RIGHT?
PLEASE. EVERYONE LOVES YOU.
YEAH BUT I DON'T LIKE *THEM.* YOU? YOU'RE THE COOLEST CHICK I KNOW.
WELL, DUH.
WHERE DID YOU GET ALL THIS MONEY?
I DIPPED INTO MY RETIREMENT FUND. SHUSH.
LUCKILY I'M JUST DRUNK ENOUGH TO LET IT SLIDE.
I NEED YOU TO DO SOMETHING FOR ME.
EVERYONE WANTS FAVORS TODAY. DOES IT INVOLVE ME ALMOST DYING?
NO. THINK OF IT LIKE A VACATION.
ALL EXPENSES PAID.
WHAT DO I HAVE TO DO?

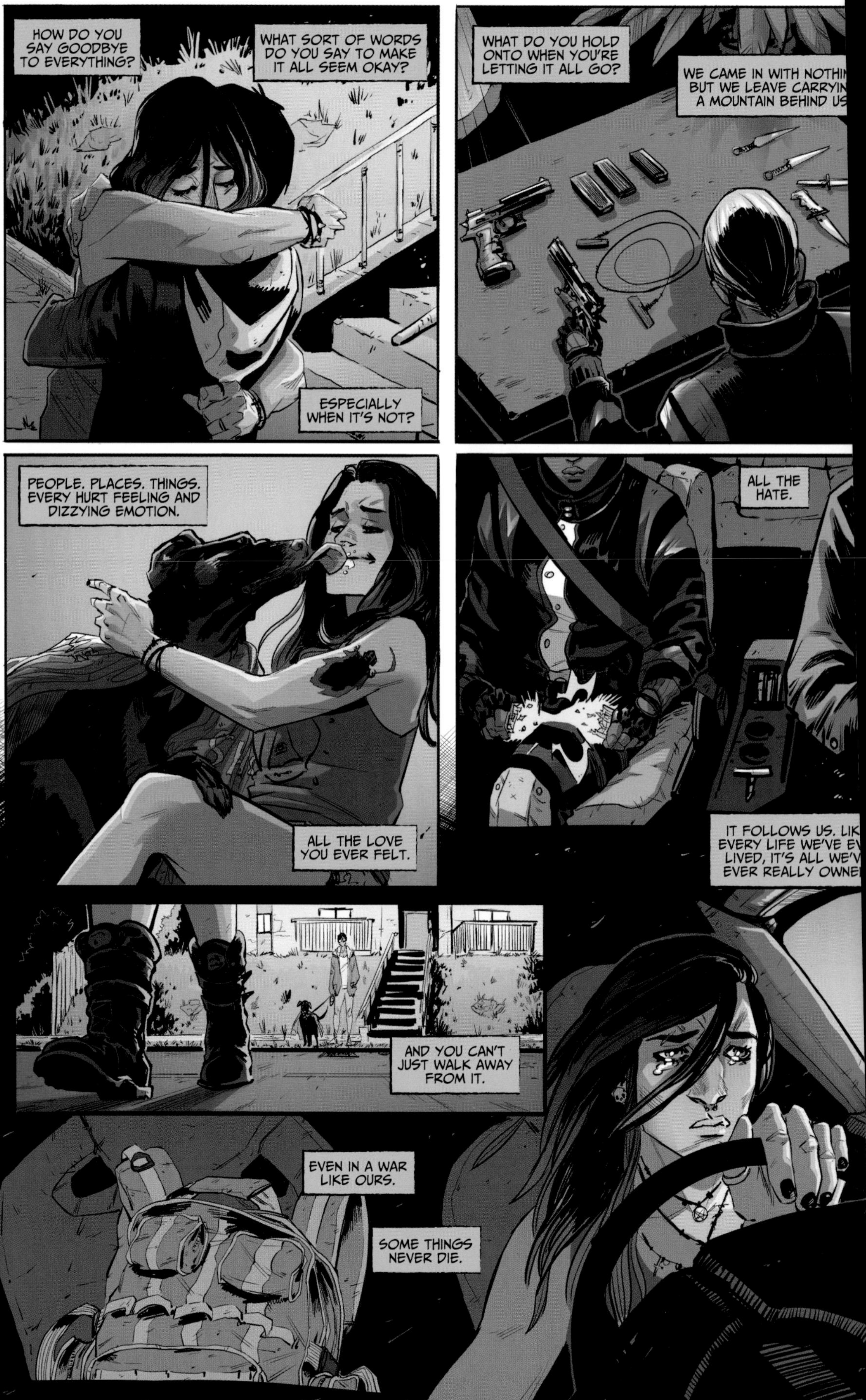
HOW DO YOU SAY GOODBYE TO EVERYTHING?
WHAT SORT OF WORDS DO YOU SAY TO MAKE IT ALL SEEM OKAY?
ESPECIALLY WHEN IT'S NOT?
WHAT DO YOU HOLD ONTO WHEN YOU'RE LETTING IT ALL GO?
WE CAME IN WITH NOTHIN
BUT WE LEAVE CARRYIN
A MOUNTAIN BEHIND US
PEOPLE. PLACES. THINGS. EVERY HURT FEELING AND DIZZYING EMOTION.
ALL THE LOVE YOU EVER FELT.
ALL THE HATE.
IT FOLLOWS US. LIK
EVERY LIFE WE'VE EV
LIVED, IT'S ALL WE'V
EVER REALLY OWNE
AND YOU CAN'T JUST WALK AWAY FROM IT.
EVEN IN A WAR LIKE OURS.
SOME THINGS NEVER DIE.

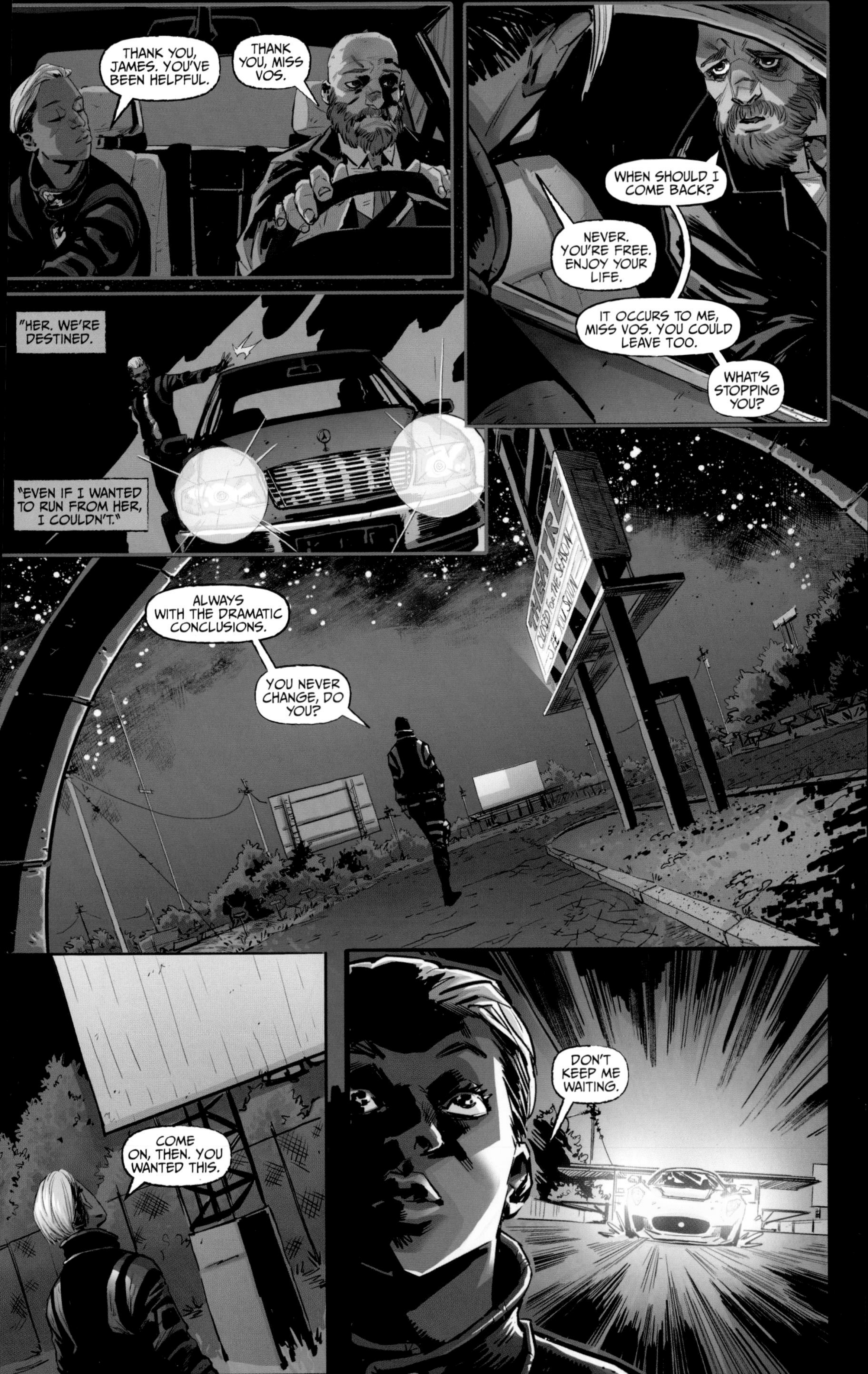
THANK YOU, JAMES. YOU'VE BEEN HELPFUL.
THANK YOU, MISS VOS.
WHEN SHOULD I COME BACK?
NEVER. YOU'RE FREE. ENJOY YOUR LIFE.
IT OCCURS TO ME, MISS VOS. YOU COULD LEAVE TOO.
WHAT'S STOPPING YOU?
"HER. WE'RE DESTINED.
"EVEN IF I WANTED TO RUN FROM HER, I COULDN'T."
THEATRE
CLOSED FOR THE SEASON
SEE YOU SOON
ALWAYS WITH THE DRAMATIC CONCLUSIONS.
YOU NEVER CHANGE, DO YOU?
COME ON, THEN. YOU WANTED THIS.
DON'T KEEP ME WAITING.

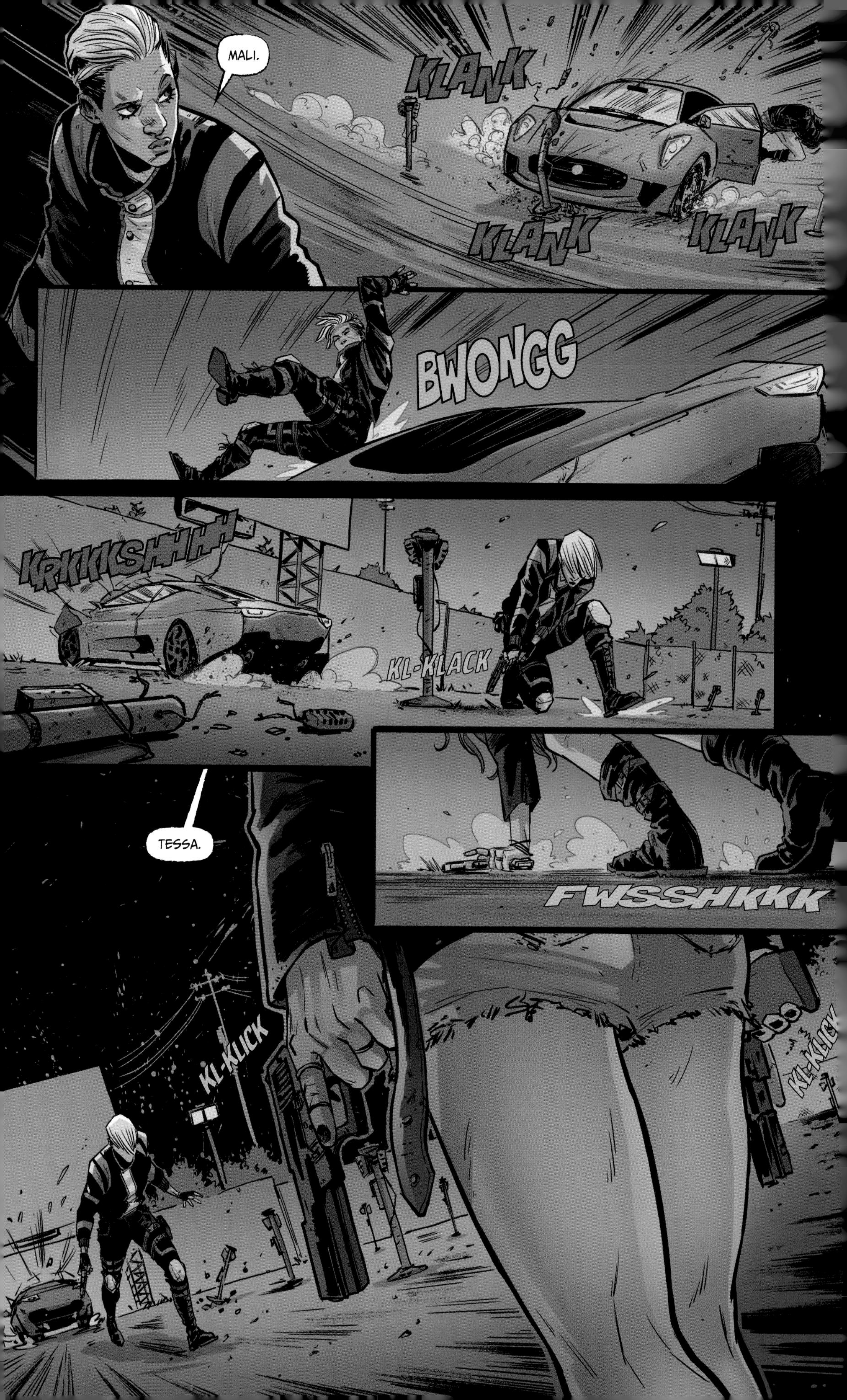
MALI.
KLANK
KLANK
KLANK
BWONGG
KRKKKSHHHH
KL-KLACK
TESSA.
FWSSHKKK
KL-KLICK
KL-KLICK

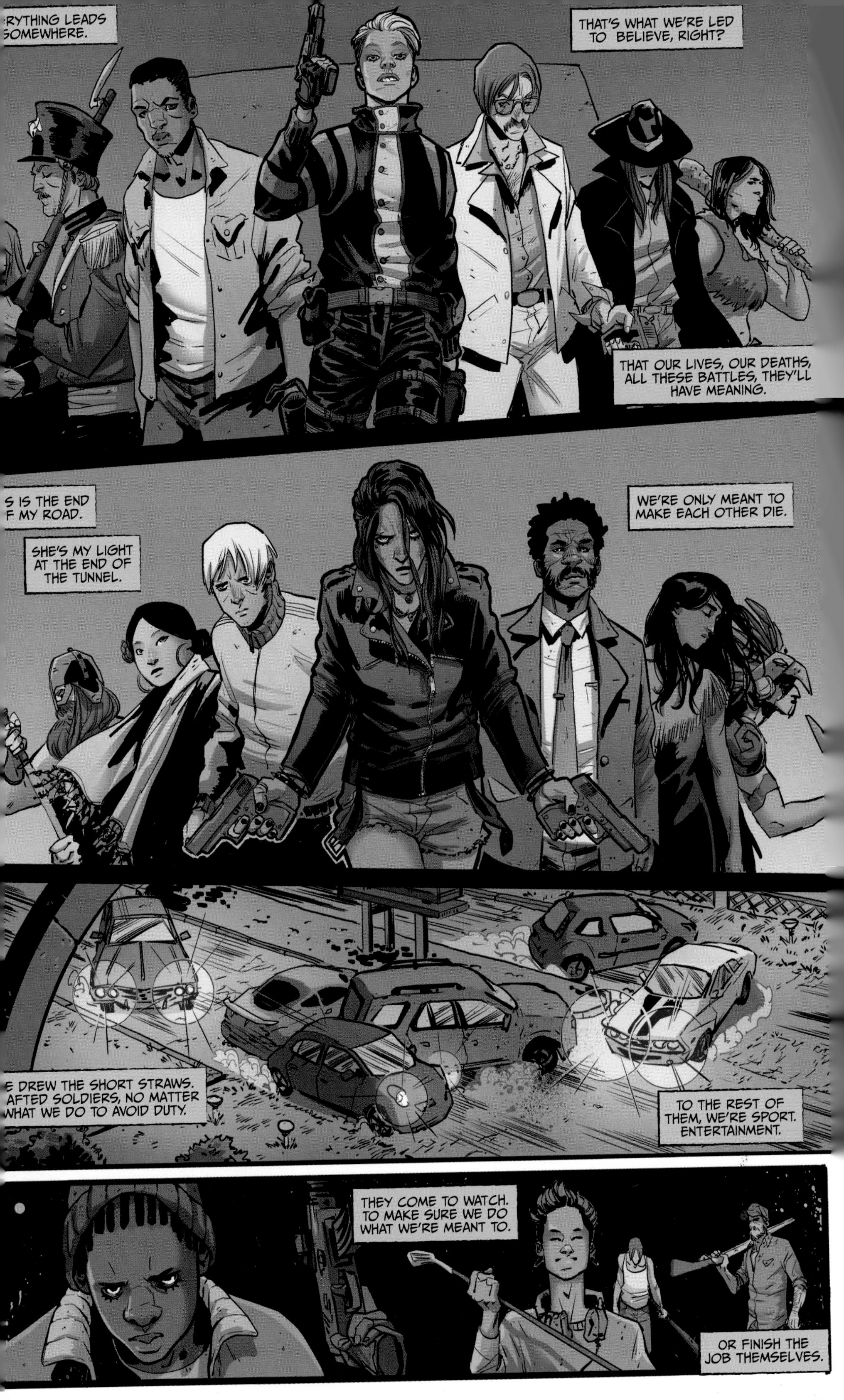

RYTHING LEADS
SOMEWHERE.
THAT'S WHAT WE'RE LED TO BELIEVE, RIGHT?
THAT OUR LIVES, OUR DEATHS, ALL THESE BATTLES, THEY'LL HAVE MEANING.
S IS THE END
F MY ROAD.
SHE'S MY LIGHT AT THE END OF THE TUNNEL.
WE'RE ONLY MEANT TO MAKE EACH OTHER DIE.
E DREW THE SHORT STRAWS.
AFTED SOLDIERS, NO MATTER
WHAT WE DO TO AVOID DUTY.
TO THE REST OF THEM, WE'RE SPORT. ENTERTAINMENT.
THEY COME TO WATCH. TO MAKE SURE WE DO WHAT WE'RE MEANT TO.
OR FINISH THE JOB THEMSELVES.

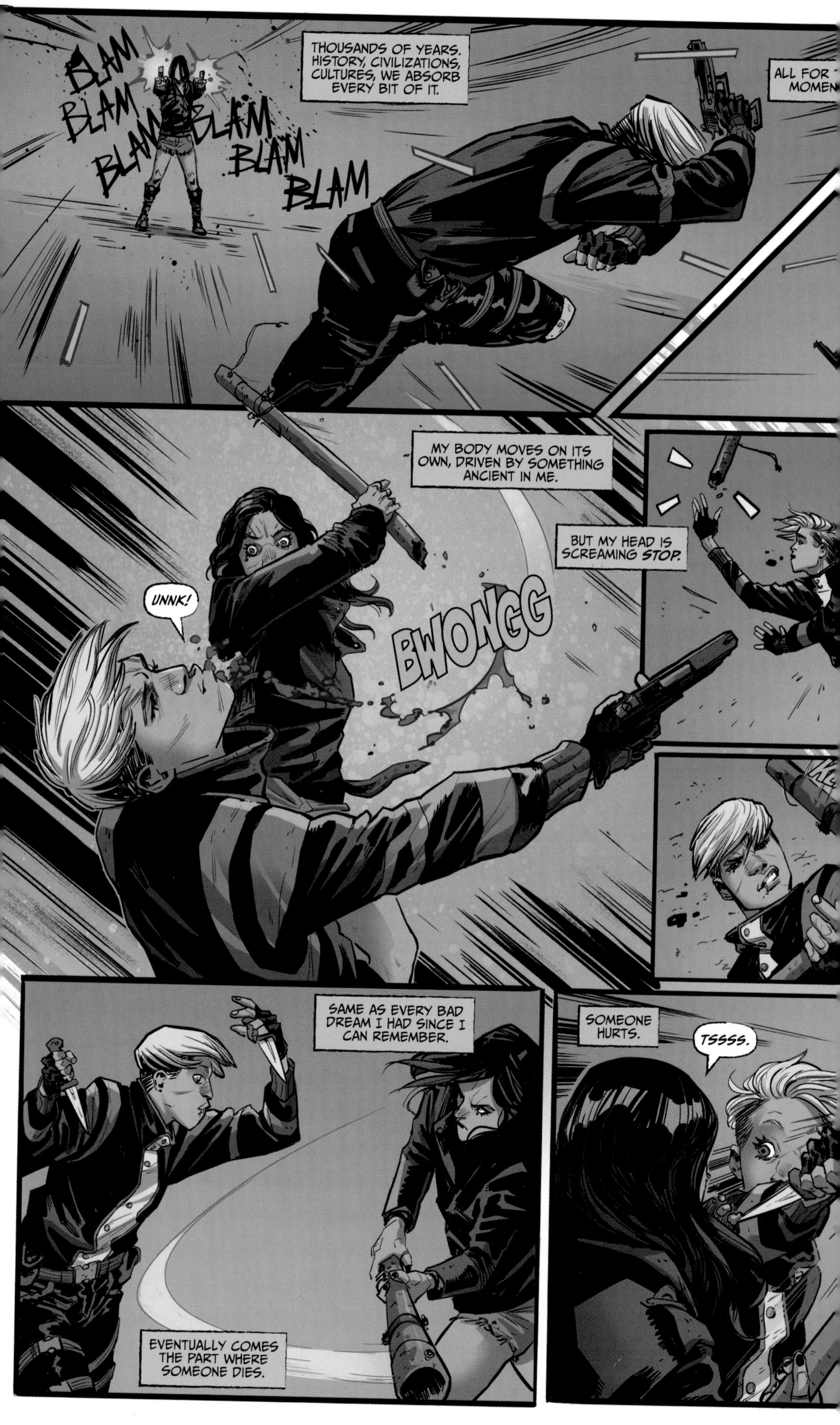
BLAM
BLAM
BLAM BLAM
BLAM
BLAM
BLAM
THOUSANDS OF YEARS. HISTORY, CIVILIZATIONS, CULTURES, WE ABSORB EVERY BIT OF IT.
ALL FOR
MOMEN
MY BODY MOVES ON ITS OWN, DRIVEN BY SOMETHING ANCIENT IN ME.
UNNK!
BWONGG
BUT MY HEAD IS SCREAMING *STOP.*
SAME AS EVERY BAD DREAM I HAD SINCE I CAN REMEMBER.
EVENTUALLY COMES THE PART WHERE SOMEONE DIES.
SOMEONE HURTS.
TSSSS.

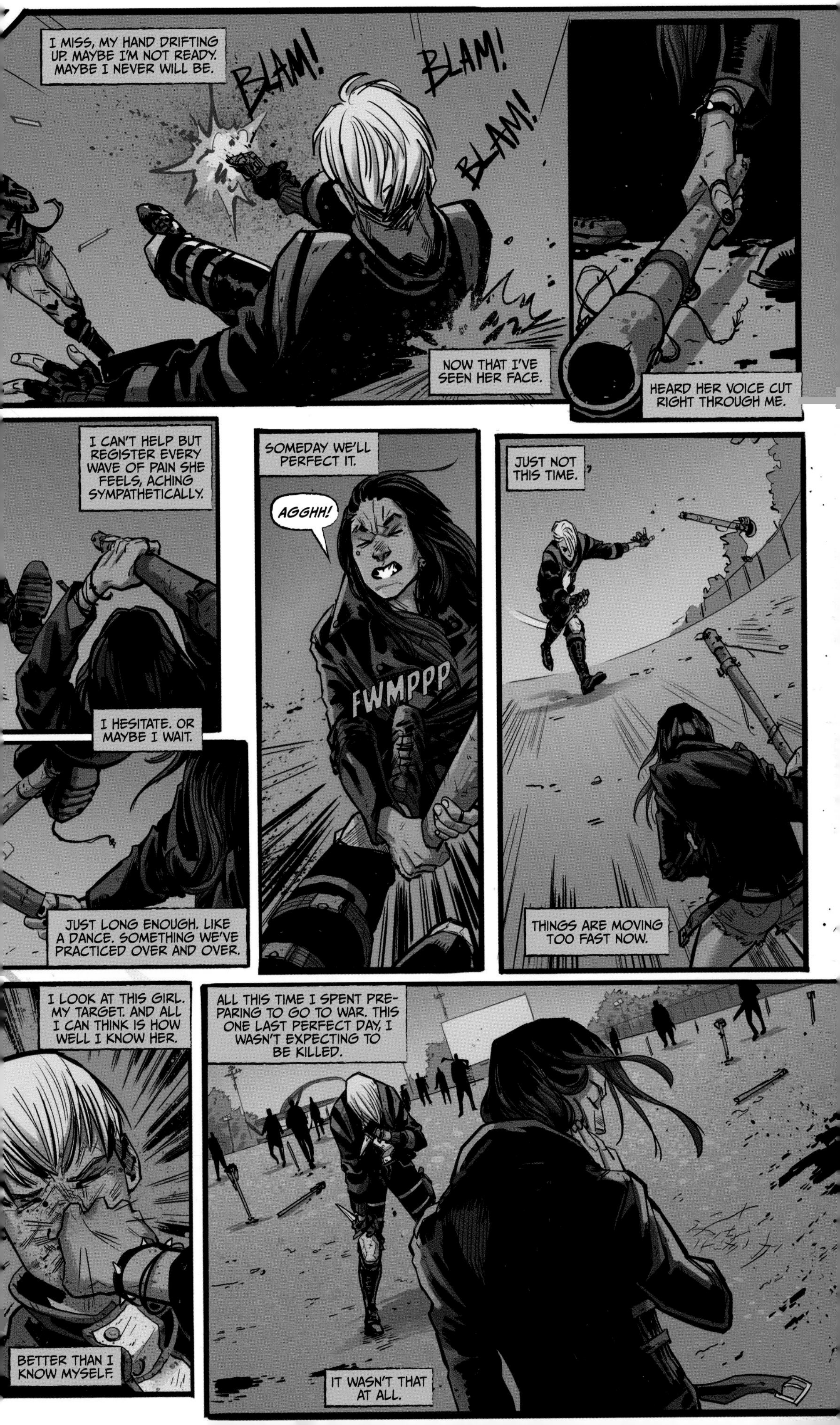
I MISS, MY HAND DRIFTING UP. MAYBE I'M NOT READY. MAYBE I NEVER WILL BE.
BLAM!
BLAM!
BLAM!
NOW THAT I'VE SEEN HER FACE.
HEARD HER VOICE CUT RIGHT THROUGH ME.
I CAN'T HELP BUT REGISTER EVERY WAVE OF PAIN SHE FEELS, ACHING SYMPATHETICALLY.
I HESITATE. OR MAYBE I WAIT.
JUST LONG ENOUGH. LIKE A DANCE. SOMETHING WE'VE PRACTICED OVER AND OVER.
SOMEDAY WE'LL PERFECT IT.
AGGHH!
FWMPPP
JUST NOT THIS TIME.
THINGS ARE MOVING TOO FAST NOW.
I LOOK AT THIS GIRL. MY TARGET. AND ALL I CAN THINK IS HOW WELL I KNOW HER.
BETTER THAN I KNOW MYSELF.
ALL THIS TIME I SPENT PREPARING TO GO TO WAR. THIS ONE LAST PERFECT DAY, I WASN'T EXPECTING TO BE KILLED.
IT WASN'T THAT AT ALL.

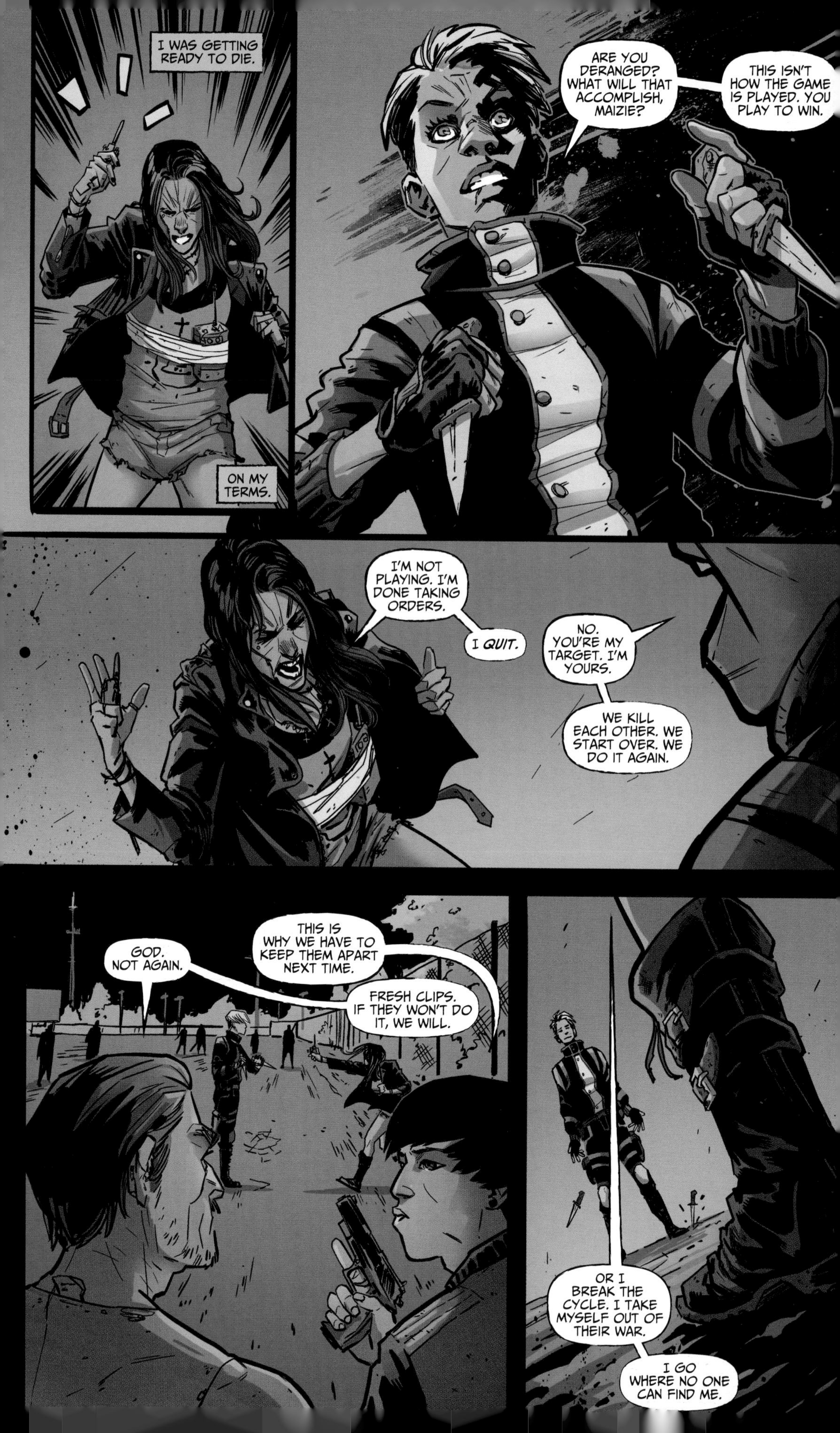
I WAS GETTING READY TO DIE.
ON MY TERMS.
ARE YOU DERANGED? WHAT WILL THAT ACCOMPLISH, MAIZIE?
THIS ISN'T HOW THE GAME IS PLAYED. YOU PLAY TO WIN.
I'M NOT PLAYING. I'M DONE TAKING ORDERS.
I *QUIT*.
NO. YOU'RE MY TARGET. I'M YOURS.
WE KILL EACH OTHER. WE START OVER. WE DO IT AGAIN.
GOD. NOT AGAIN.
THIS IS WHY WE HAVE TO KEEP THEM APART NEXT TIME.
FRESH CLIPS. IF THEY WON'T DO IT, WE WILL.
OR I BREAK THE CYCLE. I TAKE MYSELF OUT OF THEIR WAR.
I GO WHERE NO ONE CAN FIND ME.

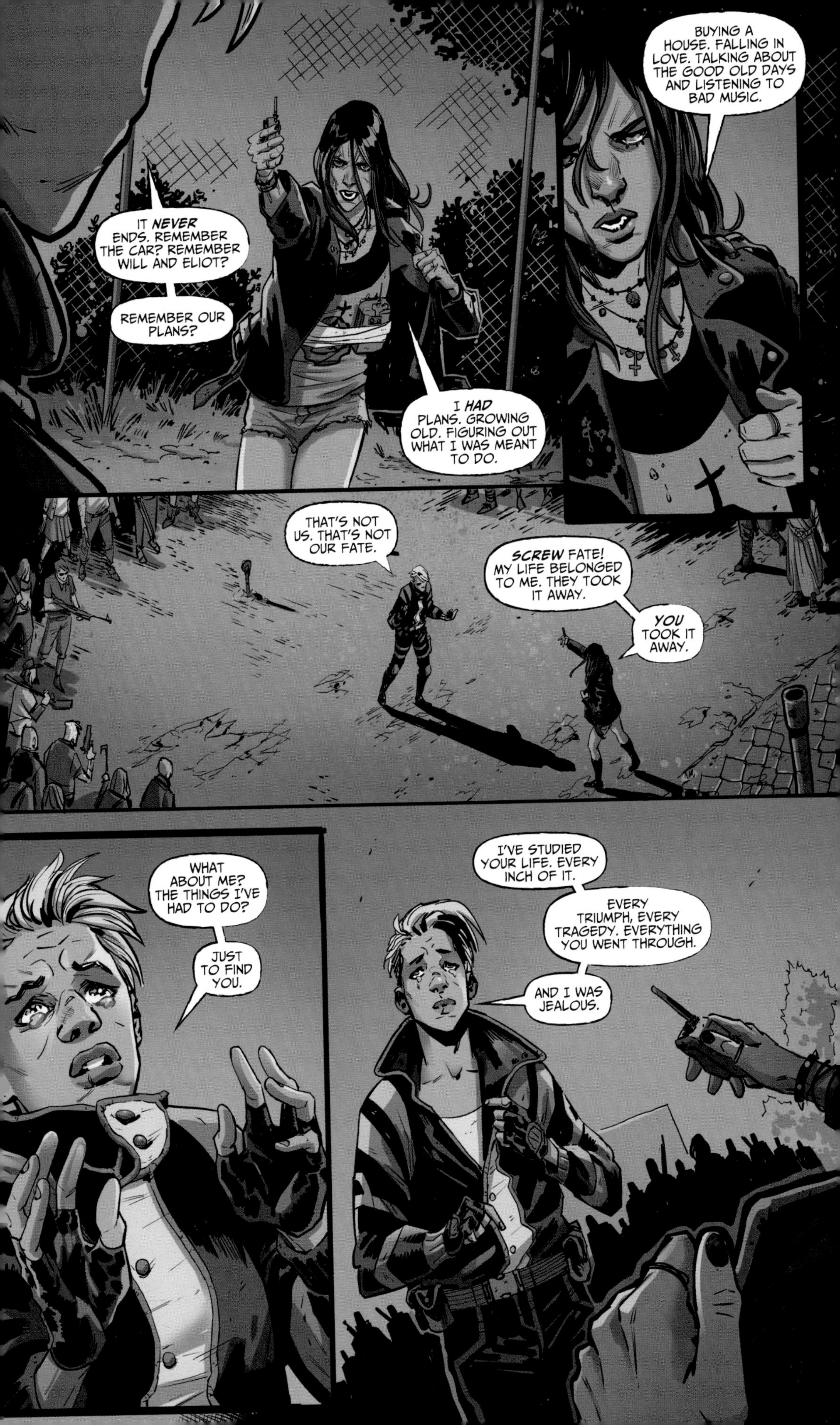
IT NEVER ENDS. REMEMBER THE CAR? REMEMBER WILL AND ELIOT?
REMEMBER OUR PLANS?
I HAD PLANS. GROWING OLD. FIGURING OUT WHAT I WAS MEANT TO DO.
BUYING A HOUSE. FALLING IN LOVE. TALKING ABOUT THE GOOD OLD DAYS AND LISTENING TO BAD MUSIC.
THAT'S NOT US. THAT'S NOT OUR FATE.
SCREW FATE! MY LIFE BELONGED TO ME. THEY TOOK IT AWAY.
YOU TOOK IT AWAY.
WHAT ABOUT ME? THE THINGS I'VE HAD TO DO?
JUST TO FIND YOU.
I'VE STUDIED YOUR LIFE. EVERY INCH OF IT.
EVERY TRIUMPH, EVERY TRAGEDY. EVERYTHING YOU WENT THROUGH.
AND I WAS JEALOUS.

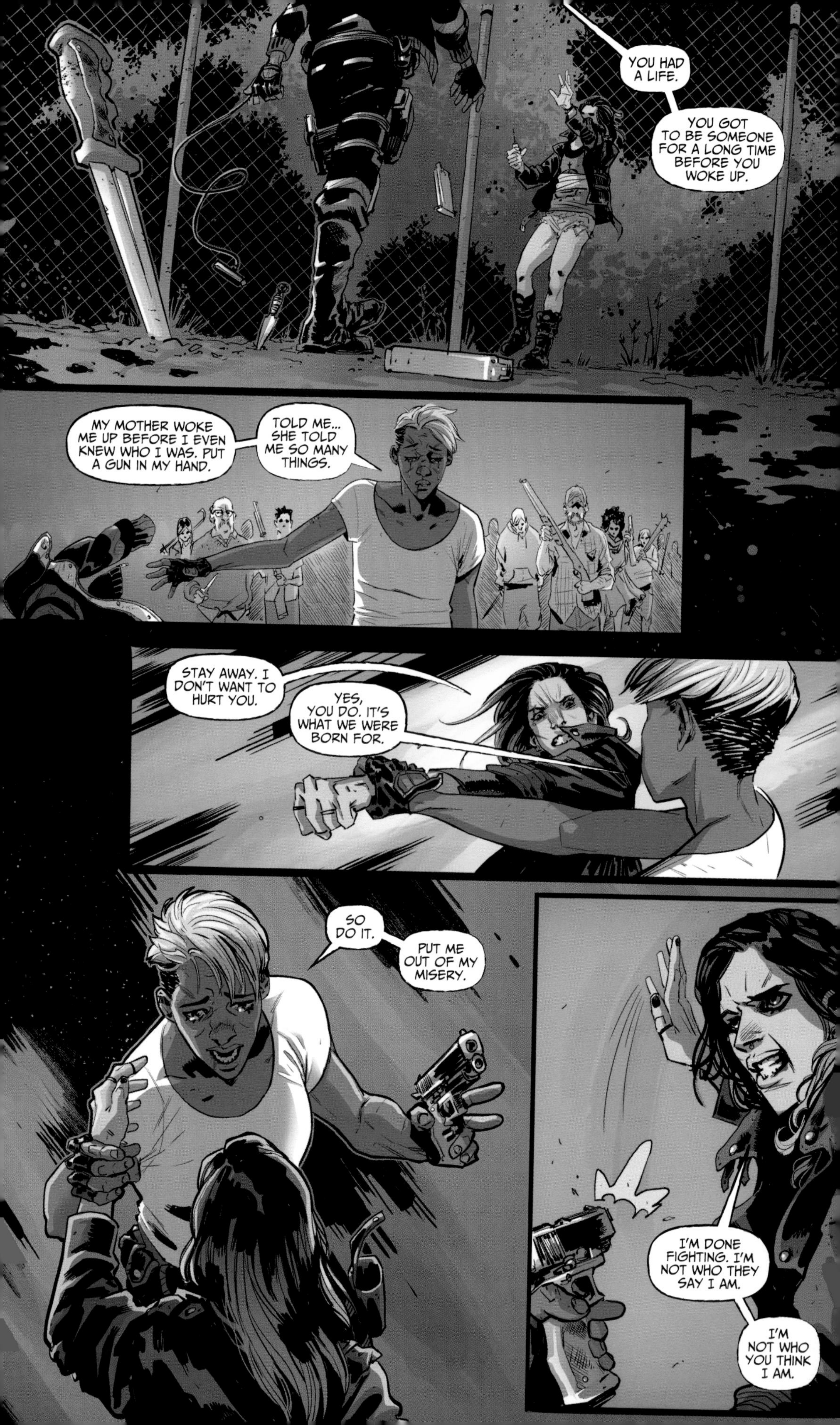
YOU HAD A LIFE.
YOU GOT TO BE SOMEONE FOR A LONG TIME BEFORE YOU WOKE UP.
MY MOTHER WOKE ME UP BEFORE I EVEN KNEW WHO I WAS. PUT A GUN IN MY HAND.
TOLD ME... SHE TOLD ME SO MANY THINGS.
STAY AWAY. I DON'T WANT TO HURT YOU.
YES, YOU DO. IT'S WHAT WE WERE BORN FOR.
SO DO IT.
PUT ME OUT OF MY MISERY.
I'M DONE FIGHTING. I'M NOT WHO THEY SAY I AM.
I'M NOT WHO YOU THINK I AM.

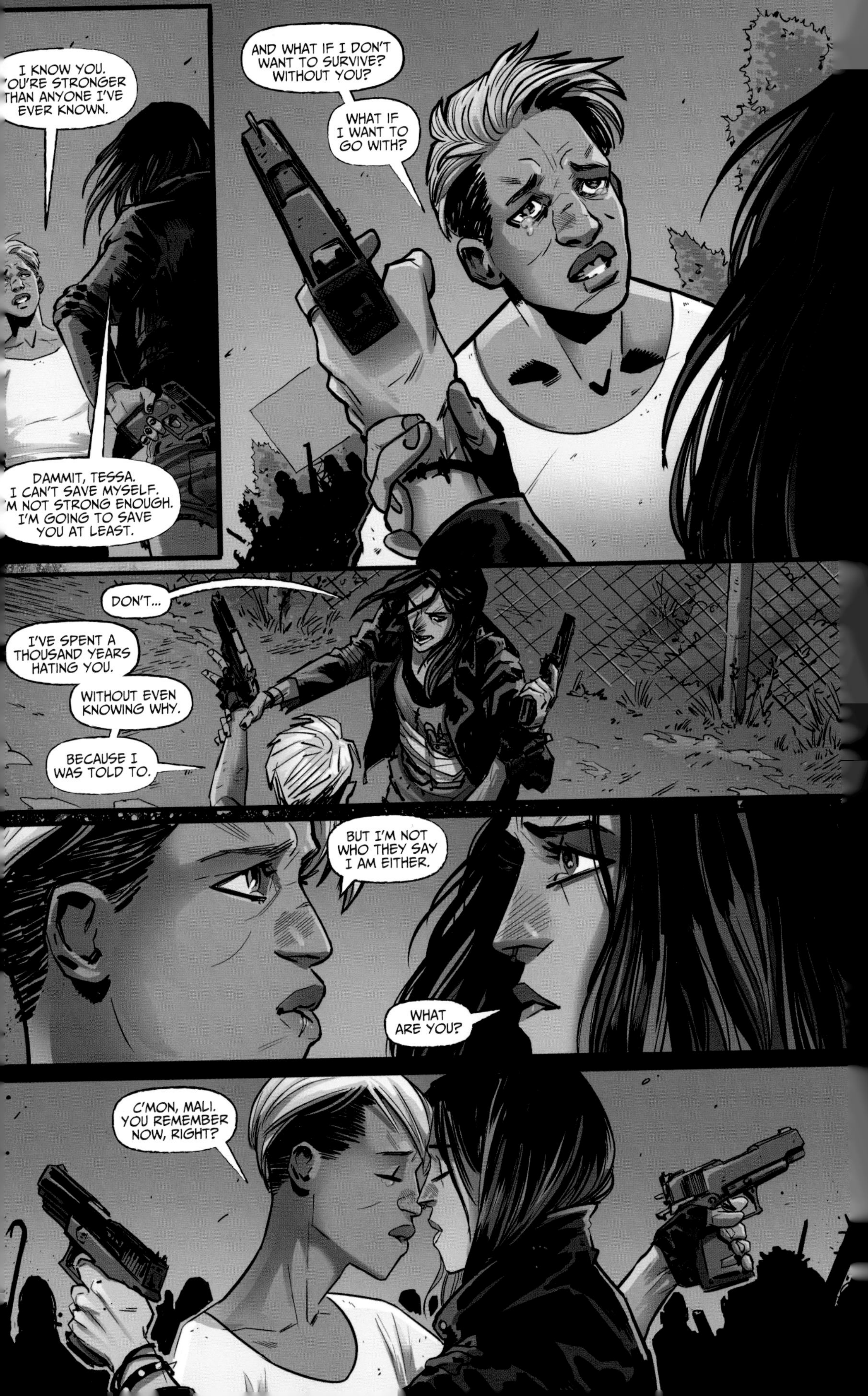
I KNOW YOU. OU'RE STRONGER HAN ANYONE I'VE EVER KNOWN.
AND WHAT IF I DON'T WANT TO SURVIVE? WITHOUT YOU?
WHAT IF I WANT TO GO WITH?
DAMMIT, TESSA. I CAN'T SAVE MYSELF. 'M NOT STRONG ENOUGH. I'M GOING TO SAVE YOU AT LEAST.
DON'T...
I'VE SPENT A THOUSAND YEARS HATING YOU.
WITHOUT EVEN KNOWING WHY.
BECAUSE I WAS TOLD TO.
BUT I'M NOT WHO THEY SAY I AM EITHER.
WHAT ARE YOU?
C'MON, MALI. YOU REMEMBER NOW, RIGHT?

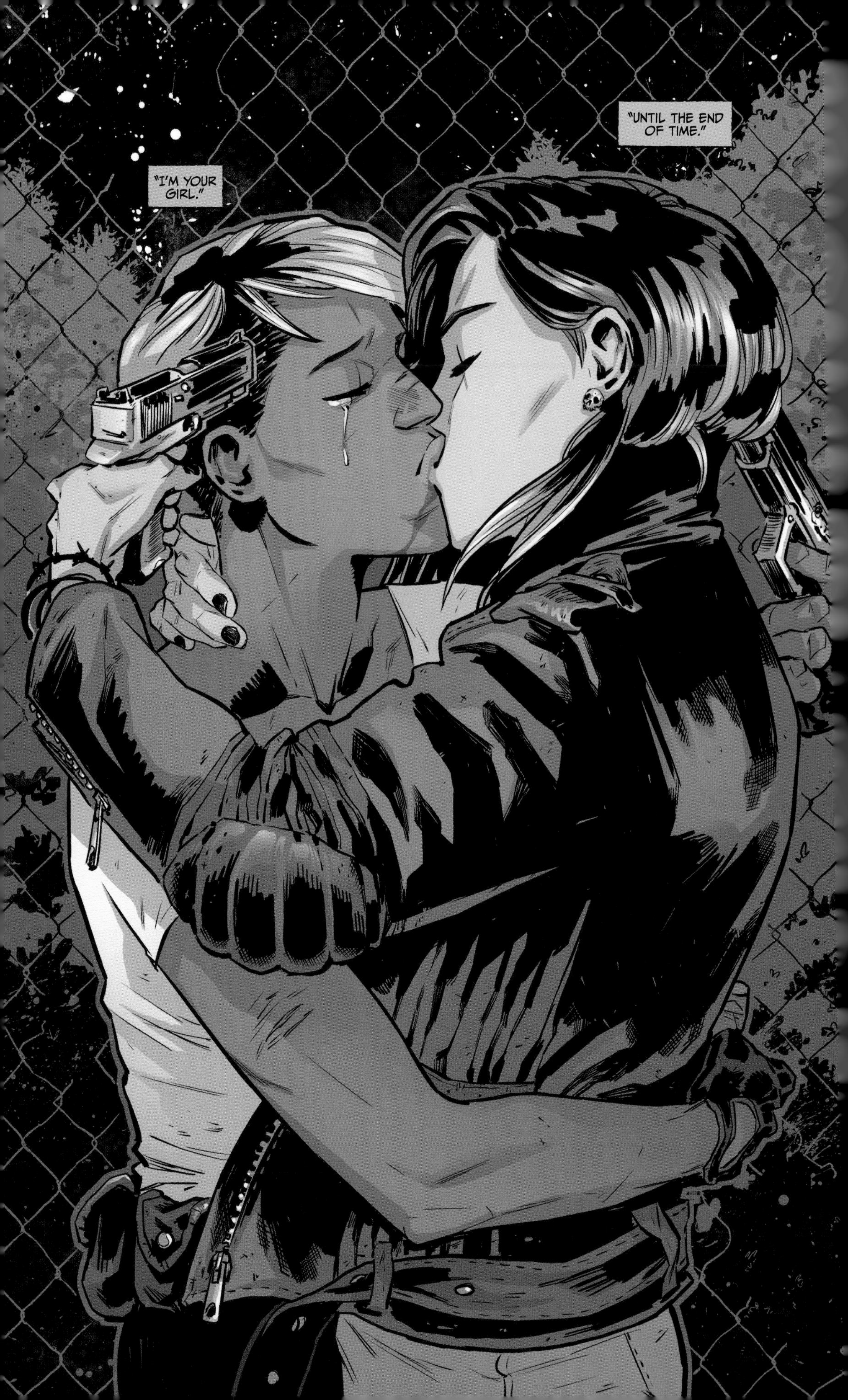
"I'M YOUR GIRL."
"UNTIL THE END OF TIME."

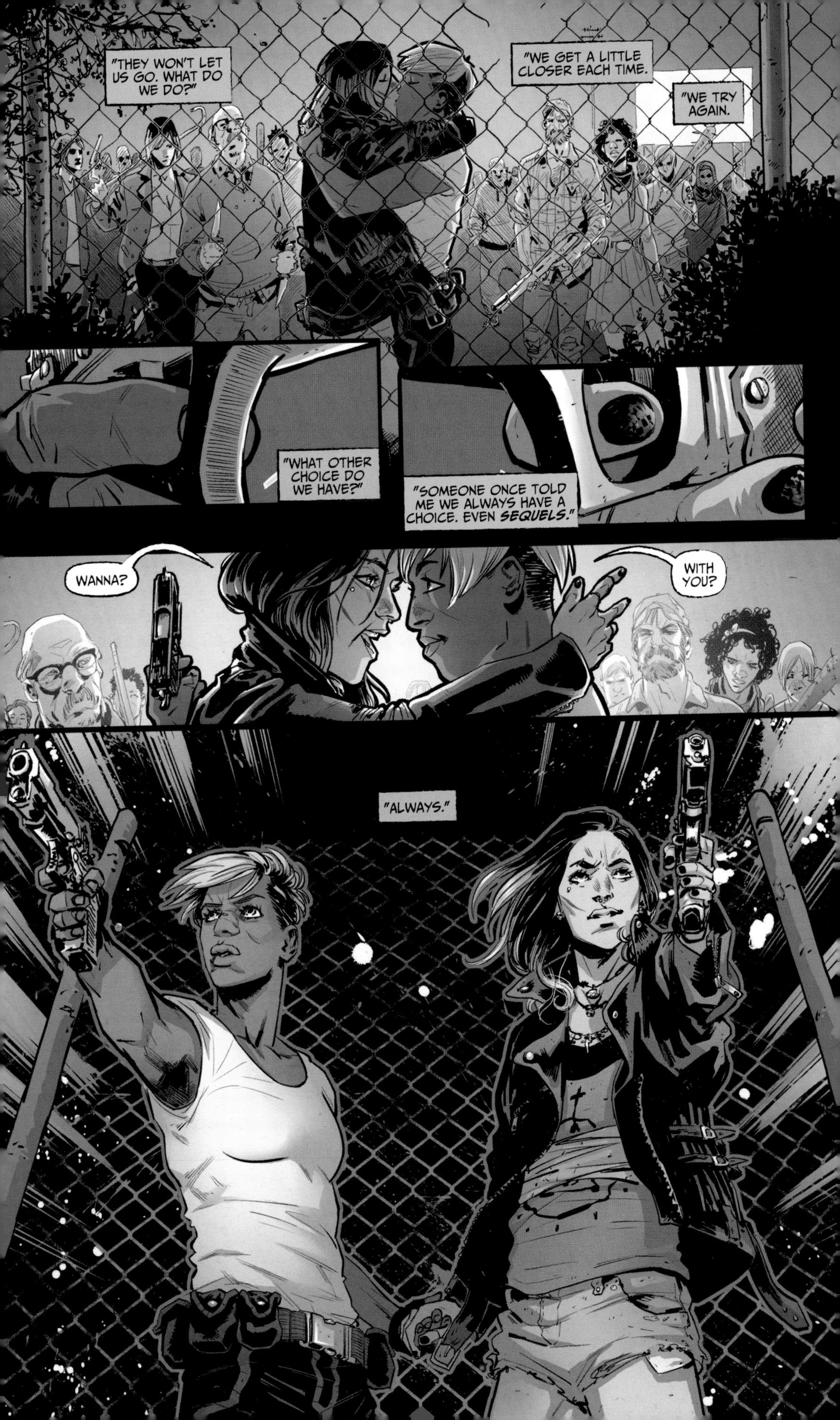
"THEY WON'T LET US GO. WHAT DO WE DO?"
"WE GET A LITTLE CLOSER EACH TIME.
"WE TRY AGAIN.
"WHAT OTHER CHOICE DO WE HAVE?"
"SOMEONE ONCE TOLD ME WE ALWAYS HAVE A CHOICE. EVEN SEQUELS."
WANNA?
WITH YOU?
"ALWAYS."

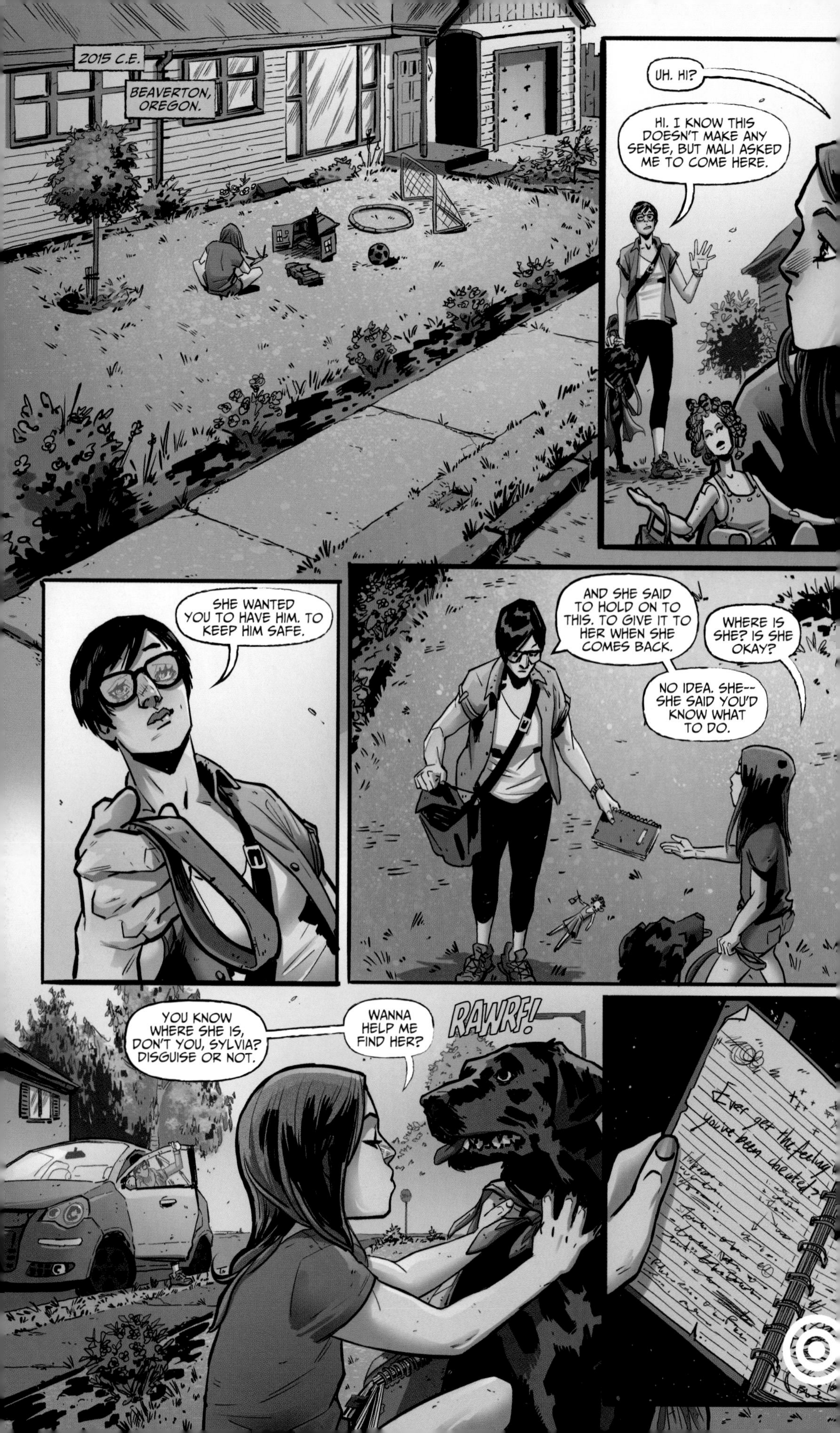
2015 C.E.
BEAVERTON, OREGON.
UH. HI?
HI. I KNOW THIS DOESN'T MAKE ANY SENSE, BUT MALI ASKED ME TO COME HERE.
SHE WANTED YOU TO HAVE HIM. TO KEEP HIM SAFE.
AND SHE SAID TO HOLD ON TO THIS. TO GIVE IT TO HER WHEN SHE COMES BACK.
WHERE IS SHE? IS SHE OKAY?
NO IDEA. SHE-- SHE SAID YOU'D KNOW WHAT TO DO.
YOU KNOW WHERE SHE IS, DON'T YOU, SYLVIA? DISGUISE OR NOT.
WANNA HELP ME FIND HER?
RAWRF!
Ever get the feeling you've been cheated?

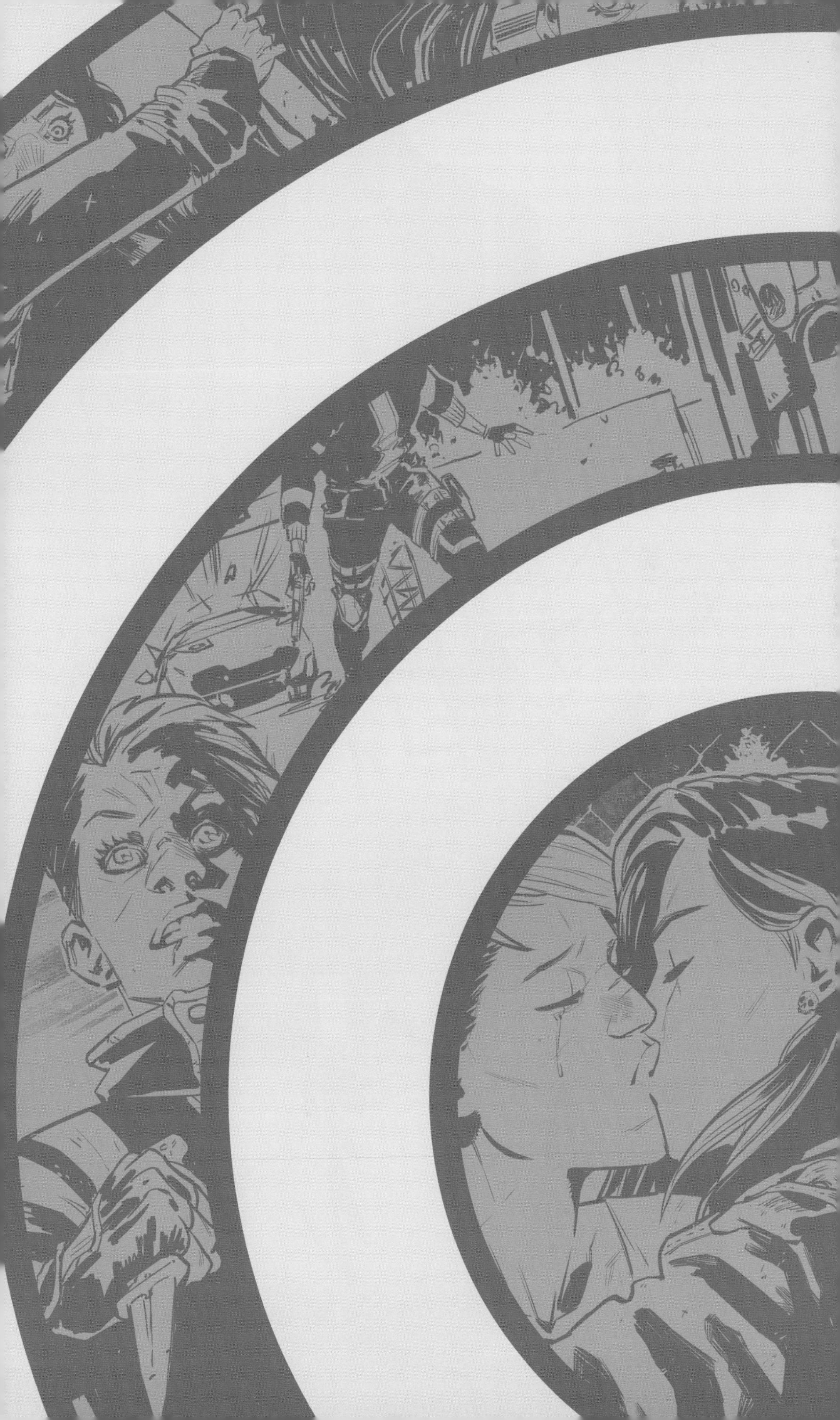

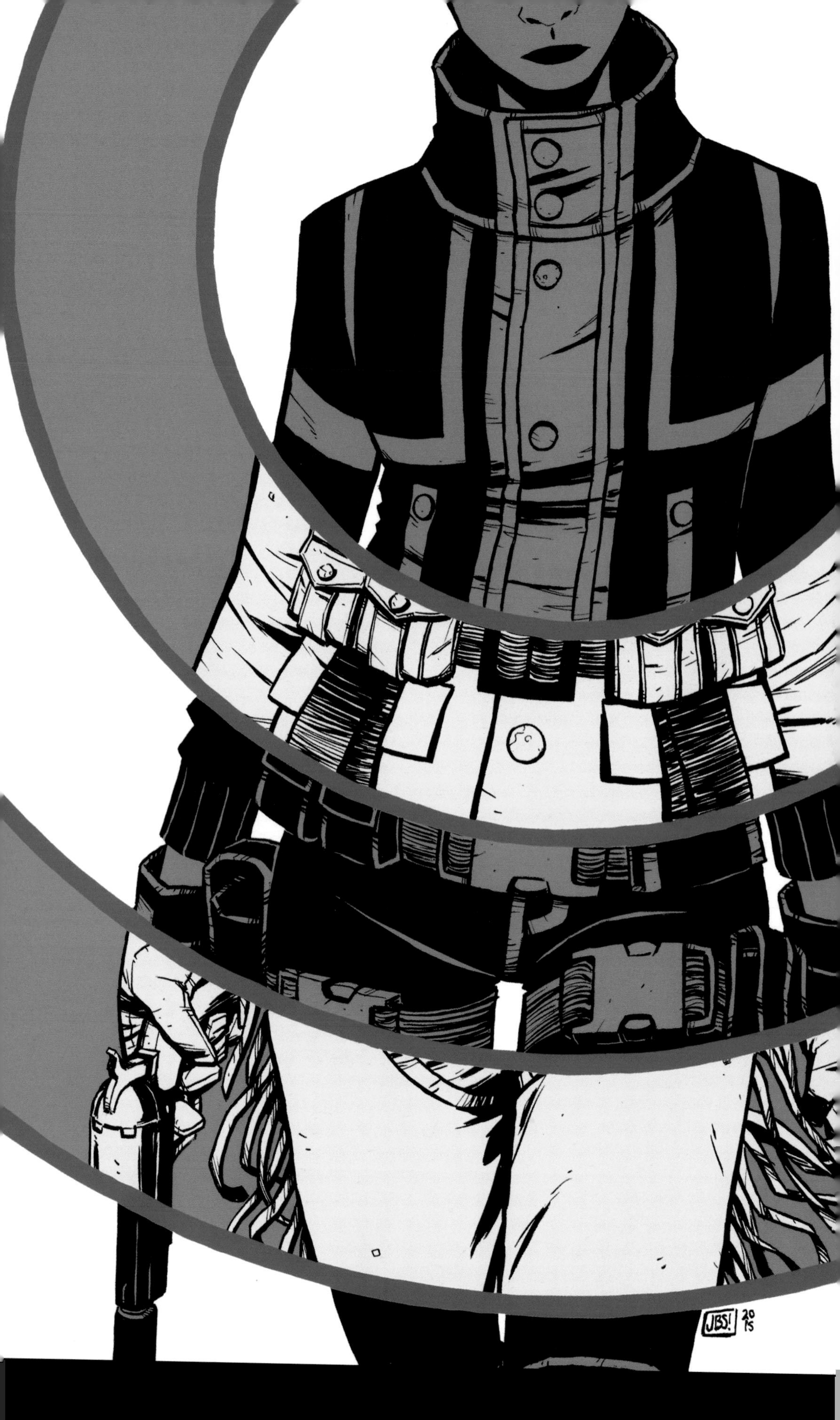
JBS! 20 15

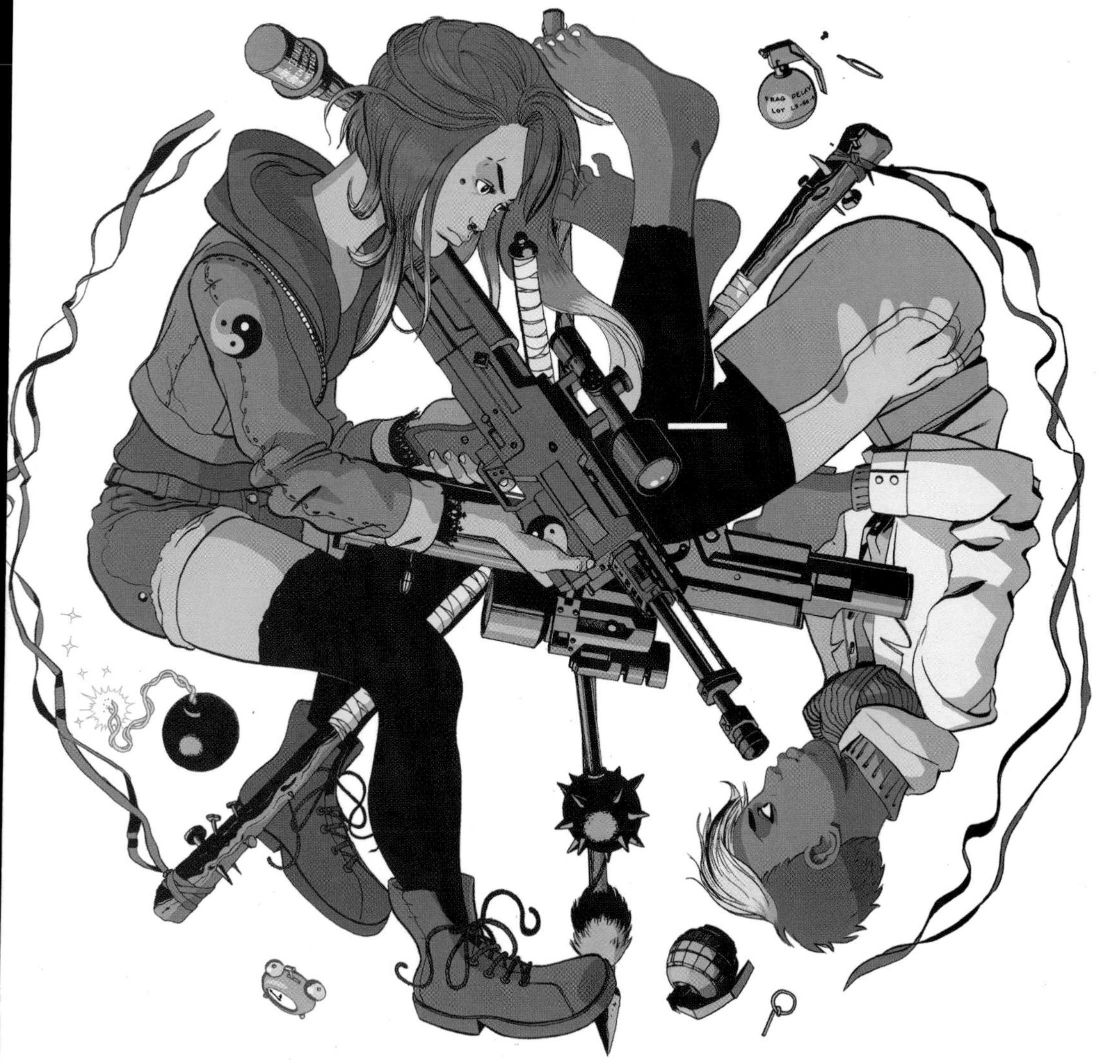
FRAG DELAY

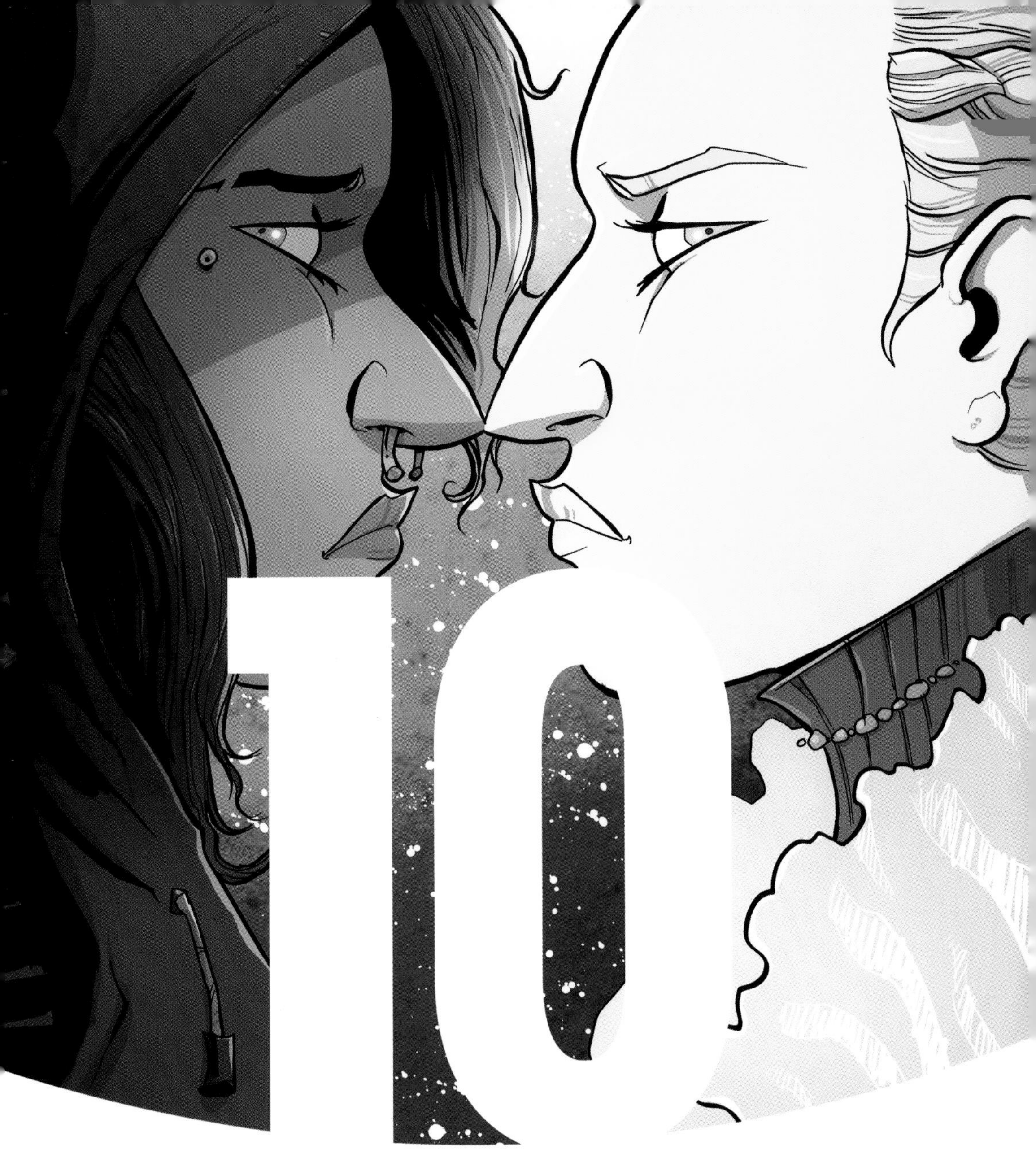

10

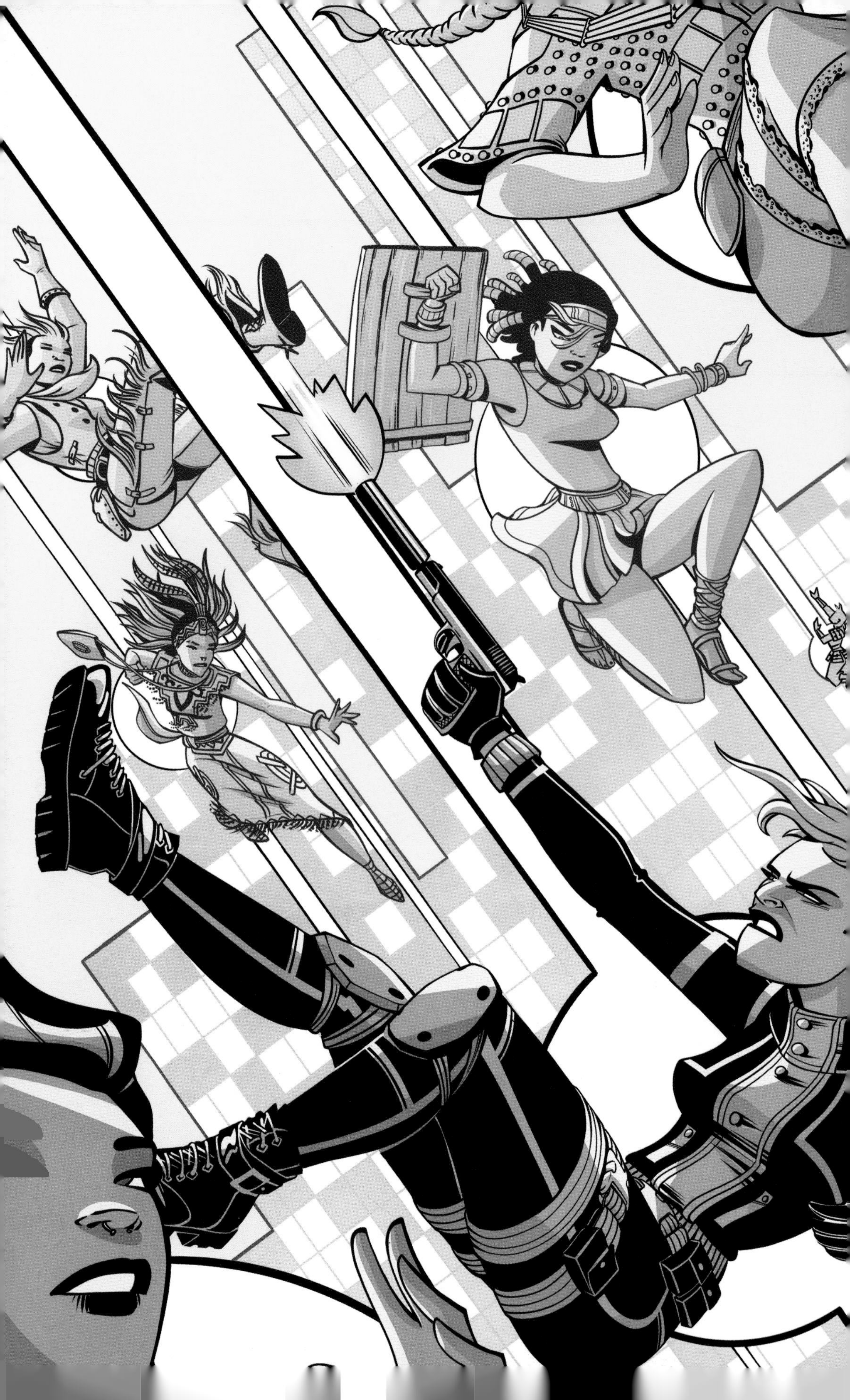

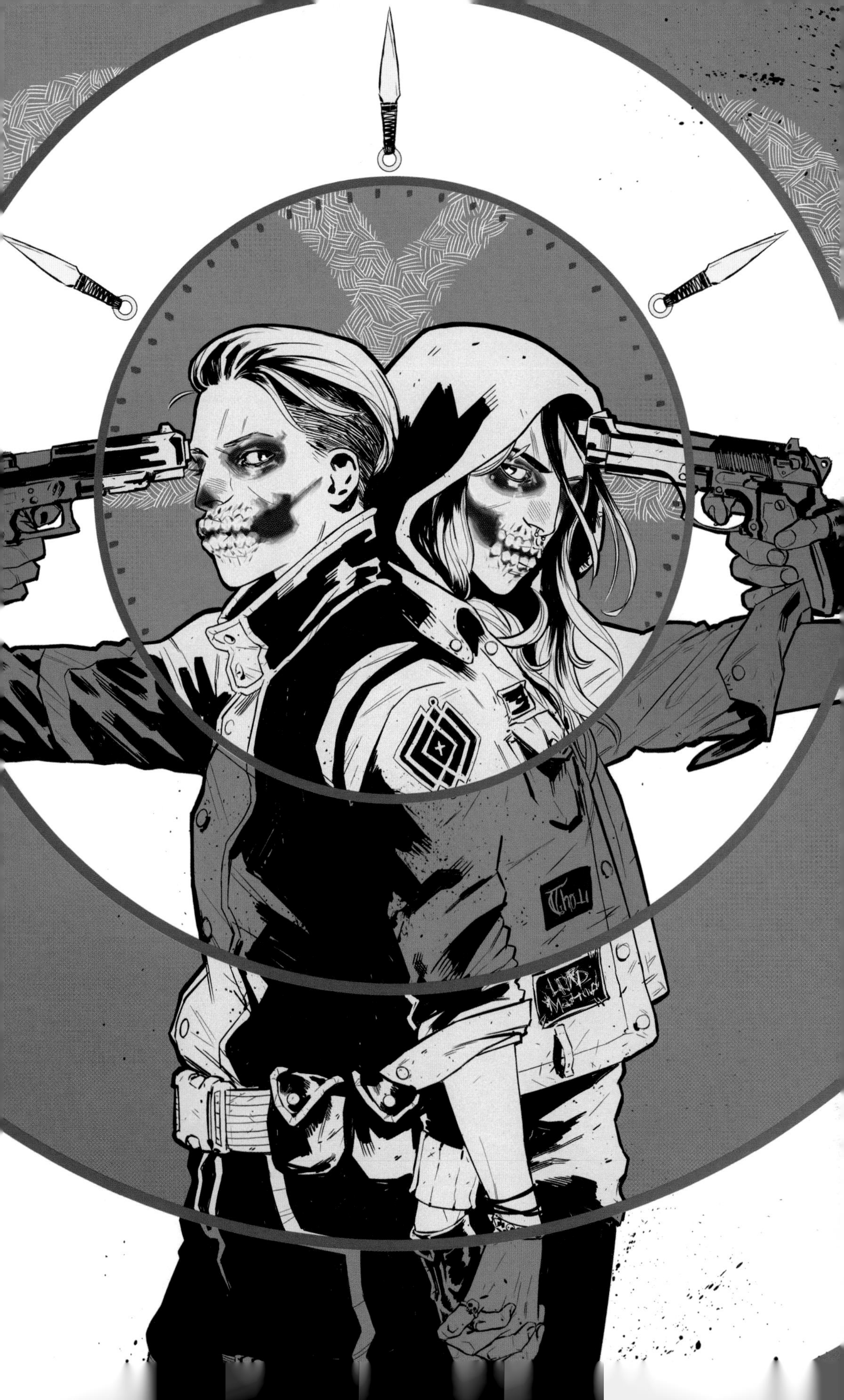

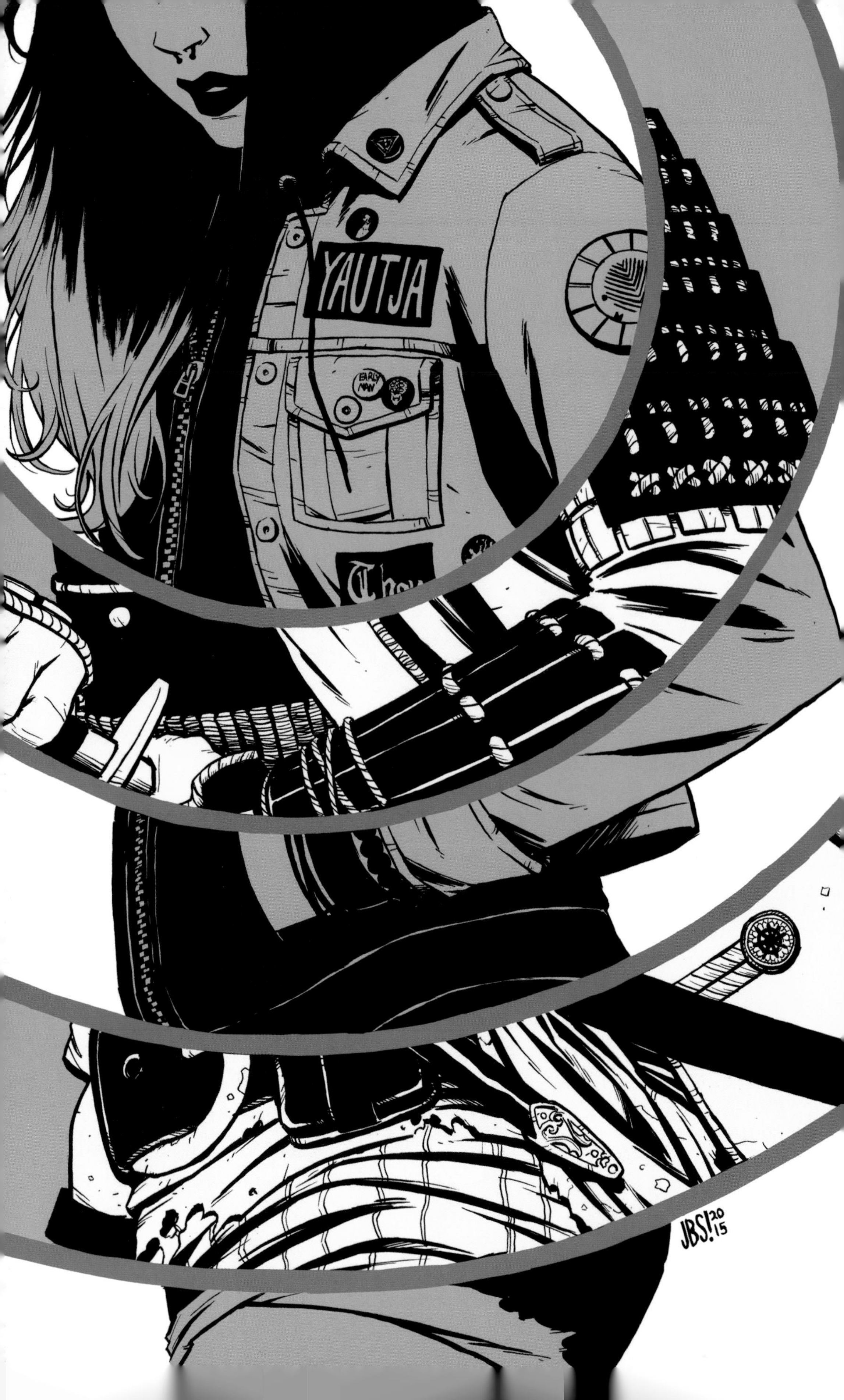
YAUTJA
EARLY MAN
JBS! 20 15

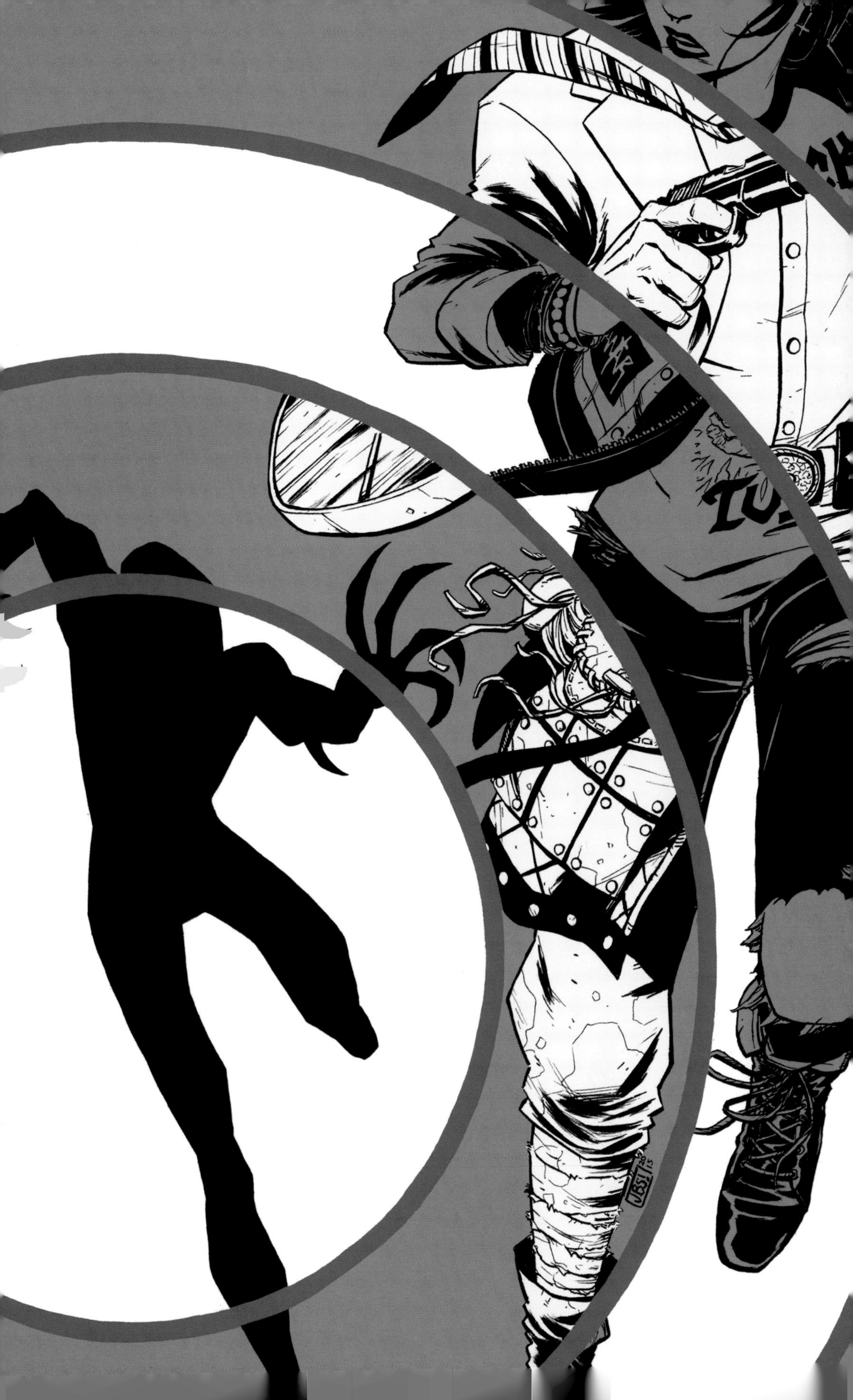

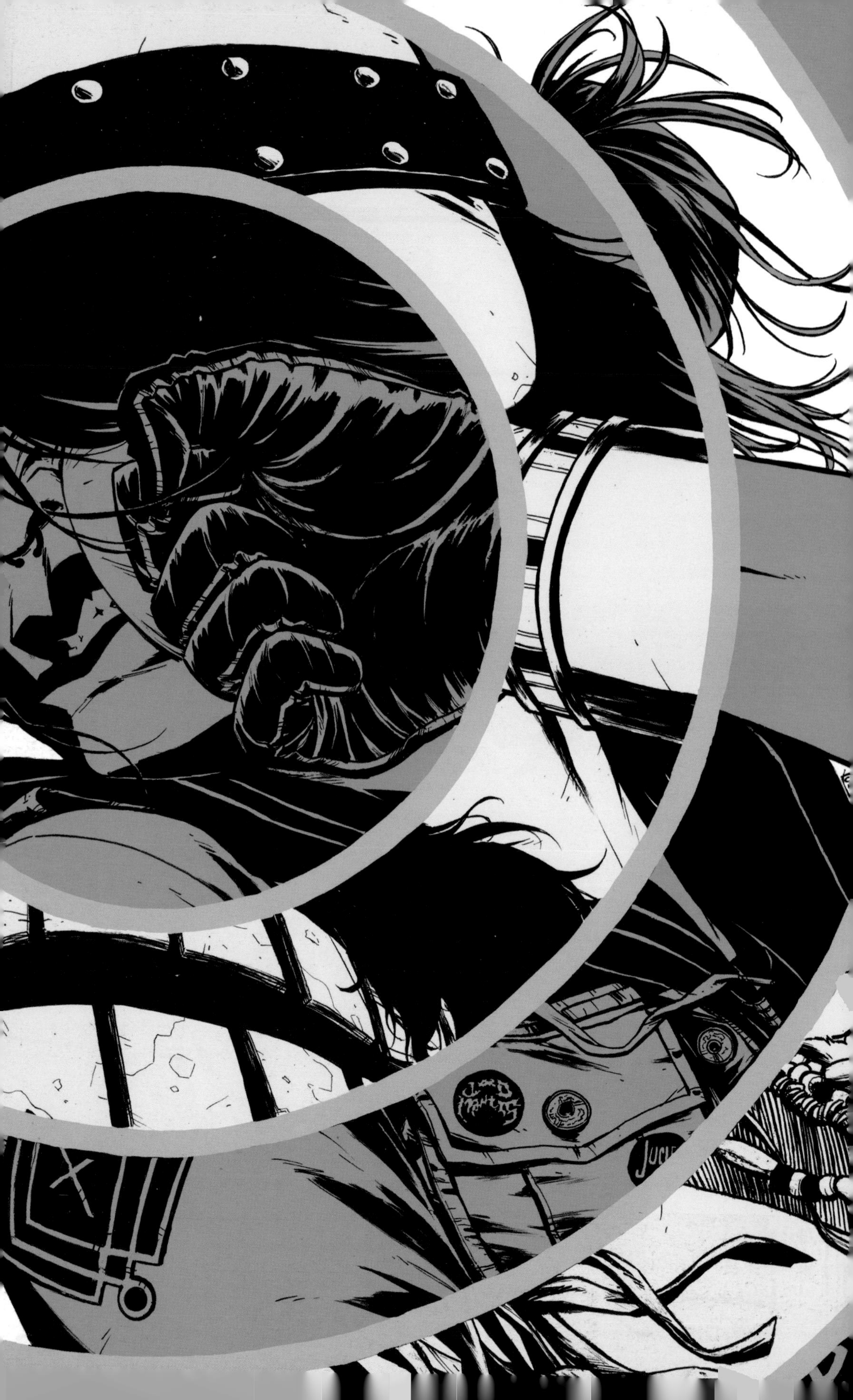

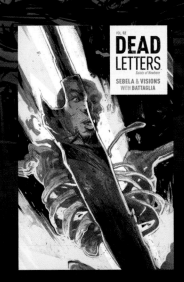

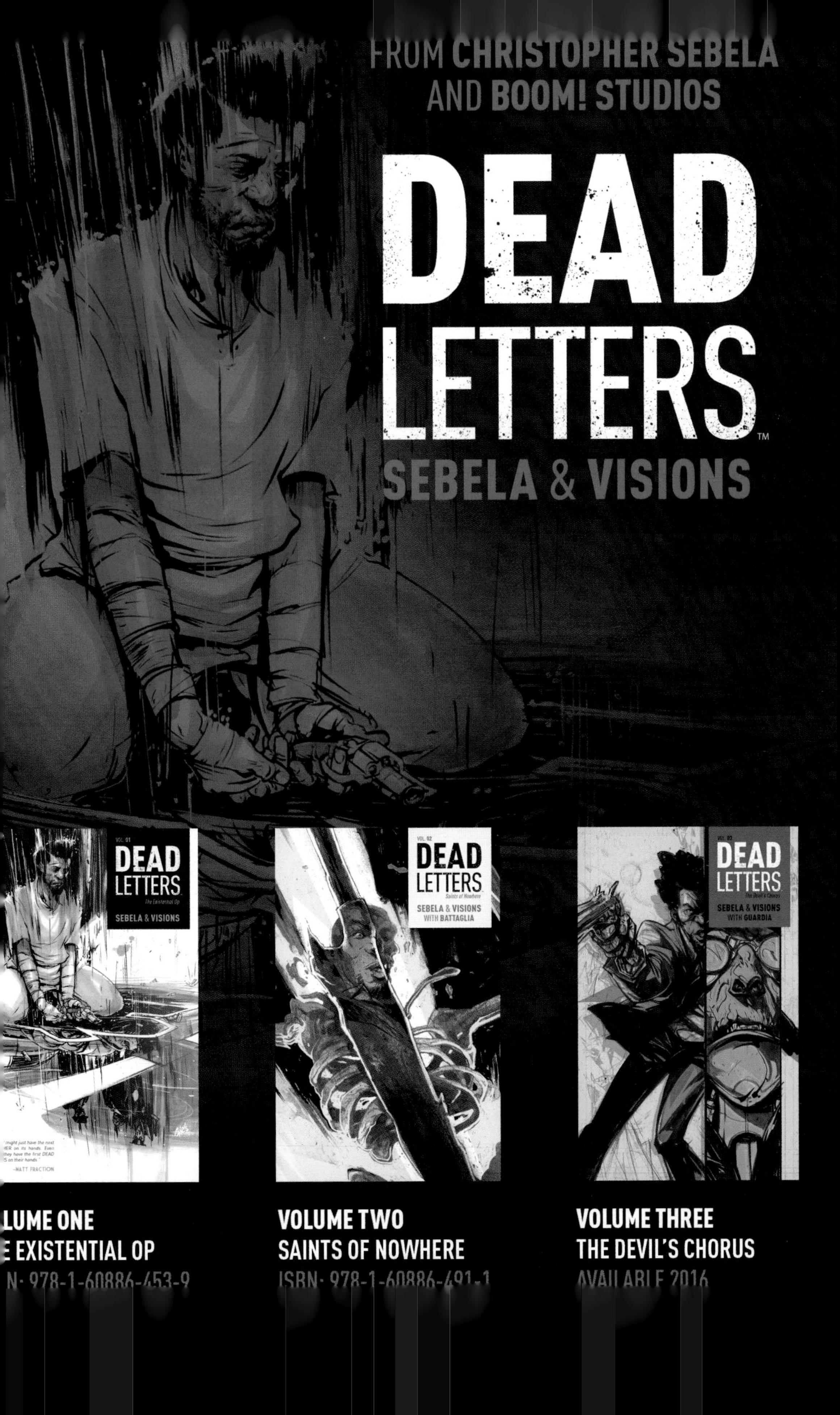

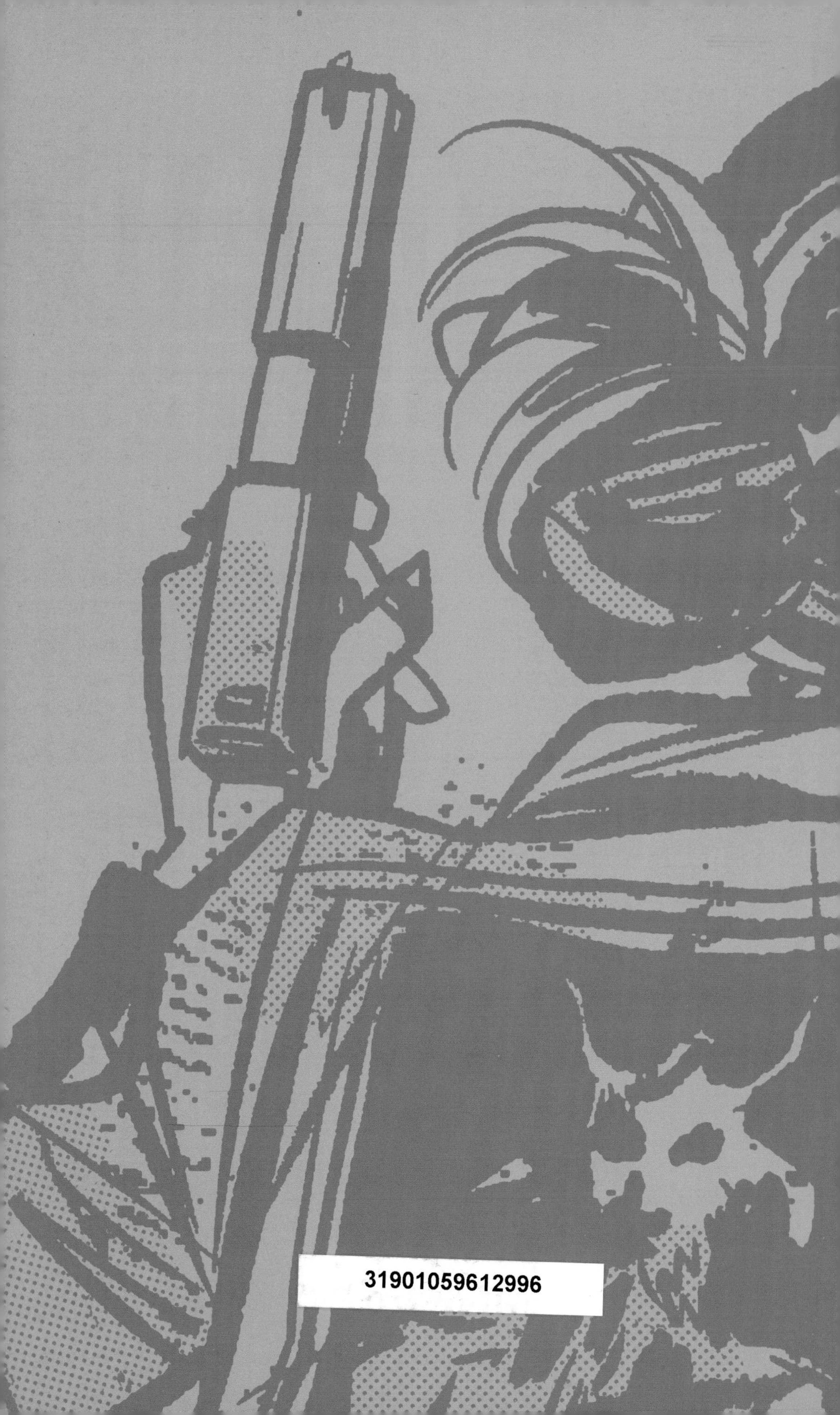